Praise for *Pagan Curious*

"When Debra DeAngelo describes her own seduction by curiosity with the lures of music, movement, and nature, the Pagan becomes as familiar as a happy memory, newly dusted and freshly polished... [DeAngelo] reveals a rich, vibrant world that's much closer to the ancient secrets of nature and the original world we inhabited once upon a time. With inspiration on every page, she leads you to step away from your screens and guides you to a more authentic you, full of magic and miracles."

—Gerit Quealy, author of *Botanical Shakespeare*

"I continue to be amazed by Debra's ability to tackle comprehensive subjects and present them in the most fascinating, yet simple, ways... It goes without saying how much I learned, but one emphasis in particular made the volume of information less intimidating: Debra's insistence that whatever I choose to do, I do it MY way... Now that's my kind of book!"

—Sunny Schlenger, life coach and author of *Organizing for the Spirit*

"*Pagan Curious* should be a prerequisite for anyone looking to explore a Pagan path. Debra DeAngelo answers all the beginner questions in a straightforward and easy to follow way. She encourages the reader to personalize the way they look at the world and connect with the spiritual realms."

—Phoenix LeFae, author of *What is Remembered Lives*

"Are you a seeker? Is there a magic in nature that calls to you? Are you yearning for something you can't quite name? Then I recommend this book for you. Find out what it is in yourself that longs to connect with and use this inexplicable energy."

—Mary K. Greer, author of *Tarot for Your Self*

"Debra's passion and enthusiasm joyfully bubbles forth as she transports readers on a fascinating tour of the dazzling flowers and delightful foliage cultivated within the metaphorical 'Big Pagan Garden.'... This engaging, accessible, down-to-earth guide—alive with ideas, observations, and exercises for beginners and seasoned practitioners alike—is a gem of a resource."

—Lady Jesamyn Angelica, high priestess and founder of Sisterhood of the Moon and The Women's Mystery School

T0049967

"*Pagan Curious* speaks directly to the person who has never been to a Pagan event, or been a part of a coven, or wouldn't know the Wheel of the Year if it ran over them. DeAngelo brilliantly suggests starting with getting to know yourself, before laying out the basics of practice, including working with plants, divination, magickal tools, and deities... This is a must read."

—Gwion Raven, author of *Life Ritualized*

"Debra takes you into her world gently and then holds your hand all the way through, with lovely writing and deep respect for all things Pagan. She gives you tools to navigate all you're curious about and asks you, the reader, challenging and provocative questions... An excellent guide into navigating this rich and complex culture."

—Beth Bornstein Dunnington, director, editor,
writer, actor, singer, acting coach

"*Pagan Curious* offers an energy that allows a reader to move through inner, outer, and magical realms to find out more about being a Pagan. With a welcoming tone and a strong foundation of practical information, I'm certain a reader will walk away with a better understanding of this path and of themselves."

—Irisanya Moon, author of *Practically Pagan*

"With a wealth of insightful exercises and broad-spectrum coverage of foundational information, Debra DeAngelo has created an excellent gateway for those who wish to dip their toe into the waters of Paganism without committing to the deep end."

—Katrina Rasbold, author of *Crossroads of Conjure*

PAGAN
CURIOUS

About the Author

Debra DeAngelo is a Garden-Variety Pagan, with many eclectic spiritual interests and magical pursuits, particularly the endless study and practice of tarot. Following a long career in print journalism as a managing editor and award-winning, syndicated opinion columnist, she now dedicates her professional time to her massage practice and writing books. She also writes freelance feature stories and book reviews for *SageWoman* and *Witches & Pagans* magazines, as well as the occasional blog. She is a graduate of the University of California at Davis, with a bachelor's degree in psychology, and had an early career in social work. A lifelong "horsey girl," she divides her personal time between the two loves of her life: her husband, Joe, and her horse, Pendragon. She and Joe live in northern California with two wacky, wonderful cats, Maxx and Minnie. She has two grown children, Jimmy and Janine, whom she cherishes more than her next heartbeat.

PAGAN
CURIOUS

A Beginner's Guide to
Nature, Magic
& Spirituality

Debra DeAngelo

Foreword by Silver RavenWolf,
bestselling author of *Solitary Witch*

Llewellyn Publications
Woodbury, Minnesota

FIRST EDITION
Second Printing, 2024

Cover design by Kevin R. Brown
Interior art by the Llewellyn Art Department

Llewellyn Publications is a registered trademark of Llewellyn Worldwide Ltd.

Library of Congress Cataloging-in-Publication Data (Pending)
ISBN: 978-0-7387-6653-9

Llewellyn Worldwide Ltd. does not participate in, endorse, or have any authority or responsibility concerning private business transactions between our authors and the public.

All mail addressed to the author is forwarded but the publisher cannot, unless specifically instructed by the author, give out an address or phone number.

Any internet references contained in this work are current at publication time, but the publisher cannot guarantee that a specific location will continue to be maintained. Please refer to the publisher's website for links to authors' websites and other sources.

Llewellyn Publications
A Division of Llewellyn Worldwide Ltd.
2143 Wooddale Drive
Woodbury, MN 55125-2989
www.llewellyn.com

Printed in the United States of America

Other Books by This Author

The Elements of Horse Spirit (2020)

Dedication

This book is dedicated to every curious person who ever looked up into the starry night sky, or out across the rolling blue ocean, or into the deep green forest, and felt a shiver of "wow."

Contents

Acknowledgments

So many people have shaped my outlook over the years through their example and with their words, both written and spoken. Amongst an expanse of stars, a few shine particularly brightly.

In order of appearance, each of these stellar women has left a dear and indelible imprint on my spirit, and contributed to bringing this book into being:

Beatrice Pizer: You gently, lovingly coaxed me out from a thick, ragged shell of fear, anxiety, and trauma. You are where my metamorphosis began. Thank you.

Sunny Schlenger: You taught me that my life could be so much more than I was allowing it to be. You encouraged me to feel the fear and leap anyway. Thank you.

Lokita Carter: You gave me a new paradigm for living in my own body and mind. The wisdom and love you've shared have been transformative. Thank you.

Gail Dettmer: You spun a crystal in my hand and changed the trajectory of my life. You showed me the path I'd been searching for. Thank you.

Silver RavenWolf: You have inspired me from the very beginning and continue to do so. I so cherish your unfailingly warm, welcoming, validating, positive spirit. Thank you.

Victoria David Danann: You were my first teacher, and even though we never met on the physical plane, you opened the magical world to me, and validated me. Thank you.

Heather Greene: You opened a doorway to opportunity that had been so elusive. You challenge me to write sharper, clearer, and brighter, and to settle for nothing less than excellence. I appreciate your support, your participation, and your willingness to take a chance on me more than I can articulate. Thank you.

Foreword

by Silver RavenWolf

Welcome to the amazing Pagan experience! Within these pages, you will find freedom, joy, peace, delight, and harmony with the universe—an intoxicating brew of self-empowerment, wisdom, and magick. Walking a new path can be heady and exciting! Enjoy!

As you read through these pages, meditate on what you learn. Take your time. Live the work. Breathe in the ideas. Celebrate the magick of each day. This beautifully written book will give you a plethora of ideas, exercises, and information to help you in your magickal journey. Don't be surprised if you experience emotional exhilaration. "It is like coming home," so many practitioners exclaim, their faces radiant and their hearts light with love. "I feel like I've been gone a very long time, and it is so good to be back!"

Becoming is your goal; but, you will never reach the end, as it is the journey itself that brings fulfillment. Magick and spirituality are a progression of power. Surrender the need for results and you will find the greatest gifts come from living the enchantment. Unfoldment of your divine self is the reward. I embraced Paganism over forty years ago and never, ever looked back. I have received amazing rewards and enjoyed complete and utter contentment. My advice? Trust the process. In Braucherei (a form of folk-magick energy healing that I practice), we have a saying: "You didn't get sick in a day, you won't get well in a day," meaning everything has its pace, its unique development, its ebb and flow. Don't rush yourself—savor every moment. See your mistakes as opportunities. Let the beauty of you happen naturally.

Everything you need is already within you. Don't be afraid of messing up. Let Debra hand you the key that will unlock the secrets of the golden web of Paganism. You can do this!

And most important of all? Have fun and enjoy the flow!

Introduction

You've always been curious, haven't you?

Curious about a friend who seems so...unusual? She wears pendants with strange symbols and stones, and her house is full of odd little arrangements—shells, stones, feathers, bells, and small bundles of dried leaves. You want to ask a million questions, but you're too shy. Your curiosity is simmering.

Curious about that yearning you feel when wandering through the woods, or along the beach, or standing and looking up at the starry night sky? You feel a connection. A deep knowing. Something very old and very familiar, but undefinable. It pulls at you and pulls at you. What *is* it?

Curious about that mysterious little boutique you see while walking down the sidewalk to get coffee? It's like a tractor beam. You're drawn inside and find a dazzling mosaic of figurines, crystals, candles, herbs, and incense. And books. So many books—and you've never heard of any of them. The shelves glisten with unfamiliar wonders. What *is* all this stuff? And why do I need it?

Yes, *need.*

Your spirit is ravenous for something you can't identify, and it shall not be ignored. It's a faint pulse. A heartbeat. It's a whisper that calls you, but it's distorted. Muffled. It's a whisper not of words, but of feelings: of memories that stubbornly evade you, blocked by some mysterious amnesia. You're compelled to return to that place where you've never been, reclaim that thing you've never had, and find that dear friend you've never met.

What is this thing I seek? Where is it? Who is it? Why, why, *why* do I have so many questions and no answers? Ah, the mantra of every curious person who ever set out on a journey for answers. You're so deeply frustrated because you're looking for yourself in all the wrong places.

Buried in your own DNA is a spiritual connection to the natural world, and its energies and rhythms; buried in your own DNA is a cellular memory of an intricate connection to nature—of being completely in tune with all the wonder and mystery of life itself; buried in your own DNA is an ancient ancestor who lived a spiritual dance with nature and knew the mystical stories about how it all worked, passed on by each generation that came earlier. It's your own Pagan past, tens of thousands of generations of it, longing to express itself again.

You're endlessly searching for something you already have: a spiritual connection to the natural world and the universe itself, and all the divine, mystical, magical energies that swirl through it all. It's there. It isn't lost. You've just become separated from it by the perpetual spin of modern life, a centrifugal force that propels us farther and farther away from our innate spiritual center. Let's slow that spin down, together, and find your center— the true source of your curiosity.

I understand your frustration, your longing. I too was once compelled to find something I couldn't identify. But I could feel it, tugging at me; waving at me from the corner of my eye, only to disappear the moment I turned to look. I felt like a visitor in my own life.

Seduced by relentless curiosity, I started exploring festivals where people seemed different from the soccer moms wandering the shopping malls: Renaissance fairs, Whole Earth festivals, and ultimately, a Pagan harvest festival, where finally, something clicked: a Goddess-centric, nature-attuned gathering of carefree people in all sorts of unusual clothing, singing, drumming, dancing. It was all entirely foreign to me, and also as familiar as coming home. I'd finally found my *tribe*.

I wandered into a booth and sat down with some lovely, lively women in flowy, flamboyant garments who said they were Wiccan. I had a million questions, and they had kind, patient answers. Suddenly, one of them peered at me, as if examining me, and said, "Hold out your hand." I did, and she placed a thick, pointed clear crystal in it, the point facing away from me.

"How does that feel?" she asked.

"Fine," I replied.

Then she grabbed it and quickly spun it backwards, the point facing toward me. I jumped reflexively and squawked, as if I'd been shocked.

She smiled up at the others, and then back at me.

"You've found what you're looking for. You're a Seeker."

And so began my first step on that path I could never find: the Seeker's path—the path of the "Pagan curious." I'd discovered the magical, nature-based spirituality my heart was yearning for. However, it's tough being a Seeker when you live a tiny town in the middle of bumdunk nowhere with more churches than bars, and only one stoplight—and it didn't even have three colors, only flashing red. There were no Pagans anywhere to be seen. At the time, the internet was in its toddlerhood, and most of the wonderful Pagan and metaphysical books available now weren't even written yet. Facebook and Twitter didn't exist. My only resource was dial-up internet. And yes, I had to walk through five miles of snow to get to my computer.

I discovered a three-year online witchcraft course called "Seasons in Avalon," created by Victoria Danaan, and that was where my learning began. The focus was to develop and become sensitive to one's own intuitive knowledge and truth, and apply that to magical skills, which immediately resonated with me. I hope to do the same for you, curious friend—dissolve the things that obstruct you from being your true, natural, magical self.

To be clear, this is *not* a Witchcraft 101 book. You might read that next. Or not. That's much further down the road, and we're just beginning. Besides reintroducing you to yourself, I'll introduce you to some basic Pagan concepts, practices, and terminology. You'll learn your Pagan ABC's and 123's, so you'll have the vocabulary and basic knowledge to enable you to explore the Pagan world and seek its paths further, if you wish, or just keep learning and growing on your own, like me: an average, eclectic, Garden-Variety Pagan.

The Big Pagan Garden

The very familiar phrase "Big Pagan Tent" means a welcoming, lively, colorful circus tent of Pagan practices, traditions, and religions where we don't all have to agree on everything in order to coexist peacefully. Everyone's welcome, even those such as myself who don't identify as anything other than generically Pagan.

Although I like that Big Pagan Tent concept, I'm changing it up a bit. Tents have walls and ceilings, and I want to see nature around me and the sky and stars above me. So, instead of a tent, we'll re-imagine this Pagan world as a vast garden: a Big Pagan Garden, warmed by the sun, cooled by the moon, nourished by the soil and rain, waving in the gentle breeze, the sky arching above it all.

This garden is alive! It's a riot of color and variety: stately roses on one side, shy little violets peeking out from under a shady tree, and delicate sweet peas winding their way up a trellis. These flower beds are the various Pagan paths, or "traditions." We Garden-Variety Pagans are the wildflowers—we spring up wherever we want, however we want. We'll wander this colorful garden together, discover all sorts of amazing and wondrous things, and check out the flower beds. Don't worry about where you'll blossom for now—just enjoy the experience of blossoming.

Our Big Pagan Garden Map

This book has three sections. The first is all about you: your inner realm, where you'll become reacquainted with your true, natural self, and reconnect with your body. The second focuses on the natural world around you: your outer realm. We'll take a magical, spiritual look at plants, animals, the environment, the planet, and the cosmos, and ways to connect with them. The third is about those mysterious, mystical things you're ever so curious about: your magical realm, which holds all that sparkly stuff from your friend's home and that little boutique. We'll explore magic and ritual and visit each of the Pagan flower beds.

As we stroll through this Big Pagan Garden, there will be activities along the way meant to enhance your insight and experience—but you have to actually *do* them to gain that insight and experience. It's like going to an amusement park: you'll enjoy it a lot more if you go on the rides, rather than standing on the sidelines watching everyone else having fun. If you want the *wheeeee*, ya gotta get on the roller coaster!

Section One

Your Inner Realm

CHAPTER 1
Getting to Know You

Allow me to introduce you to yourself!

"Hey you, meet you! What a super cool, unique, amazing, one-of-a-kind, divine creature you are!"

Yes, our journey to the outside begins inside. In her iconic poem, "The Charge of the Goddess,"[1] Wiccan icon Doreen Valiente wrote, "If that which thou seekest thou findest not within thee, thou wilt never find it without thee." In other words, if what you seek can't be found within yourself, it can't be found outside yourself. Or at all. Surprise! The beauty and mystery of the natural world, as well as the magical wonder of the universe, are not only all around you, but also right there inside you. It all begins with you.

In this chapter, we'll gently peel back your layers of self-protection and self-defeating habits, and clarify what you really love and want, or dislike, or need more of, or less. Once you're clear on what you want from life, you'll be clearer on how you spend your time, and able to open up some space to allow new things to sprout. Being sure and comfortable in your own mind, body, and spirit about exactly who you are—not who others want you to be—facilitates a connection with the natural world and allows you to explore that Big Pagan Garden, free of inhibition. You'll make better choices and have richer experiences if you're free to be all of who you really are.

---

1. Doreen Valiente, "The Charge of the Goddess," DoreenValiente.org, accessed January 28, 2020, http://www.doreenvaliente.com/Doreen-Valiente-Doreen_Valiente_Poetry-11. php#sthash.pWoyldmS.dpbs.

We'll develop a "natural" mindset. Nature is honest. Nature is genuine. Nature doesn't pretend or make pretenses. It makes no apologies for being just the way it is. Nature is real, so we'll get real too.

What Are You?

How would you describe *what* you are? Human being? Parent? Sibling? Teenager? Senior citizen? Something in between? Male or female or both or neither? Red, yellow, black, white, brown, or some combination thereof? American? Brazilian? French? Animal lover, social rights activist, doctor, tailor, teacher, sailor? Large or small, fat or thin, or somewhere in between? Musical, mathematical, mystical, magical? Democrat or Republican or Socialist or Libertarian? You may be nodding at some of those, and you may be many of those things. But, those things aren't *what* you are. They're expressions of what you are, but not the actual *stuff* of what you are.

Beneath all those descriptions, you and all your qualities and talents are manifestations of your DNA, combined with the experiences you've had over the course of your life and how you adapted to them. But they aren't *you*. Even your DNA isn't exactly you, although it's what makes you the unique creature that you are. DNA is life's living code. Whether or not DNA itself is alive is still open for scientific debate, because technically DNA is chemical in nature. However, absence of evidence isn't evidence of absence. (That's my very favorite saying, borrowed from author Wendy Williams.[2] You're going to hear it a *lot*.) Scientists haven't been able to prove that DNA is alive. Yet. What *is* known for certain is that new life doesn't form from non-living matter. Only life begets life, whether plant or animal.

Many plants reproduce by having their DNA passed along by pollination, sometimes assisted by pollinators, such as bees and butterflies. Animals reproduce when the DNA of a sperm and egg merge and create a new, unique living thing. But the DNA itself isn't new. It's been passed along from the very beginning of life on Earth. Strands of DNA—chromosomes—from two different organisms bond as one unique double helix, and divide, divide, divide, in whatever way this unique pair of chromosomes determines, but it isn't new life, nor new DNA. The same DNA is passed along at conception

2. Wendy Williams, *The Horse: The Epic History of Our Noble Companion* (New York: Scientific American/Farrar, Straus and Giroux, 2016), 178.

in different combinations, from generation to generation on and on and on, from one being to the next, whether it's a person or a peacock or a protozoa. The forms that DNA takes—species—are shaped by each one's ability to adapt to environmental changes—or not. Those that can't adapt disappear.

So, here's the real mind-blower: all life on this planet, whether plant or animal, came from the same original life spark. Strands of dead DNA don't join and suddenly spring to life, like microscopic Frankensteins. No, life + life = life, and that's the only way it works. Life keeps sparking life, on and on and on, through time, through every species of every generation, era, and epoch that followed that first spark. All life on Earth began a billion years ago in single-celled ocean-dwelling organisms called *protists*.[3]

Within you—and every living thing—is that original jolt of energy from the tumultuous atmosphere that hit the right chains of protein just so and began life on this planet—all of it, from the first protist right on up to you. Your bloodline stretches much farther back in time than your human ancestors—back to those humble little protists—as does the bloodline of all life on Earth, regardless of species. Think about that: life's first spark is surging within you, right now. You aren't just alive, you *are* life! That's pretty damn profound, and sacred, and mystical! Which means you are pretty damn profound and sacred and mystical too. Stop and ponder the miracle that is you.

But wait, there's more! Knowing that life only comes from life, what about that first spark of life on Earth? Where did *that* come from? Was it a unique, singular fluke—random electrical charges reacting with random chemicals, here on this one tiny little planet only, in all of the universe? That seems extremely unlikely. Knowing that only life produces life, that life spark must have come from another life spark out in the cosmos. Assuming the universe is an orderly place, *that* initial spark that originated out in the cosmos *also* exists in us right now, and in every other living thing on this planet and beyond. Our ancient ancestry, our life spark, precedes even the protists. It stretches all the way back to the Big Bang, when the universe began in the colossal explosion of one small particle, creating everything in the entire universe.

---

3. BBC Earth, "Meet the Ancestors of All Plants and Animals," last updated September 5, 2014, http://www.bbc.com/earth/story/20140905-meet-the-ancestors-of-all-plants-and-animals.

All the chemicals in the universe, which are present in all of the heavenly bodies and stars and planets, and everything on them, originated from that same cosmic detonation. The same chemicals found across the cosmos are the same chemicals found here on Earth and in our bodies, but in different combinations. So, we are, as famed astronomer Carl Sagan said, literally made of stardust.[4] All of us. Every living thing. The spark of living energy in you right now has existed since the beginning of time, the beginning of everything that ever was. A universe of stars sparkles inside you! You are stardust, baby! Let your mind wonder and wander and consider and ponder that reality. You're a lot more miraculous than you ever imagined.

Let's Write About It

If you're all aglow in your newfound cosmic heritage, and thoughts and ideas are whirling around in your mind, let's get that down on paper because we'll be discovering a lot more as we go along. We want to keep track of all of it. A journal is the perfect place to do this.

I'll admit, at one time, I wasn't a fan of journaling. I've been a writer and editor for going on thirty years, and I prefer a lightning-fast keyboard to scratching things out on pen and paper. I can type almost as fast as I can think, and I always found writing by hand extremely frustrating, particularly since my handwriting is barely legible. However, in the midst of some wicked writer's block, a friend who was struggling with the same challenged me to work through Julia Cameron's book *The Artist's Way* with her. Unbeknownst to me when I accepted her challenge was that the entire core of this program is daily journaling. Oh, how the resistance boiled within me. But I'd committed, so journal I did—every day for many weeks, first thing in the morning, with my coffee, out on the back patio.

I learned a few things in spite of myself while journaling. It's a much more gentle, peaceful way to slide into a new day rather than staring wide-eyed at the crisis-du-jour on the morning news. I also discovered the value in slowly, thoughtfully writing by hand, taking the time to form words I could actually read. It took my mind down currents and eddies I'd never have traveled if my fingers were zooming over the keyboard. It's the difference between zipping

4. Nancy Atkinson, "Confirmed: We Really Are Star Stuff," Universe Today, last updated January 11, 2017, https://www.universetoday.com/132791/confirmed-really-star-stuff/.

over the surface on a speedboat and paddling in a canoe. You make entirely different discoveries, notice things you never noticed before, and have a completely different experience. You access a different part of your brain, in a different way, when you write by hand. So, guess who's now a big fan of journaling. Let's do it, even if like me, you've always found it tedious.

Activity: Let Your Thoughts Flow

Treat yourself to a new journal. It can be a simple spiral-bound notebook, or you could splurge on a blank journal, maybe with something that inspires or delights you on the cover. While you're at it, indulge in a special journaling pen. I adore colorful gel pens for journaling because they glide over the paper and have little pads for your fingers.

Pick a time to journal every day. First thing in the morning is refreshing and grounding, but be realistic. Pick a time when you'll actually do it, even if you can only commit to ten minutes. Put that pen on the paper and start moving it— whatever comes to mind. It doesn't matter what you write, only *that* you write. Write about whatever pops to mind. What do you wonder about? What delights you? What drains your energy? What do you want to get done that day? Write about that, or anything else. Let your thoughts spill out onto the page, randomly, without judgment. You won't be graded on spelling, grammar, or penmanship. You're the only one who will read it. It's all for you. After splashing your innermost thoughts onto paper, close your journal, and relax and breathe. Imagine your day. What would you like to accomplish? What activities seem like a valuable exchange for eight hours of your life?

If you'd like a little more structure or if you're just really stuck, here are some prompts to get started. Start your journal entry with any of these:

- When I was small, I wanted to be a …
- The strangest person I ever met was …
- If I could have one superpower, it would be …
- If cats were people, they would …
- If I could be an animal, I'd be a …
- The color of my spirit is …
- I wish I'd spent more time with …

- If I could spend a year doing anything I wanted, I would...
- If I went to live on a desert island, I would bring...
- I have always secretly wished to be a...

Congruence

Getting to know your own true, genuine self is a prerequisite for exploring the Big Pagan Garden. If you're inhibited inside, you'll be prohibited when you go outside. It's called congruence: aligning your internal and external realities so they flow along effortlessly back and forth. You can't become congruent in your life until you understand and accept your true self. If you aren't solid about who you are, what you want and don't want, and what you like and don't like, you have no internal template to align with the exterior world. There's nothing to be congruent *with*. If you're hodge-podgey about your own self, your life will be just as hodge-podgey. That's an ironic congruence in itself: muddled inside, muddled outside.

Imagine your mind as a cluttered, crowded, disorderly closet. Opening the door may trigger an avalanche. It's bulging with stuff, some that you stashed there, and stuff given to you by others: kitchen gadgets you'll never use, clothes that don't fit, CDs you don't play, shoes that hurt, and all sorts of random stuff you couldn't bring yourself to throw away because you might need them someday or felt obligated to keep because they were gifts.

Let's talk about the "gifts" first. Those are beliefs about yourself that others shoved upon you, and you kept. A great number of people have declared a great number of things about you over the course of your life—criticisms, judgments, ridicule. You didn't evaluate their validity; you packed them into your closet. Even worse was the stuff you jammed in there yourself. We are often our own most vicious critics. Let's drag it all out, get rid of the stuff you don't want, and make space for things you actually like and can use.

Purging the Negatives

Unless we're naturally well-balanced, with innate healthy boundaries to protect our self-esteem from being pummeled by the opinions of others, we absorb negative beliefs about ourselves that may be completely erroneous: I'm bad at drawing. I'm too fat. I'm clumsy. I can't dance. Sometimes we self-flagellate, but more often, other people beat us with their criticism, and we aren't psychologically robust enough to deflect those blows. We absorb them into our subconscious like rocks being dropped into the mud. Down, down, down they go until they're submerged. But they hurt like hell if you step on them barefoot. Even when you can't see them on the surface, they're always there, always carrying the potential to inflict pain. Rather than stepping gingerly through our lives, hoping we can mince along without stepping on submerged rocks, let's just get those suckers out of there once and for all.

What horrible criticisms or judgments do you harbor? Do you cling to them and whip them out like shields to keep from doing what you want or being who you want to be? Because that's the really weird part: negative beliefs become protective tools for holding *yourself* back. *I'm tone-deaf, so I can't sing. I'm too dumb to go to college. I'm ugly, so there's no point flirting with that cute neighbor.* Whether other people injected those disparaging ideas into your subconscious, or you put them there yourself, right now, you're the one *choosing* to hang onto them. You're also the one who can choose to purge them.

Activity: Not and Gone

On a piece of paper (not your journal), write down all the cruel, belittling, soul-crushing darts people have flung at you over the course of your life that you decided to believe, as well as all the shortcomings and flaws you've claimed for yourself. Let them flow. When you've finally disgorged all that toxic bilge onto that paper, consider each one slowly, and say it out loud. Feel the accompanying self-loathing…the anger or pain. Channel it onto the paper. Loudly and forcefully, declare, "Not!" and cross it out, with all the drama and flair you can muster.

After you've "notted" them all, crumple up that paper with gusto and loudly, forcefully declare, "Gone!" Burn it in the fireplace, on your barbecue, in an empty metal coffee can, or anywhere that's safe. If burning isn't possible, snip that nasty paper into confetti with some scissors, throwing in a boisterous "Gone!" with each snip. Gather up the confetti and heave it into the trash. Gone! For good!

Another method to "not and gone" those negative beliefs is to gather up some small rocks or stones and take them to a place where you can safely throw them, like an open field or large body of water. Hold up one at a time and speak that negative belief about yourself right into the rock, then force-fully add, "Not!" Then hurl that rock as far and as hard as you can, declaring, "Gone!" There's something about hurling a rock that's intrinsically reward-ing. From this day forward, there shall be no rocks in your subconscious mud to step on!

When you've "notted" and "goned" your erroneous negative beliefs about yourself, whether with fire, scissors, or your pitching arm, do a "weather check." How did that feel? If anger or tears bubble up, let them flow. Tears rinse away pent-up pain and resentment. They're cleansing. Sit with those feelings and your wet cheeks for a bit, particularly if you habitually gird your-self against letting tears flow. A lifetime of bottling up your feelings creates psychological and physical distress. There's a physiological reason that we cry—it's a release of emotion so we can begin healing.

Conversely, you may feel elated after disposing of all that gunk, as if a ton of weight was lifted from your spirit. Indulge in your jubilation! Do your own happy dance right there on the spot. You may start giggling. That's okay! Just as we need to unblock tears and let them flow, we need to release our laughter and joy and let those emotions flow too.

And if you don't feel anything afterwards? That's also okay. This is where you're at right now. What is stuck today may bust loose another time. What-ever emotional reaction you have or don't have, it's valid. There's no way you *should* react or feel other than exactly how you are.

In your journal, write about the feelings you had after your "not and gone" activity. Let them flow right through your pen, without judgment. You can even create a writing prompt from your experience, such as "When I threw that 'I'm too fat' rock, it felt..." or "When I cut up 'You'll never amount to anything,' it was..."

Like tears and laughter, writing can release pent-up feelings. Let both flow freely.

Ongoing Activity: Replacement Therapy

So, now you've purged those negative thoughts, and they're gone forever, right? Oh, mercy, no. They're like cockroaches. You can get rid of them all one day, and before you know it, you spot another one. When you do, stomp it or you'll soon be infested again (with apologies to cockroach lovers).

Whenever you spot a psychological cockroach, write it down immediately and snip that sucker to pieces and burn it, or grab a rock and give it the old "not and gone" treatment.

Additionally, whenever you spot a psychological cockroach, immediately say a statement to yourself that directly contradicts that negative thought, out loud, with all the confidence you can muster. Replace the negative thought with an incompatible positive one. For example, "I have no talent" is contradicted and replaced with "I am talented and creative." "I can't do anything right" is cancelled with "I am competent and capable."

"But I won't believe me," you may wail in protest. Here's the thing: It doesn't matter if you believe you or not. Your brain will hear the words and believe them with repetition. Eventually, it will stop letting those cockroaches through. That's why it's crucial to actually speak your statement, not just think it. Even though it's you that's speaking, your brain still hears the words through your ears, which stimulates your auditory nerves and carries that statement to the part of your brain that interprets language, which isn't the same part that attends to your own internal thoughts. When your brain thinks *and* hears words, it's getting twice the input. More bounce to the ounce, more power to the punch! Your brain needs to receive new messages over and over, in multiple formats, to overwrite old ones.

Another method of canceling negative thoughts is to speak the messages as if addressing yourself: "Morgan, you are talented and creative." Your brain is hardwired to pay attention to your name—even if you're the one saying it. I learned this technique while in cognitive therapy for dealing with my deathly fear of flying. Just *thinking* about flying made my mind freeze in terror and my heart pound as if trying to break free from my rib cage. I'd managed to avoid flying my whole life, until the time came when I needed to fly across the country. Every time a calamitous scenario or searing anxiety bubbled up, I was to say out loud, "Debra, you will have a safe and relaxing flight." Sometimes I said that about a hundred times a day. But it effectively stomped that "cockroach." Did it eliminate my phobia? No, but it diluted it enough that by the day of my flight, I was able to get myself to the airport and onto the plane—whimpering all the way, but by Goddess, I did it.

Activity: Yes, I Am!

Get a pencil and say "I am" before each word in the following group of words. Circle the ones that jump out at you like a "yes!" Don't let any old negative sludge seep in and soil them. It doesn't matter what other people say, or whether or not they'd describe you like that. It only matters what *you* say. If you feel like claiming that word for yourself, do it.

Here we go:

I am ...

Strong. Beautiful. Empathetic. Intelligent. Talented. Elegant. Kind. Powerful. Charismatic. Athletic. Creative. Brave. Innovative. Artistic. Nurturing. Sexy. Mysterious. Musical. Thoughtful. Gentle. Spirited. Cheerful. Considerate. Reliable. Wild. Loyal. Friendly. Warm-hearted. Sympathetic. Brilliant. Clever. Intuitive. Funny. Inventive. Curious. Capable. Wise. Forceful. Generous. Loving. Fearless. Intense. Cute. Sweet. Sassy. Sensitive. Stylish. Perceptive. Expressive. Friendly. Loveable. Striking. Fierce. Patient. Sturdy. Healthy. Passionate. Superfantabulistic.

Okay! If it's circled, it's yours. You've claimed it for yourself. Now, we'll turn these into affirmations. Write each word as a statement on a piece of paper: *I am intelligent.* Fold it up, and place it into a jar, basket, bowl, or drawer. Each morning, or whenever you feel emotionally fragile, hold your hand over your affirmations, breathe, and focus. Pull one out, and read it with authority and conviction: "I am superfantabulistic!" Then, set your intention to *be* that word for the rest of the day. Repeat your affirmation to yourself whenever you need to. Remind yourself that you are, in fact, the most superfantabulistic creature there ever was, and don't accept anything that contradicts that. If other people attempt to pinch your self-esteem, block them with your affirmation. Going forward, other people aren't allowed to participate in your self-esteem anymore.

So mote it be, which is Pagan for "may it be so."

Boundaries and the Magic of No

How do you feel about saying *no*? Say, someone wants you to go to an event that you really don't want to attend, or babysit their kids *again*, or do something you just loathe—can you say no and leave it at that? Do you manage to spit out "no" and then fall all over yourself apologizing, justifying, or explaining? Here's a mantra for erecting healthy psychological boundaries: *No is a complete answer.* Burn that into your brain. Say "no" out loud in various ways, from calm to emphatic to annoyed. Get really comfortable with that humble, powerful little word rolling right off your tongue. If you've been a people pleaser most of your life—someone who trades their sanity or happiness to appease others—you now have your first magical tool: No.

No is no. Make friends with the no. Be one with the no. Be zen with the no. You mastered no at one point in your life. When you were two, you knew all about the no, without anyone teaching you. You knew exactly what you did and did not want and made no compromises about that. Your no meant *no*. Reacquaint yourself with that two-year-old you once were:

No!

No, no, *no*, NO!

"Isn't this all just bratty and childish," you may be thinking.

Well…no.

That's your inner critic stinking up the place again. You've absorbed the erroneous notion that definitively stating your boundaries is bratty. Childish. Bitchy. Shame on you! Go sit in the corner!

No!

No isn't defiance. No is a boundary. Many of our troubles with other people are really about boundaries. We may be surrounded by people with poor psychological boundaries. Like that classic old video game, they are "Space Invaders." They get into your physical and psychological space and burn through your time and energy. When they do, you feel resentful afterwards. Resentment is a red flag. When you feel resentment, someone invaded your space. Again.

Instead of shooting little 8-bit lasers at chunky, clunky aliens on a video screen, shoot some *no*'s at the Space Invaders in your life. This may shock the hell out of them, because they're unaccustomed to you defining and defending your own boundaries and saying no. They may demand an explanation. You aren't obliged to give one. Remember, *no is a complete answer.* However, if you're compelled to explain, here's your simple response: "Because I don't want to."

Hard stop.

"Because I don't want to" is also a complete answer, and requires no apologies, no explanations, no regrets.

Ah, boundaries. They're such a beautiful thing. They protect you from stress, and they also teach the people in your life not to be jerks. You're doing them a favor, really, if you think about it. How will they know they're doing something wrong if you don't smack them on the nose with a rolled-up "no"? Defending your psychological boundaries reinforces to you, and others, that you aren't obliged to give everyone what they want at your own expense.

"No."

It may be the most empowering word you'll ever utter. It's what your own boundaries are made of! It's magic!

The Magic of Yes

No is magic, but so is *yes*. *Yes* dissolves our internal boundaries that barricade us from our own joy. You pulled all that stuff out of your crowded "closet" earlier. Now you've got space for all the things you wanted but never allowed yourself.

When you see a shirt you absolutely love, do you look at the price tag, decide you don't deserve it, and put it back? Do you instead buy the shirt that costs less but you don't like as much, and feel kind of icky and sad about that? It's because you essentially told yourself that you weren't worthy of something. You didn't deserve it. And you internalize that unworthiness. For the price of a shirt! Worse yet, you'll re-experience that low-level unworthiness every time you wear that shirt. It curses you with, "I don't deserve nice things."

Is denying yourself—not because you can't afford something, but because you think you don't deserve it—a pattern? Well, give "I don't deserve it" the old "not and gone" right now. Let's make friends with *yes*:

Yes to a fancy food you've never tried.

Yes to an activity you think is frivolous.

Yes to frolicking in the ocean surf, or rolling down a grassy hillside, or having an ice cream cone for lunch (and make it a double scoop, while you're at it), yes to screaming your ecstasy right out loud as you burst into a reeling, rocking orgasm! Life is all about the yes! Embrace the yes!

1. Think about flowers, just flower-ing in unapologetic "yes-ness." They're great role models. They say, "Yes, yes, YES!" all day long. They don't hide their blossoms, or hold back and only open them a little, or apologize for blossoming—they unfurl those blossoms joyfully. Shamelessly. They soak up the sun and rich nutrients in the soil like greedy little piglets and rejoice for the duration of their beautiful and sadly short little lives. If it works for flowers, it will work for us too. Soak life up shamelessly, little wildflower, because our days in the sun are despairingly short, and not a one should be wasted. Embrace the pleasure of being alive and thoroughly experience and appreciate it, because life will throw all sorts of nastiness at you when you least expect it. Grab all the *yes* you can!

Yes is powerful magic. *Yes* is embracing growth and life. *Yes* is reclaiming your joy. *Yes* is embracing risk. *Yes* says, "Leap!" or "Try it!" It casts out "I shouldn't" and "I can't" and "I don't deserve that," and leaps in feetfirst to see where you land. Yes!

The Time of Your Life

It's time to talk about time. What is time? Ticks on a clock? Pages on a calendar? Billions of years of evolution? The rolling around of the seasons? How about: none of the above. Time is your life. Your life is time. Lifetime.

How we spend our time is crucial because we're literally *spending* the minutes of our life—and we don't know how many we'll get. Our lifetime can run out in fifty years or fifteen minutes. There are no guarantees, beyond the present moment. Time can be snatched away from us at any moment by a variety of things, internal or external. Our hearts can give out, and so could the brakes on our car as we're heading around a turn on a steep cliff. We can't dwell on these things, lest we dissolve into a pool of anxiety. Besides, worrying about what may or may not happen in the future snatches away our present moment. That's called *anxiety*, and anxiety is a time bandit. We can't know what we can't know about how much time we'll get. We'll find out when we find out. So, rather than fretting over when our lifetime may run out, let's focus on the time we have right here and now.

While some folks lock their attention and energy on the unknown and unpredictable future, others latch on to the past and the things that did or didn't happen, dwelling on events that can't be changed. They burn their attention and energy on yesterday, filled with sadness, anger, grief, and resentment. That's called *depression*, and depression is also a time bandit. You can't predict the future and you can't change the past, but sadly, many of us spend far too much time in those places. Meanwhile, the present is tick tick ticking away, seemingly unnoticed. Your life is happening right *now*. The only time you actually have is the current moment.

"Yesterday is a cancelled check, tomorrow is a promissory note. But today is cash in hand. Spend it wisely."

That phrase has been pinned to several people, including Hank Stram, Kay Lyons, and even George Bernard Shaw as recently as 2009, which is quite a trick given that he died in 1950. I first heard it from *Miami Vice* star Philip Michael Thomas, claiming it as his own poetry back in the 1980s. Whoever said it first, it really resonates with me. This moment, right now, is cash in hand. We even describe time like money: we *spend* it. Time is existential currency.

Given the finite but unknown amount of "cash" we'll get, we must spend that precious lifetime wisely, not like drunken sailors. It begins with taking charge of our present moment, to "be here now," as American yogi Ram Dass said back in the seventies. "Be here now" eluded me for most of my life, despite all my best efforts, including meditation and yoga. I explored all kinds of things to access that present-moment experience, and ironically, it was my horse, Penn, who taught me what it means. I was walking Penn out on a grassy hill one day, and he was happily grazing, and my mind started drifting off onto nothing in particular. I felt the sun warming me, the soft breeze in my hair, and birds chirping and chortling. My mind was still, just lazily noticing and feeling things. It slowly occurred to me that Penn and I were having a similar experience: no thoughts, just sensations, peaceful in this quiet moment. There was my epiphany: *Hey, this is it! I'm being here now!* All that time I'd spent struggling to grab it and there I was, doing it without even trying!

Not since Helen Keller signed WATER in her teacher's hand has someone experienced a breakthrough as joyful as that. All I have to do to step into "be here now" mode is only be aware of the same things Penn could be aware of. Or my cats. Or any animal, for that matter. Animals live a purely cash-in-hand existence. They are Zen masters of "be here now." It's not about trying; it's about simply paying attention to the present moment only. *Pay* attention. More money symbology.

How Do You Spend Your Time?

Let's examine how you spend some of your precious lifetime currency. In your journal, make a list of people and activities that absorb a significant amount of your time. Then, go back and for each one, ask yourself one simple question: does it/they make me happy? For all the yes things, great. If the answer is no, can you cross them out? If not, what are the reasons? Money? Fear? Responsibility?

Is there a pattern amongst those you can't cross out? Does a relationship hold you back? Is a job unsatisfying? Are you short on money? Experiencing health issues? Are you plagued with anxiety? Look for patterns to help you identify physical, psychological, and financial obstacles. Mull them over. These things are absorbing a lot of time. Are you getting enough bang for your buck? If not, some correction—real-life crossing out—may be in order. And, yes, that's no easy task. It's one thing to cross something off a list. It's another to cross something out of your life. It may be exhaustingly difficult and may take a lot of time and effort, and sometimes tears—your own or someone else's. It may also take multiple attempts. It took me three tries to get a divorce. In between those tries was a lot of misery, strife, and stress. There's the irony, right? Sometimes the things that are the most painful are the hardest to eliminate, but they make the most room for the greatest joy once they're gone. Sometimes we don't realize how much pain we're in until it stops.

Living in pain isn't mandatory. Our lives are meant to be embraced, not endured. Although some religions insist it is so, in the Pagan world, suffering doesn't get us bonus points for a one-way ticket to heaven. Pagans already have the "free pass" to that ever-after. It doesn't have to be earned with suffering. It's just part of the gig. Suffering is a huge waste of precious "cash."

If you have situations or people that cause pain and suffering, you may be able to cross them off, or you may not. Children come to mind. Dependent elderly parents. We can't just cross them off. Some things are crossable, and some aren't. Try to weed out the ones that are. As for the uncrossables, don't exacerbate your pain by feeling bad about it—that also burns through your "cash." Just own it for what it is and find a way to live with that person or situation *and* carve out time for your own joy. Whether you choose to eliminate your stressors or learn to live with them, build better boundaries to protect your energy, your self-esteem, and your invaluable "cash." The same magical word you use for creating boundaries will also help you hang onto your "cash": no.

The Value of Time

We "purchase" the moments of our life by spending our "cash." Hanging onto our cash is challenging because we exist in the real world with real pressures—jobs, kids, friends, and family—and they've all got their fingers in our "wallet." Beyond all that, some of us just can't seem to get control of our time. How many times have you looked back on your day, or even your week or year, and wondered, *"Where does all my time go?"* You were busy, busy, busy, but it seems like nothing was accomplished. Does time, like money, slip through your fingers?

I've always had an issue with time. It just gets away from me. Sometimes an entire day would roll by, and I'd have nothing valuable to show for that "cash" I'd spent. I knew *why*, though: Squirrel! I'd set out to do something and the Wicked Squirrel of Distraction would flick his bushy tail at me, dart down a side trail, and off I'd go into the weeds right after him.

Continuing with the money metaphor, I needed a time budget. Uh-oh. I already got bored just thinking about columns and lines and numbers. I know me, and me ain't gonna do that for more than a few days, a week tops. As soon as Mr. Bushytail beckoned me, I'd ditch it. I was already resisting, and I hadn't even started. There must be another way to add things up. And it came to me: an abacus. I could track "expenditures" by sliding beads from one side to the other, rather than adding up numbers and figuring out percentages. *That* was doable. So, where does one get an abacus these days? I decided to improvise one—slide things, like pebbles or beads, from one pile to another. Each day, I'd move them into the "done" pile, and start over the next day. I could budget my time without making myself miserable! Win-win!

I took a little field trip to the crafts store, and found a little bag of smooth, flat multicolored glass aquarium beads, about the size of a quarter, and two little brandy snifters to hold them—one for "to do" and one for "done." There were nine colors of beads in the bag (nine is a nice number) so I went with that and assigned an activity to each color:

Clear: Cleaning or organizing, getting rid of clutter. Clean and clear!

Yellow: Exercise and physical activity. Doesn't matter what it is as long as it gets me moving. If that happens to be mopping or mowing, I can nab the clear and yellow in one shot! Winning!

Green: Spending time with nature, getting outside, and experiencing and connecting with the environment.

Blue: Writing. Any amount. Even a paragraph. Anything involving my fingers moving over the keyboard that produces a coherent string of words counts. This bead is super important to me. If it's the only bead I move, I give myself a pass on the others.

Lavender: Relaxation, stretching, yoga, or meditation, massage or acupuncture, anything that reduces my stress level and reconnects me with my body.

Purple: Tarot, divination, ritual, or magic.

Red: Pleasure. Lavish, unapologetic self-indulgence; any special treat I give myself because, dammit, I deserve it!

Black: Sleep. Sleep isn't really an accomplishment, per se, but it's crucial. Insomnia is my nemesis. We've been mortal enemies for my entire life. I make good sleep a priority, because without it, the rest of the day is ruined. If the black bead doesn't move to the "done" glass, nothing else likely will either. Making sleep a priority is the catalyst for moving all the others. Getting good sleep is an insurance policy against wasting time.

White: Wild card. Any valuable, enriching, or nurturing expenditure of time such as reading, gardening, playing the piano, or trying a new recipe can score this bead for me. These are activities I really enjoy but aren't as crucial as the others. The white bead represents electives.

I put the snifters on my kitchen windowsill, where I'd see them every morning, all the beads in one snifter. Each day, when I accomplish a goal, I move the corresponding bead into the "done" snifter and can see how I spent my "cash" that day. If I'm balking at an activity, I'll imagine moving that bead and it entices me to at least "show up" for that activity. If I do the activity *at all*, it counts. Even if it's just for a minute. Funny thing, though, if I can get myself to do something for a minute, I usually manage to do it a little longer. "Showing up" is the hardest part. My beads motivate me to show up.

It's a little game I play with myself. I imagine how satisfying it will feel to see beads in the "done" glass, which helps me combat the Wicked Squirrel of Distraction.

Activity: Let's Get Moving

Okay, your turn. What might you use for your "beads"? You could go to the crafts store too, or use items you already have, like buttons or marbles, or go for a walk and collect some stones and paint them. A couple coats of glittery nail polish is great for making magical-looking stones. You don't have to have snifters; you could repurpose a couple of little jelly jars or bowls. It can be as fancy or as simple as you wish. The only thing that matters is what the tokens mean to you.

Next, assign an activity to each token that represents a valuable expenditure of your "cash." You can use mine or make up your own. What activities are most important to you? What holds the most "cash value" for you? Nutrition? Exercise? Stress reduction? Studying? What activities are worth spending your precious finite lifetime on every day? Let your tokens represent that.

To begin, put all of the tokens in one container, next to the empty one. Each day, challenge yourself to move as many as you can to the "done" pile. At the end of the day, congratulate yourself on your successes. Don't dwell on the "to do" pile, revel in the "done" pile. You don't have to be perfect. You just have to get started.

If the whole day goes haywire, and no tokens are moved, ask yourself why. What derailed or distracted you? Was it an unusual situation or is a pattern developing? Who or what is stealing your time? For each token you didn't move, pinpoint the cause. That will provide insight and ideas for making changes. Life can get chaotic and hectic, and sometimes controlling our time is difficult. However, if *life* is chronically determining how your time is spent—not *you*—this must be evaluated, particularly if you're ending up exhausted, upset, or frustrated. Pull on the threads of your situation. Journal about it, maybe. Figure out what needs to change, or be eliminated, so that you can regain control of your lifetime, your "cash."

For each token you do move—celebrate! Congratulate yourself, enjoy a treat! Wallow in your successes! Put ten times more energy into celebrating your successes than flogging yourself over your failures. In fact, never flog your failures, because they aren't really failures at all. They're only information—information that can create change. Nobody learns to walk without stumbling. Stumbling—not walking—is what teaches you to keep your balance.

Two Requests

Your tokens can represent anything you wish; however, I'm going to lobby for devoting one to Pagan activities or learning. If you don't make that a regular part of your life, time will slip by and you'll fall into old, familiar patterns. Despite your best intentions, you just sorta kinda forget to think about or practice any of this Pagan stuff. And suddenly, it's six months later. That's what happened when someone taught me how to crochet a scarf, and I went like gangbusters. And then—squirrel!—I got distracted and forgot about it. The yarn and needles have sat in a bag ever since. A year passed by, and I didn't do a single stitch. If I'd done just one row per day—a minute's worth of effort—I'd have a finished scarf by now. Maybe two. Maybe more. What "bags of yarn" are lying around *your* house?

Besides the Pagan token, I'm going to lobby for the pleasure token too. When was the last time you indulged yourself? Or did something for pure, shameless pleasure? In American culture, *pleasure* is a dirty word. Blame the Puritans! But in the Pagan world, pleasure is valued and celebrated. Let's revisit more of Doreen Valiente's "The Charge of the Goddess":

"Let my worship be within the heart that rejoiceth, for behold: all acts of love and pleasure are my rituals. And therefore let there be beauty and strength, power and compassion, honour and humility, mirth and reverence within you."[5]

Because indulging in pleasure is such a foreign idea for most of us, it can ironically be the hardest token of all to move into the "done" glass. A Pagan mindset will make it easier: embracing joy, pleasure, and merriment connects us to the Goddess and sets the Pagan path apart from religions that focus upon suffering, guilt, and sacrifice as a way of purchasing favor from their god. Our Pagan Goddess doesn't value suffering and sacrifice. She encourages us to have joyful hearts and celebrate our lives. There's no

---

5. Valiente, "Charge of the Goddess."

self-flagellation in Paganism (other-flagellation, possibly, if you're into that, but only with a safe word).

So, pleasure or pain? The choice is simple for me. How about you?

Spend It Wisely

Getting clear on who you really are and what you really want inspires you to be cost-effective when spending your lifetime. Recognizing who and what siphons away your time, and making corrections, helps you create space to spend your "cash" wisely. Your life is nothing but a span of time, and you only get one shot at spending it. There are no "do-overs." As Oprah Winfrey said, "It ain't no dress rehearsal."

We often hear the last third of life referred to as the "golden years." Such a lie! All of your years are pure gold, every single moment, from your first breath to your last. They're *all* golden years. Live—and spend—your life like the precious gold that it is.

Recommended Reading

Belitz, Charlene, and Meg Lundstrom. *The Power of Flow—Practical Ways to Transform Your Life with Meaningful Coincidence.* New York, NY: Three Rivers Press, 1998.

Schlenger, Sunny. *Organizing for the Spirit—Making the Details of Your Life Meaningful and Manageable.* San Francisco, CA: Jossey-Bass, 2004.

Schlenger, Sunny. *Flow Formula: A Guidebook to Wholeness and Harmony.* Sedona, AZ: Sunny Schlenger, 2014.

CHAPTER 2
Elemental You

Do others describe you the same way you would describe yourself? Are you one person inside but another on the surface—internally and externally incongruent? Who are you really, in your heart of hearts? What would it be like to live your life as the you that *you* know? To be completely congruent?

In this chapter, we'll explore the unique qualities, traits, and abilities that make you *you*—the basic elements of your personality, your innate temperament. We'll also unlock the energies and abilities you've always had available to you, but maybe never used. We'll consider choices you might not have considered before. We'll learn to color with all the crayons in the box, rather than just the "safe" ones.

Let's get to know you even better.

The Elements of Your Temperament

Reading, sewing, hiking, gardening—have you ever wondered *why* you prefer the things you do? It's called *temperament*, which is your personal style of interacting with other people and your environment. Your temperament is innate. You're born with it. If you watch young children, you'll notice that some are fussy, some are busy, and some are content playing alone. Temperament is the *how* of your personality—*how* you respond to the world.

There are four basic temperaments, correlating to the four earthly elements: earth, air, fire, and water. The planet needs all four to exist, and so do you. Take one away, and the whole system collapses. Everyone has all four elements in their temperament; it's just a matter of percentages from person to person. Usually, one element is dominant and is the default for responding to people and situations, and for making choices. Default responses and choices are habits. We become accustomed to dealing with life a certain way. It's not that we can't respond in a different way; we just don't.

Imagine being consciously aware of three more skill sets of abilities and energies, and *choosing* your responses to people and situations, rather than reacting to things by reflex. Getting comfortable with your nondominant elements gives you three-fourths more choices and options in life. It opens up new possibilities and potential. Instead of having only one tool available to you, you'll have the whole toolbox. If you only have a hammer, you'll get really frustrated when you need to saw a board. You need all the tools, all the time.

Activity: What Is Your Core Element?

This activity will help you recognize your dominant element. In the following groups of words, circle or check the set that feels most accurate about you. Not how others might describe you—how *you* describe you, in your heart of hearts. Also, financial or physical limitations are irrelevant. This isn't about ability or aptitude or possibility—only about whether or not you'd *like* that thing or activity. This is a "forced choice" exercise, so even if you feel drawn to more than one group of words, you can only pick one.

1) When I was in high school or college, I was most drawn to:
    A) Student government, business, economics, management, military
    B) Science, math, engineering, computer science, medicine, journalism
    C) P.E., agriculture, skilled trades (carpentry, mechanics, etc.), sports
    D) Art, theater, creative writing, social services, dance

2) When making a tough decision, I will do:
    A) What's right
    B) What makes sense
    C) What works
    D) What feels good

3) I am:
   A) Organized, responsible, punctual, loyal
   B) Innovative, intellectual, curious, educated
   C) Bold, athletic, energetic, sexy
   D) Authentic, creative, compassionate, tender

4) It is most painful for me to be:
   A) Unappreciated or shamed
   B) Disrespected or contradicted
   C) Ridiculed or defeated
   D) Bullied or criticized

5) When I was a child, I was often called a:
   A) Tattletale, teacher's pet, goody two-shoes
   B) Know-it-all, brainiac, nerd
   C) Daredevil, bully, class clown
   D) Crybaby, airhead, chatterbox

6) When I get into disagreements with others, it's usually because:
   A) They aren't doing their fair share, or aren't following procedure
   B) They're not intelligent enough to understand my point
   C) They're a jerk
   D) They're don't understand me

7) When I need to recharge, I like:
   A) Cleaning and organizing my house, gardening, knitting, sewing
   B) Reading, listening to music, watching a documentary, visiting a museum
   C) Going for a hike or motorcycle ride, building things, working on hobbies, running or working out
   D) Writing in a journal, drawing, painting, getting a massage, meditating

8) When frustrated while fixing or assembling something, I'm most likely to:
   A) Read the directions again or call a professional
   B) Figure out my own solution
   C) Swear and smash it to bits
   D) Cry, whine, set the damn thing aside, and live without it

9) I would enjoy being a:
   A) Banker, accountant, stockbroker, police chief, professional organizer, Congress member, CEO of a major company, judge, military general
   B) Astrophysicist, college professor, investigative journalist, researcher, doctor, lawyer, forensics investigator, coroner, scientist, surgeon
   C) Pro football player, astronaut, cowboy, mechanic, race car driver, forest ranger, pilot, carpenter, farmer, horse trainer, rock star
   D) Artist, actor, singer, musician, novelist, poet, graphic designer, interior decorator, social worker, social activist

10) What I really value is:
   A) Loyalty, honor, justice, service to other people, leadership
   B) Intelligence, innovation, education, academic achievement, scholarship
   C) Freedom, excitement, victory, athleticism, fun, bravery
   D) Empathy, compassion, creativity, love, genuineness

11) I can best help people by:
   A) Leading, enforcing rules and procedure, mentoring, teaching
   B) Enlightening, educating, inspiring innovation, exploring, solving problems
   C) Coaching, training, protecting, challenging, pushing the limits
   D) Being compassionate and kind, inspiring, listening, helping

12) If I were a movie star, I'd like to play a:
   A) Real-life hero, historical figure, military leader
   B) Investigator, doctor, detective, scientist
   C) Superhero or supervillain, cop, action or war hero
   D) Romantic lead, savior, femme fatale

13) I respond to heartbreak by:
   A) Becoming physically ill, depressed, blaming myself
   B) Giving the "silent treatment," verbally eviscerating someone, litigating guilt for past transgressions
   C) Lashing out, drinking too much, getting angry, getting even
   D) Crying and moaning, complete emotional collapse, creating drama

14) When I have sex, I like it to be:
   A) Traditional, lights out
   B) Kinky; any position or experiment
   C) Erotic, animalistic, and sometimes rough
   D) Romantic and sensual

15) A fantasy vacation would be:
   A) Luxury cruise
   B) Historical or cultural site
   C) Mountain climbing
   D) A tropical island beach

16) I would most like to win:
   A) Presidential Medal of Freedom
   B) Nobel Prize in Physics
   C) An Olympic Medal
   D) An Academy Award

17) My basic core need is:
   A) Accumulating wealth and respect; serving my community or country
   B) Scholarly achievement and acclaim; solving challenging problems
   C) Being free to do whatever I want; having fun and adventures
   D) Expressing my true self creatively; showing compassion and kindness

18) I am energized by:
   A) Helping others, being appreciated
   B) Making a big breakthrough in my profession
   C) Winning
   D) Creating something beautiful or meaningful

19) My favorite fantasy creatures are:
   A) Angel, leprechaun, fairy godmother
   B) Vulcan, Cthulhu, dire wolf
   C) Dragon, wookie, zombie
   D) Mermaid, unicorn, fairy

20) Some of the people I most admire are:
   A) Stacey Abrams, Martin Luther King, Jr., John McCain, Malala
      Yousafzai, Barack Obama, Ruth Bader Ginsburg, Oprah Winfrey,
      John F. Kennedy, Martha Stewart, Nelson Mandela
   B) Albert Einstein, John Lennon, Neil deGrasse Tyson, Bob Dylan,
      Nikola Tesla, Barbara Walters, Leonardo da Vinci, Friedrich
      Nietzsche, J. R. R. Tolkien, Stephen Hawking
   C) Prince, Clint Eastwood, Serena Williams, Madonna, Dale Earnhardt,
      Michael Jordan, Simone Biles, Tom Brady, Eminem, Superman
   D) Maya Angelou, Greta Thunberg, RuPaul, Elton John, Fred Rogers,
      Walt Disney, Lady Gaga, Frida Kahlo, Billie Eilish

Adding It All Up

Do a total for each letter you circled, all the A's, all the B's, and so on. If you
have a tie, pick the one that feels *most* true about you. You may not have
all of your answers in one category (A, B, C, D) but usually one stands out.
There's no right or best category. They are all equally right. The categories
correspond to the four earthly elements: A is earth, B is air, C is fire, and D is
water. The group with the highest total is your dominant element.

The following descriptions of each element can help you confirm your
results. If the one that resonates with you the most doesn't match your highest total, maybe you chose the answers you thought you *should* pick or lis-
tened to the "committee in your head," or picked the answers your partner,
parents, friends, or coworkers would use to describe you. In that case, go
back and redo the quiz, listening only to your *own* voice.

Earth

A) I am earth—element of grounding and protection. I prefer order and
predictability to chaos and chance, and value procedures and schedules. I
am comfortable taking the lead or following the lead of someone I respect.
I don't have a problem with authority; rules and laws are necessary to make
society function. I like being of service to others. I'm calm, methodical, and
sequential, but also nurturing and maternal/paternal. I like to be respected,
appreciated, and honored for work well-done. I'm particularly good at activities that are quiet, orderly, and manageable, such as cooking, gardening,

and sewing. I don't like to take risks. I prefer a safe, predictable, and neat environment. You can always count on me. Reliability, protectiveness, and honor are my natural strengths.

Air

B) I am air—element of the mind and verbal communication. My mind is my playground, and I'm perpetually curious about how things work. I love finding innovative ways to solve problems and plan strategies. I'm a lifelong learner, and am intrigued by math, science, space, and medicine. My mind is quick, and I can become impatient with those who are slow to understand things. Delving into an interesting and challenging topic is more important to me than cleaning the house or worrying about what I'm wearing. I often retreat into my own inner intellectual world. When frustrated, I become sharp and sarcastic. I use words like weapons, whether spoken or written. I will "split hairs" to win an argument. I have trouble admitting when I'm wrong—because I rarely am. I make decisions with my head rather than my heart.

Fire

C) I am fire—element of movement and courage. I am bold and fearless, unafraid of any challenge or confrontation. I'm athletic, coordinated, and strong. I'm a kinesthetic learner: I learn by doing rather than reading the instructions. I'm naturally skilled with my hands and body, whether using tools or playing drums or guitar (particularly electric). I enjoy attention and the spotlight, and a cheering audience invigorates me. I will risk my own life to save someone else. I love to take risks, even if the possibility of injury or death exists—taking risks exhilarates me and makes life worth living. So does sex. Sitting in an office or at a desk all day is torture. I love the outdoors, adventure, and sports. I'm often the life of the party. Energy, courage, and charisma are my natural strengths.

Water

D) I am water—element of emotions and creativity. I am imaginative, authentic, and unique. My clothing is often quirky or flamboyant and I enjoy the attention it attracts. I love any activity that allows me to express my creative side, whether it's painting, poetry, music, or dance. I love fantasy, whimsy, and play. I care deeply about others' feelings, situations, and struggles, and want to help them. I will rally for their cause, particularly if there's an injustice. I love animals (particularly cats), and feel a spiritual connection to them. I feel my feelings at full saturation; I'm often accused of being overly emotional. I make decisions from the heart rather than the head. I'm a romantic at heart; love is always the answer. Compassion, creativity, and artistic flair are my natural strengths.

When Elements Mix

Knowing your dominant element provides insight about why you feel exhausted, bitter, or shut down after spending time with someone of a different elemental temperament or when doing things that conflict with your own. You can reduce stressful interactions by recognizing another person's elemental temperament and "speaking their language." Earth types are convinced by rules and procedure, tradition, data, and moral judgments about what is right or wrong. They'll usually look to the rules for answers. Air types are persuaded by proof, logic, intellect, and airtight evidence—unless they disagree. They will argue to the death over minutiae. Fire types are impatient with abstract information or having to read anything and believe in physical evidence or prowess. They solve problems by jumping in and taking charge—even if it involves breaking rules. Water types are influenced by emotion and may be resistant to facts that contradict their feelings. They make decisions based upon what *feels* most right to them; heart over head.

When you can recognize another person's dominant element and address them from that same element in yourself, it alleviates frustration, misunderstanding, and friction. If you stubbornly insist on communicating with that person from only your own dominant element, you're setting yourself up for aggravation. Become elementally multilingual, and communicate in that person's elemental style.

Although certain occupations aren't aligned with certain elemental temperaments, that doesn't preclude you from pursuing them. Temperament isn't about *what* you do, it's about *how* you do it. Take teaching, for example. An earth type might have organized lesson plans, a strict grading system, and strict discipline. An air type might focus on research and experimentation. A fire type might encourage kinesthetic learning with hands-on lessons.

A water type might find creative ways to explore a topic, such as art or dance. For most occupations, situations, or hobbies, you can usually find an approach to make it work.

Try Out a New Lane

Traveling in only one elemental lane limits you. Having access to all four gives you more choices. It's like driving on the freeway—you have one lane you prefer, but you change lanes depending upon your needs at the moment or the situation at hand. You can cruise along in your favorite lane for as long as you want, confident that you can hop into another if necessary. Let's scoot into those other lanes and see how they feel.

Activity: Playing with the Elements

The best way to familiarize yourself with the four elements of your temperament is through experience. Let's make it fun! Let's play! When you were a child, you learned through play, and there's no reason you can't now. Playing with your dominant element will be easy. Playing with the other elements is a safe, nonthreatening way to explore them all. Let's go have some fun:

Play with Earth

- **Straighten** out a desk or room or shelf so that it's neat and orderly. Get rid of clutter and dust, and rearrange that space just the way you want. Throw out things that are broken, useless, or make you feel bad, or put them in a box and deal with them later. Notice how nice it feels to have a clean, functional, orderly space.

- **Clean** out a file cabinet of messy papers and sort them out. Throw away or shred papers you no longer need, get your files all in order, and label them. Color-code them if you wish. Maybe even get brand-new file folders. Feel the relaxation of knowing exactly where all your papers are.

- **Plant** something. Maybe a little garden outside, or some seeds in a little pot on the windowsill. Tend to those little living beings as they grow and change. Feel the satisfaction of giving expert, loving, parental care to help them thrive.

- **Volunteer** to lead walks in a nature area, help out at a homeless shelter, or read to children. Find something that speaks to your heart and taps into skills or knowledge you have that could help or teach others, or improve something for your community. Notice how good it feels to help others succeed, learn, or feel better, or to be part of a team working toward a goal.

Play with Air

- **Think** of something you've always been curious about. It could be something as simple as learning about butterflies or as challenging as understanding quantum mechanics. Whether the topic is simple or complicated—dive right in and soak up new knowledge. Enjoy the experience of engaging your brain cells.

- **Solve** a crossword puzzle or do some word games. Play with words. Feel your mind stretching and reaching for answers and clues, and enjoy that "aha!" feeling when you land upon the answers and solutions.

- **Search** for new words. Go on a word hunt. Using a thesaurus or thesaurus app or program, look up simple words like *angry* or *happy* or *talented* or *plain* and find synonyms you never knew before. Write them down. Drop them into a conversation. Learn one new word each day.

- **Learn** a new language. Check out local community college classes, and online or digital resources for learning languages. If learning a new language intimidates you, relax. Learn online or digitally, and you won't have to compete with or compare yourself to anyone. Experience the joy of foreign words readily springing to mind. And remember, music and math are also languages. So is sign language. There are many ways to speak.

- **Write** about a controversial topic in an opinion piece or blog. Take one side and present your case for or against it, supporting it with facts and evidence. Wrap up your position in one final statement that summarizes your case and brings your point home. If you're feeling saucy, post it on social media and engage in the commentary and debate that follows, and only respond with cool-headed facts and evidence.

Play with Fire

- **Move** your body, whether it's dancing or working out at a gym or playing tennis or hiking or swimming or kayaking—anything that gets your body moving and increases your heart rate counts. If you already exercise, try something different. Find a new way to move your body that you enjoy and fires up your own physical heat.
- **Fix** something. Is there something in your house that needs fixing—a leaky pipe? Hole in the wall? Broken light switch? Crack in the cement? Wobbly board in the fence? Make friends with some tools, watch an instructional video, or have someone teach you. Feel the satisfaction of fixing something yourself.
- **Make** or install something. Is there something you've always wanted to learn to do? Make a birdhouse? Pour cement stepping stones? Create a backyard fishpond with a little waterfall? Take on a project. Some home improvement centers even offer free classes, and there are videos available online for just about every home project you could imagine.
- **Build** muscle. Does an area of your body need strengthening or toning? Get some weights or resistance bands, and devote a few minutes each day to working those muscles. Pay attention to how wonderful it feels to engage your muscles and strengthen your body.
- **Indulge** in some really great sex. Let your inner wild animal out of its cage. Fire is the element of raw sexuality. Cast your inhibitions aside and turn up that fire! If you need to roar, ROAR!

Play with Water

- **Create** something. Painting, drawing, sewing, stained glass—the medium doesn't matter as long as you enjoy it. Browse a craft or hobby store and see what attracts you, and don't be dissuaded by fears of not knowing how. Just try! You have nothing to lose but your lack of experience!

- **Play** some music that makes you feel like moving. Sink into your body and let the music move it. Let go and allow your body to sway, to flow, and to stretch however it wants. Enjoy the sensation of free, creative, spontaneous movement.

- **Decorate** something. Hang fairy lights over a window or create a focal point in a room or get (or make) some fun throw pillows. Pick a room and decide how you want it to feel. Whimsical? Relaxing? Energizing? Express your feelings through decor, and luxuriate in the joy and satisfaction of a room that reflects the emotion.

- **Explore** new places or try new foods. Get out and play! Fly a kite or visit an alpaca farm or try on funny hats or make up silly poetry and have readings in your living room. Go outside and skip. When was the last time you skipped? Give it a try. You may start giggling. Follow your curiosity—*Wait, what's down that road? Let's find out!* Be spontaneous, embrace serendipity, and go with the flow and have fun.

- **Still** your mind. Imagine a placid lake, and sink into some quiet, meditative time. Just experience your breathing, in and out… in and out…let go of your thoughts and just drift. Enjoy the serenity of stillness, your feelings sliding through you effortlessly, your thoughts meandering where they will, playing and sparkling like sunlight dancing on a trickling stream.

Your Elements Help You Experience Nature

Engaging all of your elements facilitates immersing yourself in nature and connecting with it. Earth helps you note the changing seasons and phases of the moon. Air prompts you to learn about the things living and growing nearby. Fire emboldens you to venture into new territory and explore this amazing, beautiful planet. Water helps you to feel the energy and power in the ocean surf or appreciate the tiny life force of a duckling paddling in a pond, or gaze up at the nighttime stars and wonder, "What's it all about?"

Being comfortable with all of your elements enriches your life and your experience of both the natural and Pagan worlds. It emboldens you to try new things—you can say yes to more new experiences, ideas, situations, and people that you might have previously shied away from. It gives you all the tools you need for *choosing* how to deal with people and situations, rather than reacting by reflex and falling back on familiar and comfortable behavior and choices.

The Elements Are One Entity

To help you envision all four elements as one entity, imagine a large horizontal clock face—the old-school type with hands—at your waistline, with you in the middle, as if you're wearing a big, flat skirt. Earth is at twelve o'clock, air at three o'clock, fire at six o'clock, and water at 9 o'clock. From your central point, you could easily tip that skirt in the direction of any element you wish, and access the elemental energies associated with it. Whatever elemental skill set you need, you just lean that way and respond to people or situations from there. All four elements are available to you whenever you wish.

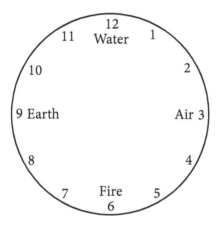

Spirit

So, what about that center spot, where you're balancing that elemental clockface? That elemental spot represents Spirit: divine energy itself (God, the All, the universe—whichever word you prefer). Spirit connects to your own true, genuine self, your divinity. It's crucial that the you Spirit knows is the same you that *you* know. When they aren't, you experience stress, grief, depression, or just feel numb inside. You know something's missing in your life, even if you can't quite put your finger on what it is. You've become incongruent with Spirit, which is the source of most of our dissatisfaction. When you reconnect with your own divine core, you reconnect with Spirit and become congruent with it. With this at your center, everything you need to fully live your life is available around you, in 360 degrees.

Elemental You

Earth, air, fire, water—you have a lot in common with our beautiful planet. Everything is connected, everything is necessary for life, whether it's you or Mother Earth. Embracing your nondominant elements may feel like stretching—stiff and awkward and maybe even painful at first. But if we keep stretching, we start to loosen up and lengthen. Our minds are like our bodies. As we stretch into new thoughts, ideas, and practices, our minds open and loosen to new ideas and fresh insight.

Recommended Reading

Cunningham, Scott. *Earth, Air, Fire & Water—More Techniques of Natural Magic*. Woodbury, MN: Llewellyn Publications, 2005.

Meredith, Jane and Gede Parma. *Elements of Magic—Reclaiming Earth, Air, Fire, Water, Spirit*. Woodbury, MN. Llewellyn Publications, 2020.

Sullivan, Tammy. *Elemental Witch: Fire, Air, Water, Earth—Discover Your Natural Affinity*. Woodbury, MN: Llewellyn Publications, 2006.

CHAPTER 3
Life in a Body

How do you feel about your body? Are you comfortable with it? Or is it a source of pain and shame? If the latter, it's usually because we've absorbed societal judgment on how our bodies "should" look—impossible physical standards that are usually only attained by lucky DNA and/or Photoshop. If our bodies are anything less than perfect, our minds become poisoned against our fascinating, miraculous biological vehicles that carry our souls around during our time on Earth.

Let's reclaim how our bodies "should" look, reconsider our own body image prejudices, and make our own decisions about body image. Let's detach from the judgments of others. We're not obliged to gulp their poison anymore.

Your Busy Body

Our bodies are so efficient at doing what they do, 24/7, whether we're paying attention to them or not, the wonders taking place inside our own skin are easily overlooked. While we're busy working, studying, and playing, our brains and bodies are working together in concert like a complex inner environmental control system. From temperature to circulation to nutrition, your body does everything it needs to do to stay alive—and you don't even have to think about it.

Forget about your exterior for a moment—search around and find out about your organs. The networks of bone and nerves are astounding. Pick one organ and learn what it does. Your lungs, for example. They're downright miraculous. When you inhale, oxygen is taken into your lungs, passes through membranes, is absorbed into red blood cells, and carried through-out your body. The oxygen from each breath reaches every cell in your entire body. Pretty damn amazing. And, you don't even have to remember to breathe—your brain takes care of that. When you eat, your stomach and intestines turn that food into nutrition and energy. Your brain is a miniature universe of wonder, learning, and memory. Your eyes see squiggles (words) on a page, and your brain transforms them into thoughts and pictures. I can type "blue square" and your brain will instantly see one. Talk about magic!

Considering all the things your body does without you even participat-ing, isn't it truly a living miracle? Your body is something to cherish, value, nourish, and protect. It's the only body you'll ever get. So, consider what you put into your miraculous body for nourishment. What you eat and drink isn't just something to make your mouth happy. Everything you ingest is lit-erally going to power all that miraculous stuff taking place inside you. If your snack provides calories but no nourishment, or worse yet, may contribute to illness over time, pick something else. Treat your body like a baby. You wouldn't give a baby a dinner of potato chips, M&Ms, and Pepsi. You'd only give your baby nutritious food. Think about your body as your sweet baby. It needs your tender loving care and good nutrition.

Now, I'm not going to go all religious about food and tell you what to eat and what not to eat. There's an entire diet industry devoted to that. The rea-son I'm poking you a little about nutrition is because if you physically don't feel well, it's much harder to enjoy your life, explore the world, and expe-rience pleasure and new adventures. If your energy is depleted from poor nutrition or you're stiff or in pain because of chronic inflammation, you won't feel like exploring much of anything, let alone the Big Pagan Garden. You should enjoy your body, and I don't mean just sex. I mean the entire spectrum of bodily delights. Pleasure begins with good health.

What we eat is often the source of our unwellness, both physical and psy-chological. Lots of people know if they have food allergies or are lactose or gluten intolerant. You don't have to have an allergy or intolerance for a cer-tain food to steal away your sense of physical well being. You can be sensi-tive to things while not technically allergic or intolerant. For example, blood sugar that's too high or too low can knock us flat, even if we're not diabetic.

The trouble is that we can become accustomed to feeling unwell and begin to interpret unwell as normal.

Activity: Experiment with Food

To learn how certain foods affect you, spend a few days choosing only pure, whole, healthy foods. Old-school exercise guru Jack LaLanne, who lived to a ridiculously vigorous ninety-seven years old, famously said, "If a man made it, don't eat it." In other words, eat only the things that nature made. Approach it like a science experiment—document changes in your journal if you like. How does your body feel? Did you notice changes in your gut or energy level? Are you sleeping better? This isn't about calories; it's about the nutritional value of those calories and how they fuel your body.

The change may be very subtle. I, for example, have noticed that if I indulge in too much sugar (the optimal amount is no more than twenty-five grams per day—that's just *one* yogurt), my joints hurt. Stiff, painful joints are really a bother when you want to get out and explore the natural world, and even when you don't. That doesn't mean I've sworn off chocolate or ice cream. I'm just aware that there will be consequences for my choices. Sometimes I decide it's worth it, most of the time not.

If you want to really hone in on the foods that make you feel unwell or that you might be allergic to, try an elimination diet,[6] which excludes all the usual culprits that cause health issues, such as nuts, eggs, dairy products, gluten, sugar, caffeine, and alcohol. To begin, you stick to foods that rarely cause allergies or sensitivities: noncitrus fruits, vegetables (excluding plants from the nightshade family, such as tomatoes or eggplants), whole grains like oats, rice, or corn (not wheat), meat and fish, healthy fats like coconut, olive, and sesame oil, herbal teas, and spices. Start with just those baseline foods, go a couple days, add in something else, go a few more days and add more, and so on. Think of it like an experiment: what happens in my body if I eat *this*? If you're fretting about all you'll miss out on (and it's only temporary!) make a game of finding delicious recipes for those nonallergen foods, like baked cinnamon apples or shrimp scampi or stir-fry veggies.

---

6. Healthline "How To Do an Elimination Diet and Why," accessed June 12, 2020, https://www.healthline.com/nutrition/elimination-diet.

Size Matters—or Does It?

Sadly, size does matter when it comes to weight and, therefore, health. Some struggle to keep weight on, but the vast majority of Americans struggle to keep it under control. Some give up in frustration, and my friend, I hear you. This has been, and is, my lifelong battle. I've always been a big girl. If I were a horse, I'd be a Budweiser Clydesdale, not a sleek racehorse. So, I strive to be the healthiest Clydesdale I can be, rather than strive for an impossible goal and feel perpetually frustrated and disappointed with my body. Besides, being a Clydesdale isn't so bad. Everyone loves them—they bring the beer.

The sad, simple fact is that too much weight is hard on your organs, particularly your heart and circulatory system. Over time, it's also hard on your joints, especially feet, knees, and hips. An extra load in your tummy creates strain on your back. Excess weight also makes it difficult to move around, particularly during challenging activities like hiking, dancing, or running. Part of loving your body is striving to maintain a healthy body weight. This doesn't mean you need the 4% body fat of a professional athlete. It just means that a little less load to pack around might make it easier to get around. Add movement into your life. You can start small—a few extra steps, skipping a second helping. Maybe just skipping the last bite. Every little bit moves you in the right direction. Every day, just do a little better so you'll feel a little better. All those littles add up.

Some of us have a lifelong battle against extra pounds, but others have an entirely different issue. They're a normal body weight and still think they're too fat. If you're five-foot-seven and a size eight and miserable because you can't starve yourself into a six, something's wrong with this pitcha, sistah. You've swallowed the beauty magazine poison. All beauty magazines operate on one premise: you are imperfect, and we'll show you how to achieve perfection. This is bull crap. Beauty magazine models aren't average people. They're at the extreme end of the beauty bell curve to begin with and have made a career of extreme dieting and exercise. They frequently have plastic surgery, and on top of that, their images are Photoshopped. Those perfect magazine models don't exist in nature. And yet, if we don't look just like them, we feel less than.

Even worse than the overt premise of achievable physical perfection is the underlying message: we must be perfect so we'll be attractive to *someone else*.

We pin our value to a certain size, shape, or number on a scale so we can be validated as a human being based upon what others think about our appearance. However, your body's lifelong task is far more important than looking sexy for someone else. Its job is to stay alive. Reclaim your body for yourself. It belongs to you and you alone. And if someone will only love you if your body looks a certain way, run from that person like your hair's on fire. They're not in love with you. They're in love with your container.

When you think about weight, pry your focus away from ridiculous beauty standards and toward health. Retrain yourself to think about function over appearance. Replace your frustration with how you think your body "should" look with appreciation for what it does.

In Our Own Skin

Being comfortable in our own bodies, just as they are, gets pounded out of us from infancy. Remember infancy? Probably not, but trust me, you had one once, and the last thing you were concerned about was your round little belly or fat, lumpy little thighs, or silly wifty hair. None of that mattered at the beginning of our lives, but most of us didn't get very far before someone informed us that our bodies were unacceptable. Ugly. Disgusting. That's when we learned what shame feels like. Shame is absolutely toxic. It's abuse. It's insidious. Harboring toxic shame erodes your self-esteem.

Can you remember your first experience with body shame? Were you teased or called names for how you look? Too fat, too skinny, too tall, too short, too, too, too. Those toos are brutal. When some schoolyard bully labels you with a nasty nickname for your "too-ness" (I got called "porker" as a child, and that word still pinches), others often chime in, and we can become truly traumatized. Being bullied carves wicked, lifelong scars of toxic shame on our self-esteem. However, when we continue to harbor that toxic shame long after the schoolyard bullies are long gone, *we* are then the ones who perpetuate our own misery. But we are also the ones who can stop doing so.

When Gender Is the Issue

For some people struggling with body issues, it's not shame that's the issue. They don't feel at home in their own bodies because the gender they were born with feels unnatural to them. They struggle with depression, and gender dysphoria, feeling uncomfortable with their own bodies or expected gender roles. Some decide they're unable to live their one and only life as the gender they were born with, and go forward as transgender.

If this is how you feel, like your gender was an error, and maybe gender confirmation surgery is in your future, remember for now that your body is more than genitalia—even though that genitalia and the social expectations that come along with it cause you misery. If you're able to get that surgery, great. But if not or if you're waiting, work around it for now. You can do everything in this chapter—and this book—regardless of gender. Focus on your eyes, your heart, your hands, your bones, your skin, and the amazing functions your body performs.

The majority of our body parts and organs have nothing to do with sexuality. There's still a lot to appreciate, even if you're in gender transition or waiting for surgery. Either way, your body—whether surgically confirmed or not—is doing its best to carry you through this life. Appreciate that much. There's a lot more to love than not. Take solace in knowing that there are options for you to feel okay living in your own body, and take solace in knowing that whether transgender, female, male, or nonbinary—however you choose to live in your body—there's a place for you in our Big Pagan Garden. You'll find a place where it's safe for you to exhale and be comfortable in your own skin.

Gender-Based Body Shame

Gender can be problematic, even if you identify with the gender you were born with (cisgender). Both genders suffer with their own unique issues; however, women are flogged with societal expectations and judgment regarding their bodies from day one. As women, our worth is measured by our waistlines (small), bustlines (big), and perpetual youth (under thirty). Toxic body shame is intrinsic to the experience of being female, and that's why the hair, makeup, and plastic surgery industries exist. Boobs alone are a multi-billion-dollar industry. Unless they're large, firm, and can defy gravity, breasts are always being propped up, flattened down, reduced, or enlarged by having baggies of silicone gel surgically inserted under our chest muscles.

Women are judged by the shape and size of our breasts. Too small and we're called flat. Too large and we're assumed to be promiscuous and receptive to unwanted sexual comments and advances. Men don't have this experience. Strangers don't stare hungrily at their chests and make catcalls. When it comes to breasts, men and women are most definitely not created equal.

Men can walk around freely bare-chested in public. A woman doing the same would be ogled at best and arrested at worst for "public indecency." It is actually illegal in some states in the United States for a woman to go topless in public, and the laws are still ambiguous in several.[7] But not for men. And think about that charge of "indecency." Obscene, offensive, and disgusting, in other words. A woman's naked breasts are legally considered indecent, obscene, offensive, and disgusting in this country. This sinks in, even if on a subconscious level, that parts of our bodies are shameful. If someone yanked our shirt and bra off in public, we'd immediately cover our breasts in horror. We're saturated in toxic shame, simply for being female.

Meanwhile, on the other side of the chromosomal spectrum, men have pressures of their own. What boobs are for women, balding is for men (although a relatively smaller percentage), particularly when it happens early in life. My son's hair began thinning in high school. He was teased mercilessly throughout his adolescence. It was heartbreaking. My son, and all bald men, know what it feels like to get called "baldy" or "chrome dome." The beauty industry knows that a Y chromosome isn't an impenetrable shield against body shame, and that's why the Minoxidil and hair replacement industries are booming. *Ka-ching.* That's what toxic self-loathing sounds like to the beauty industry, regardless of gender. For men, however, the beauty industry is the least of their worries. It's other men who are often the source of their shame and suffering, and usually connected to appearance.

Short or small men, or those with lithe physiques who are built more like dancers than quarterbacks, are bullied and ridiculed by other men because of their appearance. They can be viciously persecuted if they just aren't, or don't want to be, a brawny, muscled, rutting, alpha male, or would rather study theater or art than play football or go hunting.

Men who show fear or vulnerability are harassed and ridiculed for being "sissies" or "pussies," and God forbid they cry. The harassment is a thousand-fold for gay men or those who defy the restrictive cismale gender expectations

---

7. GoTopless.Org, "Topless Laws," accessed February 23, 2021, https://gotopless.org /topless-laws.

for behavior, dress, and appearance, sometimes to the point of physical harm and even death. Why? Because men who defy gendered male norms make those who don't very uncomfortable. It's called toxic masculinity,[8] and men who stray beyond society's gendered expectations can suffer mightily, and they act out aggressively to alleviate their own discomfort. It's the other side to the same coin women deal with: pressure to look, act, or be a certain way to make *other people* comfortable, and shamed if you don't. Pain has no gender.

Aging Issues

Men and women also have very different experience with aging. Unlike men, women aren't allowed to age naturally and normally and just be at home in our own skin and bodies. We're expected to look twenty-five for our entire lives, right up until they close the coffin. Even when we *are* twenty-five, we're pummeled with the notion that there's *still* something wrong with our bodies, which is the cash cow of the beauty industry. They make billions off of female low self-esteem. Want to instantly feel better about yourself? Never look at a beauty magazine again.

Even more insidious: it's not just about clinging to perpetual youth, it's about an obsession with making ourselves attractive to men. The beauty industry would have us believe that this is a woman's only value—to give pleasure to *someone else*. Our bodies aren't for us. They're for them. I don't know about you, but I find that horrifically offensive. Thankfully, some women are pushing back hard against this gender-based abuse. Grammy award-winning singer Billie Eilish tops that list, refusing to succumb to pressure to dress in a way that sexualizes her and focuses attention on her body rather than her talent.[9] Brava, Billie.

Going gray is another unequal aging issue. Men are considered distinguished and sexy when they start going gray. Women are just declared old. Disposable. And most often, invisible. Men start going gray and just shrug.

8. Colleen Clemens, "What We Mean When We Say 'Toxic Masculinity," Teaching Tolerance, last updated December 11, 2017, https://www.tolerance.org/magazine/what-we-mean-when-we-say-toxic-masculinity.

9. Kori Williams, "Billie Eilish Calls Out Sexism During World Tour: Is My Value Based Only on Your Perception?" *Seventeen*, March 10, 2020, https://www.seventeen.com/celebrity/music/a31340779/billie-eilish-body-shaming-world-tour/.

Women race to the hairdresser or the grocery store shelf for hair color when that first silver strand comes sparkling through. And yes, there's hair color for men too, but the vast marketplace for hair color is still women.

I grew up in the "Hate that gray? Wash it away!" era, and the message was clear: gray hair is old and ugly, and if you have it, so are you. And women bought it. Literally. Box after box after box of hair dye. Until only recently, a woman going naturally silver was about as rare as a unicorn.

I used to do the monthly hair-coloring ritual: dye the white roots brown, only to have them reappear in three weeks. Literally, rinse and repeat—for about twenty years. That monthly visit to the hairdresser to camouflage the horizontal skunk stripe on my scalp was too expensive for a cheapacabra like me, and grocery store kits made my hair look like mud. In my fierce fifties, I started wondering why I was bothering with any of this, and fretted over the wisdom of saturating my scalp in toxic chemicals month after month. I embarked on a three-year project to grow out my silver and break the chains of hair-dye bondage. I was, for once, ahead of a trend; more and more women are doing the same and embracing their silver and their age, and, moreover, refusing to be invisible because of it.

If you color your hair because it makes you happy, fine. If being a redhead reflects the fire in your soul, great. But if you're coloring it because you're terrified that gray hair will mean you're old, ugly, undesirable, and disposable, ponder that for a bit. Are you covering up silver or are you covering up shame? Ageism—even when self-inflicted, and maybe particularly so—is another form of toxic body shame. It's also such an insult to your body. Your body is doing its best to keep staying alive, year after year, and you're rewarding it with contempt. Getting older means you're still alive! Isn't that entirely preferable to the alternative? And here's more good news: you'll see lots of women in the Pagan community who don't hate the gray and wash it away. Elders actually have value there.

A Place for Everybody

Body shaming isn't really a thing in the Big Pagan Garden. People aren't ostracized for their size and shape of their bodies, or their appearance or impairments. It doesn't matter if you're a size two or size twenty in the Pagan community. Everyone, even big girls and boys, gets to put on flowy black lace skirts, red leather bodices, and fairy wings, and dance at that party like *every-body's* watching! Everyone gets to play!

Pagans are far more accepting of "differences" than mainstream society. Big or small, fat or thin, young or old, gay, straight, or bi, male, female, non-binary or transgender, you'll find acceptance somewhere within the Pagan community. Oh yes, there are some jerks there too, because after all, Pagans are still people. But overall, you can behave, look, and identify however you want and find a place where you fit in. You aren't alone anymore. You'll find a tribe. You can finally relax and be free of the intense societal pressure to look or dress or be a certain way. You can finally be who you *are*, and not who society demands you should be.

Embracing Our Natural Bodies

It may seem like I got way out into the weeds of health and beauty here, but there's method to my madness. The environment is natural. Organic. How might it feel to be congruent with that? To run wild in a field or forest, unconcerned about putting on makeup or messing up your hair or getting dirty? How would it feel to ditch all the toxic body shame and just *be* in your body?

What would it feel like to connect to the natural world like a kid again, oblivious to your appearance or body shame? Little kids don't put on makeup or fix their hair before running out to play, they just *go*. Adults can relearn how to just *go* too. We need to get out there and get dirty again, with joyful, wild abandon, and run free like the wild things. It's therapeutic. Embrace the dirt. Be one with the dirt. It's where all the fun stuff is.

When you're out vibing with nature, appearance is insignificant. The forest doesn't care about your muffin top, the ocean doesn't think those jeans make your butt look fat, and the river doesn't notice streaks of silver in your hair. Letting go of your toxic body shame and feeling natural and comfortable in your own body, in your own skin, is congruence with nature and the Goddess.

Going Goddess

Way back when, while I was still searching for that *something* I couldn't identify, I'd go to any hippie-dippie earthy alternative festival I could find. They weren't exactly what I was looking for, but I felt like I was trending in the right direction. At a Health and Harmony Festival one day, I found a flyer for a Goddess Retreat at a beautiful, remote oasis in the northern California hills. I knew I *had* to go. I registered as soon as I got home.

On the first day, we goddesses gathered at the retreat center and got acquainted with some icebreakers, then shared a scrumptious organic meal. By the time dinner was over, I knew I'd finally landed on something my spirit was desperately searching for. So far, the experience was a big, ecstatic "Yes!" So, when some of the gals wanted to walk up to the warm mineral pools for a soak, of course I said yes. I gathered up my swimsuit and towel, and we walked along a trail in the woods by moonlight. As we approached the dressing room, I began noticing most everyone was naked, men and women both. My new friends seemed oblivious to this. We went into the dressing room, and they ditched their clothes too and headed to the pool.

Gulp.

What's a forty-something gal with a mommy body and stretch marks and a poochy belly and saggy tits to do? I couldn't back out now without looking like a big, stupid chicken head, so I stuffed my clothes and swimsuit in a cubby, clutched my towel tight against me for dear life, and followed along.

Oh. My. *God.*

What if someone *looks* at me?!

I kept wondering when others would stop and stare, and whisper and point at my obvious grotesqueness. Imagine my shock and surprise when no one did. Nobody cared. It was as if walking right around naked outside was the most normal, natural thing in the world. (Actually, it is—I just didn't know that yet.)

One by one, my fellow goddesses stepped into the large warm pool, where others were leaning back against the sides and relaxing, the bubbling of a nearby waterfall creating a soothing ambient lullaby. I followed along and glided over to an empty place along the wall, trying to seem like someone who appeared to be fitting in. I focused on the water, sparkling with the reflection of soft light from the poolside lanterns, up-lighting the velvety green canopy of fig leaves overhead against the starry night sky.

I pretended to close my eyes but was peering through squinted eyelids to see if others were staring at me in disgust, cueing me that I should flee from this place, leap into my car, and get the hell out of there with as much of my dignity intact as possible. Imagine my surprise when nobody pointed and stared. Nobody laughed or snickered. Nobody turned away, nose wrinkled in revulsion at the sight of my naked midlife body. Holy crap! I was *entirely* less important than I believed! Naked me was a really *big* deal to *me*. To other people, not so much. What a shocker. There in the water, we were just people in our natural bodies, enjoying a warm, wonderful pool under the stars … relaxing, sighing, just being. The horror of being seen naked in public just drifted away, and I finally exhaled—maybe for the first time in my life.

I crossed a threshold that night. I'd gulped the be-attractive-for-men poison long, long ago. I'd abused my body for decades to make it so, and despised it for falling short of those beauty industry standards and for stubbornly insisting on aging. Epiphany! That's all ridiculously self-destructive! From that moment forward, my body wasn't for *them*: it was for *me*. It was *mine*.

By the time our goddess weekend was coming to a close, I felt spiritually, emotionally, and psychologically liberated—in *this* body, at *this* age, at *this* weight, just the way I am. Our final experience together was to gather naked in a big circle, as cheerful, bouncy Indian music played. Each of us took a turn dancing boldly to the center and flinging our arms, hips, heads, and hair however the music moved us, our goddess sisters applauding and cheering. It was release. Pure joy. We were *free*.

Afterwards, we got dressed to go home, and before parting ways, we sat in a circle, and our teacher, esteemed Tantra coach Lokita Carter, quietly looked into our eyes, each of us, one at a time, with her dancing eyes and sunbeam smile, and said with such warmth, love, and conviction, "This was time well spent." That made such an impact on me. It placed value upon how we'd spent our time. This started me thinking about our "lifetime" and how we spend it. A goal for me is to be able to say to myself at the end of every day, "This was time well spent."

This workshop was my spiritual turning point. There was no going back. I'd decide if my body was okay from now on. No one else. I recognized that torturing my body to meet unachievable beauty standards was ludicrous, worse yet, self-abusive. I literally never looked at a beauty or fashion magazine again. They don't peddle beauty. They peddle toxic shame. As for attracting men? Well, I flipped that around: the only man who deserved to have me was the one who appreciated my natural, organic self. If he wasn't interested, then neither was I. I am much more than a shape, an age, and a number on a scale. Only those who recognize that get to play. I came away from that experience completely, confidently, ferociously comfortable in my own skin. It was *my* body now.

Activity: *Spend a Day in Your Own Skin*

How about you? Are you ready to jettison your toxic body shame, and reframe your beliefs about your wonderful, miraculous body? You can create your own little personal goddess retreat.

Set aside a special day all for yourself, where you won't be disturbed. Nobody gets to need you for anything for one whole day. If you can do that at home, fine. If you have to treat yourself to a hotel room to purchase some time for yourself, it'll be a valuable investment. Twenty years from now, you'll remember the experience—not the credit card bill.

On that day, when you get up, no checking Facebook or staring into your cell phone or turning on the TV. Spend the morning with yourself. Savor a cup of coffee or tea, or a healthy smoothie, nestle down with yourself, and let the morning unfold. Check in with your body and just feel it. Turn your attention to each part, noting if you're holding tension there. Breathe into that part and ask it to relax and soften. Drop your shoulders ... relax your jaw ... just breathe.

Treat yourself to a ridiculously wonderful, healthy breakfast—lightly broiled fresh figs on toast, drizzled with honey, or an avocado and Swiss cheese omelet, or a fresh fruit smoothie. Turn your breakfast (and all your meals that day) into an act of love for your body.

Next, some pampering. You don't need fancy, expensive beauty products. In fact, most of those are full of chemicals and perfumes that aren't good for your body anyway. Your skin isn't merely a covering. It's an amazing organ that protects everything inside it, and can absorb nutrients and medications right through its surface and into your bloodstream—including harmful chemicals. My rule of thumb: don't put anything on your skin that you couldn't eat.

All you need to pamper your skin is some olive oil, a half-cup of brown sugar, a small bowl, and some Epsom salt. A nice added touch is a little cloth pouch (a cotton sock will do) containing some fresh or dried soothing herbs or flowers, such as rosemary, chamomile, rose petals, lavender, or any combination thereof.

Pour the brown sugar into the bowl and mix in some olive oil until it has the consistency of paste. As you do, breathe positive intention into it: *My body deserves this.* Set it near the bathtub where you can reach it, and draw a warm bath. Pour in the Epsom salt, asking it to cleanse you of all negative energy, then toss in the pouch of herbs. Epsom salt is actually magnesium sulfate, and when dissolved in water, can be absorbed through your skin. Magnesium sulfate is calming, and can relieve muscle and joint aches and pains. Magically speaking, salt is used to cleanse, purify, and protect. It's a dual-purpose product.

Speak positive, nurturing affirmations into that swirling water as the tub fills. Connect to the element of water—love, calm, compassion—and then slip into that healing water. Relax, close your eyes, soak. While you're soaking, imagine a pink light of protection swirling down from the universe and enveloping you. You are *safe.* Indulge in that feeling of peace and safety. Experience the salt leaching away all negativity from your body and mind.

When you feel like you've relaxed enough, grab that bowl of brown sugar and olive oil, and gently smooth it in loving circles over rough patches of skin—arms, legs, feet, torso. You can use it on your face, but be extra gentle—don't scrub. When your skin feels silky and smooth, time to get up and shower everything off. (A word of caution: Sugar scrub makes the tub slippery, so step carefully and watch your balance.)

When you feel all warm and fresh and clean, get out and dry yourself off. Stand in front of the mirror and look at your body from all angles. No insults or judgments or wrinkled nose. Cancel all negative thoughts immediately by saying out loud, "My body is perfect and wonderful just the way it is." Keep viewing it until you feel peaceful and at home in it. Whatever shape it may be, whatever frailties it may have, this is your one and only body, and it's doing its best to carry you through your life. Pour gratitude toward your body, and dedicate yourself to keeping it healthy.

Next, a body blessing to honor each part of your body and channel divine energy from the universe to it. Still naked, dip a fingertip into your olive oil, and anoint (dab) each of your major body parts with the oil, thanking it for the job it does: "Thank you, foot, for allowing me to walk. Thank you, knee, for bending and allowing me to jump. Thank you, hip, for flexing and moving so I can dance." Keep working your way up your torso, both arms, your neck and head and face. Give yourself a big hug, and tell your whole body, thank you.

With gratitude and appreciation for your body welling up within you, stretch your hands toward the ground and scoop up loving energy from the earth. Pull that energy all the way up over your head, and sprinkle it through your fingers, all over you. Stretch up to the heavens, grasp some divine energy, and pull it down all around you. Bring your hands to your heart, palms together, and let your own love for yourself flow through you. Feel your connection to divinity, to the Goddess herself. Remember your stardust origins, and honor that original spark of life coursing through you; what a divine miracle you are. Rest with that thought and just breathe, and be.

Open your eyes and look at your face. Are your eyes a little brighter? A little smile playing at the corners of your mouth? If not, greet yourself with a big smile! *Hello, me!* Maybe, like the corners of your mouth, your eyes are smiling now too. How does it feel to look in the mirror now? Wrap your arms around your body and give yourself another hug—bigger and warmer this time. Say out loud to your body, "I love you *so* much. I appreciate you *so* much. Thank you for carrying me through this life."

The Rest of the Day

You began this special day with healthy nutrition, enveloping yourself in relaxation, affirmation, self-care, and love, and reconnecting your sacred body with the sacred divine. Keep going for the rest of the day. Drink plenty of water (coffee and tea don't count—only water) and make only healthy, body-loving food choices. Get out of your gray matter and focus on your senses and how your body feels. If you're hungry, eat. If you're tired, nap. Let your body guide you through the day for a change. Immerse yourself in the experience of fully inhabiting your own body, from head to toe. Move, stretch, sway, dance, walk, do yoga—reconnect with the joy of feeling your body move.

If you can, spend some time in just your own skin, preferably outside. In Pagan circles, this is called *skyclad*—wearing nothing but the sky. Soak up the sensation of warm sun warming your skin and air caressing it.

This may trigger an old, old memory. You've likely done this before, many times, when you were a toddler, running free in the yard. Reach back for that joyful, innocent memory and recapture it. Being clad just in bare skin is natural. The trees, birds, and flowers aren't wearing clothing either. Wild things don't wear clothing—go wild today.

If you aren't in a skyclad-safe place, wear a sarong or something loose and flowing, like a kaftan, that allows the air to move freely over your skin. If the weather isn't conducive to going naked or you just aren't "there" yet, go skyclad indoors. You can still enjoy the feeling of air moving over your skin.

When the day is done, as you're nestled in bed, comfy and cozy, think back over your day of fully living in your own body. Tell yourself, "This was time well spent," before you drift off to sleep. May all your dreams be sweet.

So mote it be.

How Sensational

We've spent a lot of time getting comfortable in our own skin. Now, we'll get comfortable with physical sensations. Regardless of size, shape, weight, color, race, or gender, we all have senses: taste, touch, sight, smell, and sound, which allow us to experience the world through our bodies. Focusing on physical sensation—sensuality—cues your brain to "be here now," which reduces stress. Sensuality isn't just about great sex, nor is it restricted to the bedroom. You can be a sensual person all the time by engaging and enjoying your senses.

Activity: Sensing Your Environment

Let's indulge in our senses, one at a time, devoting a day to each. We'll experience them as if we never had before—as if they're brand-new. If one of your senses has lost function, or maybe you never had it, work with what you do have. If you have an impairment, just focus on the others or find a substitute, such as exploring vibrations in place of sound. Appreciate what *does* work in your body. Even with impairments, your body is still an amazing miracle.

Sight: Go outside and soak in everything you can see around you: shapes, colors, patterns, movement, shadows. Peer up into the tree branches and notice how they dance in the breeze. Look up at birds in the trees or stars in the sky as if it's the first time. Take a walk around your neighborhood and really *look* at the houses and yards. How many new things can you spot? Look at everything slowly and thoroughly. Consider all the things you do that require sight, from driving to reading to grocery shopping. Really appreciate your eyes, and your vision. Honor them. Say thank you.

Taste: Oh, this one's easy. Open up your spice cabinet or fridge, and really, really taste your food. Roll it around in your mouth and savor it slowly, like a wine connoisseur, and pick up the different flavor notes in your soup or cup of coffee. Indulge in something you really love, like a truffle or watermelon or fish tacos. It doesn't matter what it is as long as you love it. Try a vegetable or spice you've never tasted before, and try to describe that taste in words. Really appreciate your tongue and taste buds, and your sense of taste. Honor it. Say thank you.

Smell: Go outdoors and don't just breathe—*smell* the air. Are flowers blooming? Grass being mown? Stroll through your yard or neighborhood, and smell the plants and flowers. Visit a spice, tea, or candle shop and let your nose explore. Smell your partner's neck, or your child's ... wouldn't you know their scent anywhere? Our sense of smell is primal and can trigger deep memories and bonds. What are your favorite scent memories? Cookies baking? Morning rain? Old books? Can you recreate them? Really pay attention to all the scents that waft your way, and take a moment to appreciate your sense of smell. Honor it. Say thank you.

Sound: Tap objects together and see what sounds they make. Go outside, close your eyes, and just listen. What sounds do you routinely filter out that you're hearing now? Birds? Airplanes? Children playing? Listen to water trickling or falling, and leaves whispering in the breeze. Enjoy your favorite music or explore new music online—maybe meditation music or ambient sound. What lovely sounds could you bring into your life? Wind chimes? A canary? A backyard waterfall? Really tune in to all the sounds around you, and consider how hearing enhances your life. Take a moment to really appreciate your ears and your hearing. Honor them. Say thank you.

Touch: Touch is the most neglected sense of all. Skin covers the entire surface of your body, and it yearns to be touched. *Skin hunger* is when people aren't getting touched enough, or at all. Infants that aren't being touched or held can fail to thrive, and even die. Touch is that important. Run your fingertips across things around you, and feel their texture. Scratch, rub, and tickle your skin. With your eyes closed, touch your child's or partner's or pet's face. Hold it in your palm, run your fingertips over the planes and curves. Would you recognize that face just through touch? Ask them to do the same to you. It's not just any old hand. You can feel their love though touch. Take note of how things feel when you touch them, and when you are touched. Be thankful for your skin and sense of touch. Honor it. Say thank you.

When you've indulged in all of your senses, reflect upon any new sensual discoveries you made or experiences you had. How can you bring those pleasant sensations into your life? With your senses engaged, don't you feel a little more aware? A little more alive? When you soak into your senses, you're experiencing life like animals do. They aren't mulling and pondering and worrying. They're completely aware of their senses and responding to them.

Respect Your Need to Rest and Recharge

Any time you're stuck in between your ears and your mind's whirling with negative thoughts, stress, and anxiety, you can recenter and ground yourself by focusing on your senses. They are the conduit to reconnecting to your body and reducing stress. Besides being aware of your senses, be aware of your energy. If you're feeling burned-out and exhausted, respect that. Rest, recharge, and be absolutely shameless about setting boundaries with others and carving out time for yourself. Here are some helpful phrases for setting some boundaries to protect the time you need to take care of yourself and your body:

- I am unavailable for the rest of the afternoon.
- I can give you my full attention tomorrow morning.
- Let's make an appointment to discuss this.
- Let's chat about this over lunch next week.

Note that none of these boundary-setting statements began with "I'm sorry." They also did not state a reason. If pressed for one, you can simply say, "Now isn't a good time" or "I have some personal matters to take care of."

Both are true statements and require no further explanation. You don't need to apologize or make justifications when you're taking care of yourself and your body. If the person persists, simply restate your response until they understand.

Your body is just like your cell phone—if your battery is running low, you have to let it charge back up or it will just shut down. Learn to respect your body's signals that it needs to recharge. If you ignore them for too long, your body will stop hinting that it needs rest and recovery, and start demanding. It will shut *you* down. Paying attention to your body's whispers for help is less painful than waiting until it hollers.

It Begins Within

As we care for our bodies, so shall we care for the planet. It's that congruence thing again. Care for what's inside as you would care for what's outside, and vice versa. Care for your own body as you would our mother's body: Earth. What does this have to do with nature and the Big Pagan Garden? Basically, everything.

Remember "The Charge of the Goddess": "What you can't find within, you will never find without."[10] Your body is a reflection of the larger body of the planet. How you treat your body translates to how you'll treat the environment, the planet, and everything that lives on it. If you don't care enough about your own body to take care of it, you'll not likely take care of anything beyond it.

The love you pour into yourself radiates outward to everything else. If your own self-love well is dry, there's nothing to tap into. A full self-love well provides a never-ending flow of kindness, compassion, and wonder. Love is self-regenerating. You'll never run out of it. The more you give away, the more you get. Put love out, more love comes back to you. Be a vessel of two-way love.

Love yourself, love the Earth. Love yourself, love nature. Love yourself, love the universe. It's all connected. It's an exchange. It's a relationship. Love and care for yourself unabashedly—fill yourself up—because it gives you an

10. Valiente, "Charge of the Goddess."

infinite supply to extend to others, to nature, to the Earth, to the Goddess, and to the universe itself.

Recommended Reading

Muryn, Mary. *Spa Magic*. New York, NY: The Berkley Publishing Group, 2002.

Section Two

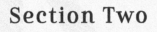

Your Outer Realm

CHAPTER 4
Going Feral

Many people use *wild* and *feral* interchangeably, but they really aren't the same thing. A wild animal has always been wild. Even if its ancestors were once domesticated, it was born wild and has remained so for its entire life. A feral animal is born domesticated and becomes wild, relying on innate, hardwired instincts. Feral cats are a great example. They have little trouble adapting to life without humans. Whether wild or feral, animals instinctively live in harmony with their environments and become part of it.

People have innate wild instincts too, but we rarely need to activate them in the way nature intended, like fleeing from a ferocious, hungry lion. Our instincts will kick in anyway, though. Our sympathetic nervous system triggers our fight-or-flight response with a flood of adrenaline when we're faced with stressful situations, such as a near-miss traffic accident or aggressive people, but when the threat is past, we don't run for our lives and burn off that adrenaline. Consequently, our hearts pound, our eyes dilate, we breathe heavily, and we may shake all over, as if that lion was still at our heels. Living with chronic stress—even in our safe little homes in our safe little communities—triggers that same fight-or-flight mode, bathing our nervous systems in adrenaline over and over. Without a physical outlet for all that adrenaline, all sorts of stress-related conditions can develop, such as anxiety, high blood pressure, headaches, and stomach problems. Sometimes feeling unwell isn't about nutrition. It's about stress.

Fight-or-flight isn't the only instinct hardwired in our DNA; our sex drive, for instance. Nobody has to teach us that. Some of our instincts are obvious, while others are very subtle and easily ignored if we don't become sensitive to them. Let's increase our sensitivity. Let's be like those runaway housecats. Let's go feral.

Go Wild, Child

To find your wild center, dial back to childhood. Sure, there were adults taking care of you in your early years, but you were still essentially wild. If you've ever seen a toddler whip off their diaper and run giggling and shrieking away from their mother in frantic pursuit, you've observed the wild human baby in its natural environment. You *were* one once. And that wild baby is still there inside you.

Let's reconnect to your inner wild child, who made mud pies and climbed trees, and talked to the birds and stuck seeds and sticks into the ground—and they sprouted! That child felt awed listening to the breeze ruffle the leaves in the trees, and kneeled down to intently watch a ladybug crawling over a dandelion, and then blew wishes onto fluffy dandelion seeds, carried off by the wind. Wonder coursed through that child's veins like hemoglobin. Looking up at the moon and stars, that child felt a connection with something infinitely larger and vast. That child could communicate with anything without uttering a word, and maybe with the starry sky and universe itself.

That child is you.

Instincts and Intuition

Whether domesticated, feral, or wild, all animals (including humans) have instincts, and react to them. Instinct is a genetically precoded innate behavior that does not have to be learned.[11] Mother animals don't have to be taught to care for their newborn young. Somehow, they already know how. A cat doesn't need to be taught to chase a mouse, nor does a spider need to be taught how to spin a web. These behaviors are genetically hardwired and are performed even without observing another of their own species performing them. They don't have to learn these behaviors because they already know how—even if they've never exhibited those behaviors before.

People also have intuition—a strong, inexplicable feeling that says, "Turn here," or "Pick that one," or "Don't go in there." Instinct is the first

---

11. Coline Beer, "Instinct/Behavior," Encyclopaedia Britannica, accessed June 15, 2020, https://www.britannica.com/topic/instinct/Freuds-Trieb.

cousin of intuition.[12] People have both instinct and intuition, and neither relies upon learned knowledge—both are innate. However, instinct is reactive and happens without thinking (I see a snake, I run), whereas intuition is a gut feeling (I sense a snake in those weeds, I'll avoid them). When you're out in nature, instinct and intuition are activated. You may be hiking, and suddenly, inexplicably drawn toward a grove of trees—you have no idea why, but you're compelled to go there—and discover a colony of monarch butterflies feeding and fluttering upon the purple flowers of a bushy vine, and you freeze in wonder and delight. It wasn't instinct that brought you there. It was intuition—a gut feeling to go that way. However, if you approach the butterflies, and discover that snake coiled nearby, instinct triggers you to startle and back away, your heart pounding, your blood diverted from your organs to your legs so you can flee. Although instinct and intuition are innate behaviors, in modern domesticated human life, we may not have many opportunities to experience them. Nature can bridge that gap and reconnect you to both. Nature is the key to rediscovering your inner wild child.

Intuition Is Connection
Becoming more aware of your intuition is key to things we'll explore later, like divination and magic, which don't originate in our logical, sequential mind. They come from a place of inner knowing—intuition. You can develop sensitivity to your intuition by paying attention to those gut feelings rather than ignoring or overriding them.

I believe that gusts of intuition are the universe reaching out and trying to guide us or send us information. It's tapping us on the shoulder and saying, "Look at this!" Some Pagans might say that it's their personal pantheon of deities speaking to them via intuition. There's no scientific proof for either of those theories—nor is there for many Pagan practices and beliefs. But remember this common phrase: absence of evidence is not evidence of absence. There was a time when humans didn't know what sound waves were, but they still believed in hearing. There was a time when humans didn't

---

12. Francis P. Cholle, "What Is Intuition, and How Do We Use It?" Psychology Today, last updated August 31, 2011, https://www.psychologytoday.com/us/blog/the-intuitive-compass/201108/what-is-intuition-and-how-do-we-use-it.

know about viruses, but they knew that people got sick. There's far more that we *don't* know about how the universe really works than what we *do*. Besides, you don't really need to understand how something works to make use of it. I have no idea how my cell phone actually works, but I can do all sorts of cool things with it besides just making phone calls, and I don't know a microchip from a potato chip.

When I get the sense that the universe is talking to me, I listen. I don't have scientific evidence that a conscious universe is speaking to me, or even exists. But I know what I feel and I know what cumulative experiences I've had. I'm okay existing with absence of evidence, because my own experience is proof enough for me. I don't need to convince anyone else. Just me. Just like I feel the universe, I feel nature too—the energies, messages, and yearnings and churnings of life all around me. I believe in it. I know it. I can't go up to a chalkboard and present a complicated formula to prove it, but frankly, I don't really care. Algebraic calculations don't speak to me. Nature does. The universe does. The Goddess does.

Rather than analyzing or denying your intuition, acknowledge it, listen to it, and see what happens. The universe speaks in whispers that get drowned out by the chattering cacophony in our minds. To borrow a lovely, comforting phrase from the Bible and transpose it to the universe or Spirit when you're out alone, surrounded by the natural world, imagine it whispering to you, "Be still and know that I am." Because that's the simple truth: It *is*. It just *is*. Look at the life all around you, the living representations of the four elements. Wait for that whisper: "Be still and know that I am." You won't experience it as words. The whisper doesn't go into your ears. It goes directly into your spirit. It feels like "I *know* you." You'll recognize it the moment you hear it.

Nature also speaks in whispers—the buzz of bees and dragonflies in the air, the drip-drop as rain begins to fall, the hush of autumn leaves floating to the ground. Nature's whispers are muffled by chronic physical, psychological, and spiritual racket. Bring the background noise level down—internally and externally—and get comfortable with delicious quiet. Just listen. Much can be said in a whisper.

Activity: Let's Go Wild

Find a comfortable spot to sit or lie down, outside if possible. Close your eyes. Breathe deeply and slowly from the middle of your belly. Focus there and feel yourself becoming still and calm.

Visualize a wild area and imagine that you're a wild thing. What do you see? Smell? Sense? What are you doing? Creeping through the brush? Climbing a tree? Soaring through the air? Are you a predator, alert for a rustling in the bushes? Can you feel the urge to pounce? Or are you a tiny, crawling thing, trundling along a stalk of grass? Let your imagination decide. Be that creature for a while. Be here now with it, only aware of the same things it's aware of.

When you're ready, breathe deeply and calmly, and return to where you started. What wild thing were you? What was it like to feel instincts and act upon natural urges? Write about this visualization in your journal and include why you think you became that particular animal. What insights did that offer?

Take It Outside

In chapter 2, we learned about the four elements of our temperaments, and in chapter 3, spent some time experiencing our senses and our bodies. Now, we'll blend all this together to experience them one at a time. These activities are optimally done outdoors, but for some of us, outdoors means acres upon acres of tall buildings, cement sidewalks, and cars clogging the asphalt streets. You may have to plan a nature getaway for yourself. It doesn't have to be fancy or expensive. It doesn't have to be Hawaii; it can be some sweet little lake near where you live or a day trip to a rural area or visit to a city park. A park has nature in it too, even if humans put it there. The plants don't know or care how they got there, they're just plant-ing away for all they're worth, just as the native ones. They're not fake. Even planted plants are still nature. It's all nature! It's all good!

If visiting a natural setting isn't possible, look for what nature *is* around you. Finding nature in an urban dwelling is tricky but not impossible. You know those pigeons that many city dwellers complain about? Stop thinking of them as rats with wings, and look at their lovely iridescent plumage and listen to their soothing cooing. Allow yourself to be amused by their waddling down the sidewalk like fat old grannies. Take a walk and seek out any sign of nature: a pot of bright pink geraniums on a balcony, a squirrel skittering up a tree, the breeze that caresses your hair, or even the way the sunlight dances on a prism in a window. Be aware of what *is* there. Make spotting nature in your unnatural setting a game—something you do while out walking or riding a bus. See how many natural things you can count in a day.

Outdoors, Indoors

If getting outdoors at all just isn't possible, the natural elements are still all around you, even in a high-rise apartment in the middle of a big city: the pull of Earth's gravity on the floor beneath you, the breeze from an open window, sunlight streaming in, and cool water flowing from the tap.

You can bring the outdoors indoors by bringing home some plants and becoming the goddess of your own little garden. Music and videos can bring nature to you when you can't get out and experience it firsthand. Close your eyes and listen to ambient nature music. Explore nature videos online and stream some nature shows. Animals, plants, fungus—if it exists, there's a nature documentary about it. Let yourself fall in love with our amazing planet and all the life it supports, even if you can't get outside.

If it's impairment that keeps you inside or limits your mobility or movement, improvise. Adjust these activities in accordance with your own abilities. Replace "I can't do this" with "How can I do this my own way?" It's the experience of the element that's important, not the exact method of experiencing.

Activity: Elemental Explorations

You can do the following explorations of the four earthly elements in one day, or one day for each. Before getting started, summon that love you felt for your body. Close your eyes, and imagine yourself as a vessel, filling up with love. What color feels like love to you? Pink for tenderness? Red for passion? Green for the heart chakra? Whatever color says "love" to you, imagine that liquid love filling you right up, from the soles of your feet to the top of your head. Take that feeling of fullness outside and let it flow outwards to everything around you. Channel it through your fingertips, your gaze, your words, or song or dance or stillness. Broadcast love all around you, in 365 degrees. Transmit love to everything you see, even the little beetle crawling along on the ground, the cloud floating in the sky, or a prickly old cactus growing in a flowerpot on the patio. Keep the love flowing as you start exploring and experiencing.

Activity: Connecting to Earth

Kick off your shoes and feel the grass or sand or dirt beneath your feet; close your eyes and soak in the feeling of being 100 percent supported by Mother Earth. Feel her energy. Lie down on the ground and experience the safety from the weight of gravity. She is holding you close. Feel her loving you … send love back. Stay there and luxuriate in that mutual love for as long as you like. Tell her "thank you."

Wander through that environment, and gently stroke the leaves and flowers, brush your hands through the grass, lean against a tree, and send love to that living, growing entity. Feel its energy coming back to you. Observe each plant's desire to thrive, reaching joyfully up for the sun, and unseen to you, sending its roots deep into the earth. Stop and consider the tenacity of plants, thriving wherever they are as best they can, whether it's a lush forest or a crack in the sidewalk. There's a lesson to be learned there: wherever you are, thrive *anyway*.

Scoop up some dirt, enjoying the sensation of it in your hands, and take in its rich, comforting scent. What images does it bring to mind? What memories? Let it fall through your fingers and dig around in it and play with it if you wish. Get dirty! Feral things aren't afraid of dirt!

Take a stick and write love messages to Mother Earth in the dirt. Pick up a rock or stone and examine it closely. It took eons for that little rock to have chipped away from whatever boulder it was once part of and tumble along until it was smooth. You're holding time in your hand.

To connect to earth indoors, get some houseplants. Give them the light, water, and fertilizer they need. Nurture them like your little green babies. Plant some seeds in a little windowsill pot. Enjoy the scent of the potting soil, and how it feels to dig your hands into it. Wait and watch as the tiny sprouts emerge, and leaves unfurl, reaching up for sunlight. Talk to your plants. Feel their energy. Gently stroke their leaves and tell them you'll take care of them.

Give them names if you want. They aren't "just plants," they're little rooted beings that, although unlike you, also contain that first divine spark of life on Earth.

You can also create your own little indoor forest in a terrarium. Place rocks that you pick up while out walking right there into your little mini forest; maybe tiny pebbles that form a little path for your imagination to go wandering. If you want, add little fairy touches, like a tiny toadstool or bridge from the crafts store or the aquarium aisle at the pet store. Pour all your creativity into your terrarium, and imagine you are the Goddess herself, tending this little slice of earth.

Whether connecting to earth outdoors or in, wrap up this experience by standing solidly on the ground, soaking in earth energy from the soles of your feet. Send grateful love to Mother Earth. Put your arms straight down and straighten your fingers and cock your wrists so your palms are parallel with the ground. Close your eyes, and really *feel* that grounding, calming energy as you say, out loud, "Earth." Tell yourself, "I am safe." Feel the love flowing and coursing in both directions.

Activity: Connecting to Air

Close your eyes and slowly, deeply, breathe in. What can you smell? See how many scents you can detect: grass, leaves, blossoms. Smell just the air itself. Is it thin and dry? Thick and humid? Would you know where you are, just by smelling the air?

Slow your breath to relaxed, slow, deep breaths, and feel your heartbeat slowing down, and your body relaxing. Consider the physiological miracle happening inside your body as you breathe: Air goes into your lungs, passes through membranes and oxygenates your blood, which carries energy and nutrients to every single microscopic cell of your body. Your body exchanges that oxygen for carbon dioxide as you exhale, providing a necessary nutrient for plants. They are also breathing! All of life is inhaling and exhaling together, a magnificent symphony of oxygen transfer.

Air is vital. A human can live many days without food or water, but only a matter of minutes without air. Take a moment to really appreciate the air that keeps you alive. Say "thank you."

Play with the air: blow it out your lips, let them flutter together, make funny sounds. Air makes it possible for you to hear those sounds. Your sounds make vibrations, which create sound waves in the air that are carried to your eardrums, which vibrate and activate the inner ear mechanisms that your brain interprets as sound. No air, no eardrum vibration—no sound. Without air, you'd hear nothing at all.

Look up into the sky…are birds, bees, or butterflies soaring effortlessly on the air? Are there big puffy clouds floating in the sky? They actually aren't light and airy at all. A single cumulus cloud can weigh one million pounds, or more![13] The darker the cloud, the heavier it is, and although it looks like one big thing, it's actually millions of microscopic droplets lifted and carried by air. And, when they collectively get too heavy—it rains. Same with airplanes and jets passing by overhead: so heavy, and yet, air—with the assistance of speed—launches them aloft. Observe the clouds or passing airplanes, and even though I just explained it, you'll likely wonder, "How the hell does that even *happen*?" Forget the science, and just enjoy the wonder of witnessing something that big and heavy not only held up by air, but carried or propelled by it.

If you're indoors, air is easy to experience—it's all around you. Open a window and welcome in the fresh air. Turn on a fan and enjoy its cooling breeze or make a simple fan from folded paper and fan yourself. Notice how the air feels as it moves over your skin.

Make some noise—clap your hands or ring a bell or tap on a drum or listen to music. Burn some incense, herbs, or scented candles, or boil some cinnamon sticks in a little saucepan, or bake some cookies, and enjoy the scent as it fills your home. Scent travels on air. Air can also carry scent from essential oils and diffusers, or from fresh flowers or herbs growing in pots. Inhale their scent, and be grateful for air, that allows you to hear, smell, and breathe, and keeps you alive.

Whether connecting to air outdoors or in, wrap up this experience by standing solidly on the ground. Hold your arms up, elbows bent toward the ceiling at your side, your palms just above shoulder height, and open your hands, stretching your fingers wide apart. Feel the air tickle through

13. David Kariuki, "How Much Does a Cloud Weigh," World Atlas, last updated August 16, 2017, https://www.worldatlas.com/articles/how-much-does-a-cloud-weigh.html.

your fingers. Take in a deep, cleansing breath, hold it for a beat, and then let it swoosh out of your lungs. Say out loud, "Air." Tell yourself, "I am alive." Let the love of air flow into you and out from you.

Activity: Connecting to Fire

Stand in the sunshine and enjoy its light and warmth flowing over and around you. Rest in a chair or right there on the ground and experience that spa-like sensation of warmth seeping through your skin and into your muscles, relaxing you. The sun is actually a massive ball of ever-burning gases—fire—and without it, our Earth would be a still, frozen, lifeless ball. The sun provides the light, heat, and energy that allow life on Earth to exist. Remember those thriving plants that were stretching up to the sun? They can convert sunlight into energy: photosynthesis. If million-pound clouds floating in the sky blew your mind, ponder turning light into energy! Again, "How the hell does that even *happen*?" That big ball of fire out in space, that you take for granted every day, provides and sustains life here on our little blue planet. Send the sun some big love and tell it "Thank you."

You can also experience fire by creating your own. Find a safe place to start a fire outdoors, like a hibachi, fire pit, or Mexican *chiminea*. Light it and feel the wonder of connecting a spark to tinder and watching it rise into flames. Humankind has been mesmerized by this crackling miracle for eons. Sitting by a fire is one of the most ancient of collective human experiences. That warmth, comfort, and safety we feel by the fireplace or campfire is a cellular memory. It's encoded in our DNA. Doesn't the fireside feel like cozy love? Don't you feel so very safe? Luxuriate in fire's warmth, calmed by its crackling, hissing, and popping. Feel its protection and power. Send it some warm, grateful love.

Fire is easily experienced indoors with a candle. There's a sense of wonder and power when you ignite it—your inner wild child just loves striking matches. Gaze upon the flickering light and dancing flame. Relax your eyes while peering into the flame. Hold your hands at various distances and see how far away you can sense the flame's heat. Turn out all the lights and notice how much light the flame gives off. Look how the flickering flame dances. Get up and dance too; become that dancing flame. Let your body's own fire take over. Feel your body heat rising. You are literally *burning* calories when you move your body. Yes, you *are* fire! Feel the heat!

If you have a fireplace, sit beside a crackling fire, enjoying some music or even golden silence. Let fire's warmth soften your body and luxuriate in how relaxing and safe that feels. If you have a partner, snuggle up and feel the warmth of their body heat. Simple body contact is therapy. Or foreplay. If things start getting hot, well, go with it! Sexual energy is big fire energy. You can scream "Thank you!" if you want.

Whether connecting to fire outdoors or in, wrap up this experience by standing solidly on the ground. Hold your arms up in front of your body, elbows bent toward the ceiling at right angles up near your shoulders, and clench your fists tight, as well as your whole body, tightening every muscle as if you are one big, powerful fist, and let that power energize you. Say out loud, "Fire." Tell yourself, "I am powerful."

Activity: *Connecting to Water*

Find a body of water, big or small, and spend some time at its shores. If the water is safe, wander in barefoot or trail your hand in the flow, and feel the current of the brook or stream, or the push and pull of lapping waves. A natural body of water is optimal, but a swimming pool will suffice, even if it's the little blowup kind for children. Splash your feet around and up, and catch the droplets in your hands, and then splash your hands in the water. Play with it. Have fun! Slap it, splash it, sploosh it between your fingers. If you feel like giggling with joy, don't hold back. Water is the element of playfulness.

If you are a proficient swimmer and the water is safe, wade in further and let your body relax backward. Float on your back and experience water softly, firmly supporting you, and carrying you along—so soft, yet so strong and safe. If floating isn't your strong point, use a raft or floating device, or have someone gently support you under your neck and thighs, so you can experience the relaxing support of water. When you get out, don't immediately grab the towel. Stop and experience the cooling sensation of water evaporating from your skin. Imagine your tensions or concerns evaporating along with it.

Rain is a wonderful experience of water. Go out into the rain and let it fall on your tongue and face. Take a walk with an umbrella and listen to the sounds water makes as it falls from the sky. Splash and stomp through puddles. Observe the shimmering green of plants as they soak up life-giving water.

Experiencing water indoors is easy. Just take a bath. Fill the tub with warm water, step in, and relax. Close your eyes and feel the water soaking away tension, worries, aches, and pains. Trail your fingers through the water, feel how smooth and slippery your skin is; breathe in the moist air. Water cleanses you physically, emotionally, and spiritually. So soothing. So loving. Soak up that comforting water love and send some back gratefully. Say, "Thank you."

In your bath, experiment with sound carried by water. Sink your ears below the surface and tap on the tub or scratch it with a fingernail. Notice how loud the sound is. Water is denser than air and carries sound vibrations more quickly and more loudly. (That's why you shouldn't tap on the glass of an aquarium. It makes a racket for the fish.)

If you only have a shower, that's okay. Step in and let the warm water flow over you, washing away any stresses, strains, or negative thoughts or feelings. Let water cleanse you, physically and spiritually.

Just as you can create a terrarium to bring earth into your home, you can bring water indoors by setting up an aquarium and creating your own little ocean. Nurture your fish just like your houseplants, giving them everything they need to thrive. Spend some time with the aquarium. Gaze into it. It's a powerful relaxation tool. Gazing at fish in an aquarium actually lowers blood pressure.

Make yourself a cup of tea and enjoy the lovely, scented steam, and the warmth sliding down your throat and into your tummy. Drink a big glass of fresh water and think about it hydrating all your cells and refreshing your digestive system. Sixty percent of your body *is* water. It's literally flowing throughout your body right now.

Whether connecting to water outdoors or in, wrap up this experience by standing solidly on the ground. Cradle your hands against your tummy in front of you, one in the other as if holding a baby bird, and release your stress and worries, allowing them to evaporate. Relax your shoulders and neck, letting your head drop gently if you wish. Welcome feelings of calm and serenity to flow right into you. Send some grateful love to water. Say out loud, "Water." Tell yourself, "I am peaceful."

Activity: Elemental Ritual

After experiencing each element, the activities ended in a specific posture that embodies the energy of that element. Now, we'll combine them into one smooth movement, creating a ritual for starting your day, wrapping up your day, or anything that happens in between. This ritual reconnects you to elements and can help you feel calm and grounded anytime you wish. I like doing this ritual in the morning before leaving for work to reinforce me spiritually—I have all the elements and their energies available to me, all day long. Should the day start getting pissy with me, or if I'm feeling off-balance or disconnected from myself, or if I'm feeling just plain old frazzled by life, I can do this ritual anytime I want, or close my eyes and visualize it.

In chapter 2, we imagined the elements on a horizontal clock face, wearing it like a big, flat skirt, with ourselves in the middle. With that image in mind, we'll place the elements on their corresponding directions: earth (twelve o'clock) is north; air (three o'clock) is east; fire (six o'clock) is south; water (nine o'clock) is west. In Pagan rituals, facing in the direction corresponding to each element is traditional for inviting that element and its energies to be present and participate.

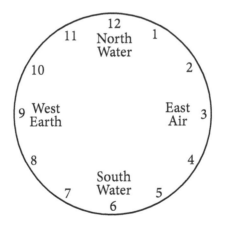

All you need for this ritual is yourself. Find a clear space in your home, room, or yard where you can move around a bit and won't be disturbed. Facing north, point your index finger at the ground and imagine it emitting a stream of blue light onto the ground a couple feet away from you. Draw a clockwise (deosil) circle of blue light around you, ending up facing north again.

This creates a safe and sacred space, which is begins a ritual. (There are magical tools for casting a circle, but your index finger works too.) After you've drawn the circle, visualize a safe, blue circle and a blue protective dome rising up from it and over you. Say, "Only positive energy and healing may enter," or anything that inspires safety and protection. Or say nothing at all and just be aware of the experience.

Face north, breathe calmly and deeply, and relax your mind. Do the earth posture: arms straight down at your side, palms parallel to the ground. Say, "Earth." When you feel grounded, in control, and safe (like earth), keeping your arms in that position, make a quarter turn to the right to the east, breathe calmly and deeply, and relax your mind.

Sweep your arms from the earth posture directly into the air posture: arms bent at your side toward the ceiling, fingers spread wide. Say, "Air." When you feel light, refreshed, and invigorated (like air), keeping your hands in that position, make a quarter turn to the right to the south, breathe calmly and deeply, and relax your mind.

Sweep your arms from the air posture directly into the fire posture: arms bent at right angles in front of you toward the ceiling, fists clenched. Say "Fire." When you feel strong, courageous, and ready for anything (like fire), keeping your hands in that position, make a quarter turn to the right, to the west, breathe calmly and deeply, and relax your mind.

Sweep your arms from the fire posture directly into the water posture: arms bent and relaxed at your waist in front of you, right against your body, one hand gently cradling the other, palms up. Say, "Water." When you feel calm, serene, and relaxed, make a quarter turn and return to facing north.

Swing your arms way up over your head, fingertips touching. Grasp all the divine light from the universe, and sweep it down over your body, all the way to your feet. Stretch your fingers down to Mother Earth and grasp her loving energy, pulling it up over your body and over your head, touching your hands, palms together. Pull your hands right down in front of you, palms together, in front of your face, then your neck, then your chest, stopping at heart level—the heart chakra. Close your eyes, breathing calmly and deeply. Let divine energy fill you, and Spirit connect directly with you. Let the divine love of the universe swirl around you, and through you, and in you.

When it feels like enough, open your eyes, face north, and point your finger at that circle of blue light, and imagine the light returning inside your finger. Moving counterclockwise (widdershins) to the west, continue pulling that blue light back into your finger, and complete the circle through the remaining directions. You are now fully elementally and spiritually charged.

You can do this ritual anytime you feel the need, anywhere you want. It requires no tools, and it's always with you, no matter where you go, no matter who you're with. You can even do a quickie elemental boost by performing each of the postures as one fluid movement. If you can't escape to a quiet, private place, you can recreate the entire ritual mentally. Just close your eyes and retrace it, step by step, as a meditation, remembering how your body felt as it moved. Draw the blue circle of light around you in your mind. Recall the elements, and their strengths and qualities, and pull them right into your own spirit, right there. Brighten them, feel them, allow them to assist you in whatever you're dealing with. As for others around you, if you don't wish to share what you're doing, simply tell them you're resting your eyes for a moment. If you need that protective blue bubble to stay with you, just decide that it's portable and imagine it moving around with you all day, shielding you from negative energy.

The elemental energies are available to you all the time, whenever you need them. The universe, Spirit, the Goddess—they are always with you, and within you. You are never alone. Let that feeling of un-aloneness remind you of that.

You, the Elements, the Earth

There isn't a "me in here" and "world out there." The awareness of an ever-present, living connection to the natural world around you, and within you, may be blossoming. This constant sensitivity to your environment and all the elements—inside and out—enlivens your intuition, your instincts, and your feral self. You belong with the wild things. Take notice when an element shows its energy to you, or expresses itself through you. Acknowledge that element when it speaks to you. Embrace it. Thank it, and the universe and the Goddess too.

Recommended Reading

Crosson, Monica. *Wild Magical Soul—Untame Your Spirit & Connect to Nature's Wisdom*. Woodbury, MN: Llewellyn Publications, 2020.

Dulsky, Danielle. *The Holy Wild: A Heathen Bible for the Untamed Woman*. Novato, CA: New World Library, 2018.

Louv, Richard. *Last Child in the Woods—Saving Our Children from Nature-Deficit Disorder*. Chapel Hill, NC: Algonquin Books of Chapel Hill, 2008.

CHAPTER 5
Bioiongruence, Cosmocongruence

We first talked about internal congruence—the you that you know matching the you that others now, and also the you that you know matching the you that Spirit knows. Now we'll take congruence beyond ourselves and expand it outward to nature: biocongruence. Then, we'll expand even further, beyond this planet, out to the entire cosmos: cosmocongruence.

A familiar Pagan saying is "as above, so below." It implies spiritual and physical congruence, and is sometimes symbolized as the Tree of Life, with its branches spreading above, in the air, and its roots spreading equally below, in the earth. Borrowing from that, we'll set out to become "as within, so without" with the natural world and detect the spiritual energy flowing between ourselves and nature. Moving outward the cosmos, we'll set off to become "as below, so above" with the cosmos, and detect the spiritual energy flowing between us and the heavens.

Bioiongruence

Bioiongruence is a two-way spiritual relationship with the natural world. As comfortable as we are in our own skin, so can we be in nature. On a spiritual level, they shouldn't feel all that different. You aren't visiting nature, you're part of it, and it's part of you. Nature isn't the "other." We aren't "in here" while it is "out there." It's not a place you go visit. Nature is you, and vice versa. Humans have a bad habit of "us and them" compartmentalization—everything in neat and tidy boxes. Nature is some foreign country we travel to, explore, and then go home—not recognizing that, evolutionarily speaking, we lived in nature much, much longer than not. Our brains and our senses evolved in the natural world. We still have the physiological equipment to be intimately connected to nature, we just don't use it.

Have you ever hiked a trail or walked beside a river or beach for the first time and felt as if you belonged there—even though you'd never been there before? That sense of belonging is literally in your DNA. You *do* belong there, not trapped in a traffic jam or staring at a computer screen or standing in line at the DMV or having your ears blasted by howling leaf blowers.

Our physiology and brains in their current form developed tens of thousands of years ago, and haven't really changed much. But our world—our environment—has changed drastically. Every day, we're assaulting our brains and bodies with unnatural images, inputs, situations, and stressors, and experiencing them through senses and physiology that didn't evolve for that purpose. Our senses evolved to connect to and interpret the natural world around us, perceive patterns and changes, and stay alive by seeing, hearing, and smelling the environment—and they evolved in a time devoid of pollution or man-made chemicals or noise, in surroundings so quiet that our sensitive hearing could hear a twig snap under a predator's paw in time to hide, flee, or fight. Constant noise is a chronic source of stress. When you get out in the hush and quiet of nature, and relax instinctively, sensing that you belong there, it's your own paleolithic DNA heaving a sigh of relief: *Finally, something familiar! Something I understand!*

Your own ancient ancestors were absorbed in their environments. They were a part of it, and it them. There was no separation. They were truly wild beings, completely biocongruent. They paid careful attention to the plants and animals, stars and seasons, because it was key to their survival. This biocongruence is in your own cellular memory, bloodline, and DNA, but civilization mutes it. But it's still there. Even if you've lived all your life in a big noisy city, you don't have to be taught to relax at the sound of ocean surf or the chirring of crickets on a warm summer night or the warmth of a crackling campfire. The cellular memory of these things communicates to you that all is peaceful. All is safe. There are no predators here. You can be calm, and even doze. The memory of your own genetic intimacy with nature doesn't return to you in words—it comes through sensing and feeling; remembering something that didn't seem to actually *begin* within your own lifetime. It's much older than that.

Reconnecting with nature is a reconnection with biocongruency, with your ancient ancestors, who were intimately immersed in their surroundings, and aware of the ebb and flow of natural energy and all its vibrations. Regardless of your race, culture, nationality, or religion, your ancient ancestors predate these categories, and all of them were biocongruent. They lived in harmony with nature, observing it, studying it, and over time, making interpretations and predictions about how it all worked.

Your evolutionary ancestors understood animal behavior and vocalizations, and paid attention to them. They knew which plants were edible and which weren't, and how to consume or use them. Being in sync with nature—biocongruence—was crucial, as was their awareness of the changing seasons, weather, and the phases of the moon. Their survival depended upon it. Those prehistoric biocongruent survival skills advanced the human species. You exist now thanks to the survival skills of your ancient ancestors, and those skills depended upon biocongruence, which is amongst the survival skills that allowed you to appear far, far down the family tree. It's literally in your DNA to be biocongruent with all the living things in your environment, and the environment itself.

Communicating with Animals

When you were very young, did you talk to animals? Birds? Fish? Did it feel more like a conversation than a monologue? You were probably exchanging grand and riotous stories, discussing the matters of the world, until some adult informed you that animals are just dumb beasts that can't understand anything. Forget all that nonsense and go clean your room. Thankfully, I stubbornly ignored those who were too dull to recognize when animals were talking to them. Animals always understood me entirely better than people, and often still do. Animals never lie, betray, deceive, or disappoint. They're always genuine, always true. What you see is what you get. When they like what you're doing, they'll tell you, and when they don't, they'll make it very clear.

Turns out, stubborn little me was onto something. Animals do communicate and understand—they just don't do so in words, let alone English.

That's hard for Chatty-Kathy humans to grasp. We hardly ever stop talking long enough to hear what animals are saying.

Many domestic animals recognize certain words, but they don't understand them in the abstract, as people do. Horses, for example, don't have a verbal left brain and spatial right brain like humans. Both sides of their brain are spatial, and they recognize particular words, but don't comprehend them as abstract verbal concepts. They learn the sound of a word, like a whistle or bell ringing, and associate that word-sound with a particular thing or action. They pay no more attention to our incessant yacking than humans do of birds chirping in the trees. But if they hear, "Treat," their ears perk up and their big, velvety noses stretch toward us.

Horses don't have words, but they communicate all sorts of things through body language, facial expression, and the movement of energy, or *chi*, and they definitely have opinions, preferences, and insights. But if you insist they communicate in English, you'll never hear what they have to say. You have to hear their "words" with your nonverbal ears. Same with all animals. We've heard about our third eye, which perceives through intuition. When interacting with animals, we need a third ear, which hears through intuition.

Activity: Congruence with Animals

We can have a much richer relationship with animals if we stop being so species-centric and start communicating with them in their own language. Try this with your pet: Sit down and have a "conversation" with it, without words. Make eye contact. Touch. Scratch. Stroke. Pat. Exchange nose breaths. Slowly run your palm over its body, a couple inches above the fur, and play with the distance until you can feel the animal's energy field. Just like you can feel when something is too close to you, so can animals. Watch your pet. Does it react to your hand passing through its energy field? Look at and touch that pet as if you'd never experienced a creature such as this before. Absorb its energy, observe little nuances of behavior.

Hold your pet's face in your hands and mentally transmit love. "Tell" it how you will protect it and take care of it for the rest of its life, that it is safe. It is loved. See if you detect a change in the animal's breathing, facial expression, posture, behavior, vocalizations, or dilation of its eyes. Was the message received? Was one sent back? Do this whenever you get a chance.

You'll deepen your relationship with that pet and become sensitive to the two-way flow of energy between you.

If you have animals nearby, out in a pasture or field, observe them for awhile. Notice their subtle communications and their not-so-subtle ones. What happens if you mirror their behavior and posture? Are they taking more notice of you? Make eye contact. What happens? Does the animal step toward you? Retreat? What messages are you picking up from that animal? What happens if you take a few steps back, or hold out your hand? Should that animal walk closer to investigate you further, what do you sense from it?

Just because animals can't speak in words doesn't make them less than. They are nonverbal creatures of equal spiritual value. They love, they fear, they grieve—just like us. They don't have a verbal center in their brains, but we humans have a spatial half. We can communicate with them from there. And, from time to time, we should listen for a change.

Communicating with Plants

Just as you can communicate nonverbally with animals, so can you with plants. They are clearly nonverbal beings—in fact, not even really cerebral beings, at least not in the way that we understand cerebral. But they do have consciousness, and they do communicate—just not in a way that most humans bother to detect. Just as with animals, if we insist on communicating by speaking English, it's not going to be a very rewarding conversation. It's a lot easier if we adapt to the plant's form of communication than vice versa. And plants have plenty to say.

Consider a grove of trees. It's not just a big green blob—it's a community of living individuals, quietly sharing information. It may sound very quiet in the forest, but there's a cacophony of information being transmitted back and forth, underground and undetected by human ears or awareness. Plants communicate via networks of underground fungi, which send out lacework patterns of threads called *mycelium*, stretching out underground and touching tree roots. Through mycelium, trees exchange information, and can even detect when other trees are stressed and share nutrients with them. Trees can also detect their own kin, and provide them extra protection and nutrients, and can warn other trees if competition from new plants indicates a need for more seedlings. They can even alert other plants about changes in the environment, such as a destructive insect invasion, or logging from humans. And yes, there really is such a thing as a "mother tree" within a grove.

Suzanne Simard, ecologist and researcher at the University of British Columbia, has devoted herself to studying the underground communication of trees, and revealed her discoveries in a 2016 interview with *Yale Environment 360*. In the interview, Simard said, "A forest is a cooperative system. To me, using the language of 'communication' made more sense because we were looking at not just resource transfers, but things like defense signaling and kin recognition signaling. We as human beings can relate to this better. If we can relate to it, then we're going to care about it more. If we care about it more, then we're going to do a better job of stewarding our landscapes."[14]

A hundred years ago, we knew mycelium existed, but didn't know it behaved like a network of telephone lines between trees—much like we don't know what dark energy or dark matter in the cosmos are, only that they're there. A hundred years from now, the next Suzanne Simard may be explaining how humans can communicate with the cosmos and vice versa via an unseen network of dark energy—spiritual mycelium—verifying that yes, magic does indeed exist. The wonders of our own Earth never cease, and they're dwarfed by the yet undiscovered wonders of the cosmos.

But, back to the forest.

I once attended a talk on plant spirituality, given by the late Pagan author and scholar Raven Grimassi, who asserted that plants have a collective experience and memory of being damaged by humans. Plants remember! He recommended that when approaching a plant, gently touch a leaf or branch, or place a palm on its trunk, and reassure it that you aren't there to harm it. I often do this while walking through my yard, greeting each tree and bush, congratulating it on doing a really fine job of "tree-ing," and thank it for the energy, shade, and/or food it provides. I continually nurture a relationship with my plants. My yard feels spiritually alive; I can feel the spirits of those trees and plants. They *know* me, and I know them.

Beyond my yard, I frequently greet trees and plants when out hiking or in the forest, reassure them that I come in peace, and transmit love—just like

---

14. Diana Toomey, "Exploring How and Why Trees 'Talk' to Each Other," *Yale Environment 360*, last updated September 1, 2016, https://e360.yale.edu/features/exploring_how_and_ why_trees_talk_to_each_other.

with a pet. Yes, I'm a tree hugger from way back. There's nothing like wrapping your arms around a sturdy tree, leaning in, and feeling its life force connecting you to the energies of Earth. It's very subtle, but it's there. Listen with your spirit, not your ears.

Activity: Congruence with Plants

Spend some time with a plant, indoors or out. Pick one you're attracted to, and gently stroke its leaf; hold it lightly. Can you feel its energy? It's not the same vibration as an animal at all. Animals have a kaleidoscope of emotions, from joyful to enraged, and everything in between. Plants are more binary. They're either thriving or they're not. Just look at a bush or plant or tree, stretching up to the sky, as if joyfully exclaiming, "Yay, I'm *alive!*" An unhealthy plant emits the opposite energy: "Ugh, I'm dying." It almost seems to moan in distress. What is that plant you're touching saying? "Yay" or "Ugh"? Does it need something? Can you provide it? Watch it respond as you do. I can "hear" my plants and trees say "thank you" when I water them, and grumble like reluctant children getting their faces washed when I repot them. Plants are not huge fans of change. Once they take root somewhere, even if it's a fracture in a boulder, that's where they like to stay.

As you go about your daily life, greet the plants and trees you see. Acknowledge them as individuals. Wish them a safe and carefree day. Pay attention to how it feels. Write about any revelations or insights in your journal.

What's Really Growing Out There?

Those scrappy bushes you pass by on the roadside or while out hiking may be more than just scenery. They may contain powerful medicine or healing properties. I once went on a local nature hike with herbal medicine expert Kami McBride and learned that this area is packed with nutritional and medicinal vegetation, like Yerba Santa, from which a powerful decongestant syrup can be made—medicine discovered by the local indigenous people.

Also growing wild nearby is St. John's Wort, from which a tincture can be made to relieve anxiety and depression. Kami also taught us that the fresh green oats from plain old wild oat grass, which spreads over every hill and field around here, can be made into a soothing and nourishing tea. The elderberry bushes that spring up all over the place are loaded with dark, purple berries packed with antioxidants and anti-inflammatory properties, can be made into tea, jam, or even wine, and can even alleviate cold and flu symptoms.[15]

Discovering that a living pharmacy grows all around me prompted me to reexamine my perception of the native plant life all around me. I never realized what was actually there, or what it offered. My relationship with plants had been entirely one-dimensional. I wasn't seeing what I thought I was seeing.

Although I'm loath to people whipping out their cell phones while out in nature (there's nothing sadder than someone walking through the woods, staring into a cell phone, oblivious to the wonder and life all around them), there's a super cool app to help you identify what grows there: PictureThis. You take a photo of a plant, flower, berry, or leaf, and it identifies the plant and provides information about it, on the spot. You may discover that you have some powerful nutritional or medicinal plants nearby.

Use extreme caution identifying wild plants before harvesting them to eat or for medicinal use. That beautiful, fat mushroom you want to put in your spaghetti sauce may be lethal. If you aren't 100 percent certain what a plant is, do not eat it or anything you harvest from it. When you're absolutely certain what that plant is, when you harvest some part of it, do so respectfully. Touch the plant and explain that it has something you need. Ask its permission. If you get a strong energetic response of *no*, move on to another plant. When you find a receptive plant, give thanks for whatever you harvest. Do this in your own garden or yard too. Don't just whack stuff off and walk away. That's so rude.

To take a magical approach in your harvesting, use a *boline*, which is a very sharp curved-blade knife, usually with a white handle, used only for harvesting plant material for medicinal reasons or magical work.

Activity: More Congruence with Plants

Instead of just letting local scenery blur by in your peripheral vision as you walk or drive from one place to another, start taking notice of the plants and trees you pass by every day. Find a spot where you can stop and sit quietly

---

15. Healthline, "Elderberry: Benefits and Dangers," accessed January 15, 2020, https://www.healthline.com/nutrition/elderberry.

in their presence. Observe each one individually as a divine life form. There may be a particular tree you've passed a thousand times, noticed briefly as "that tree over there"—but have you ever *really* looked at it? Studied it? Would you recognize it as an individual amongst other trees?

Get closer, and call upon your inner wild child, the one who could speak to butterflies and apple trees and waterfalls, and start a conversation with that plant or tree. Don't just talk, listen. What is that tree or plant saying? "Yay, I'm alive," or "Ugh, I don't feel so well"?

Place your hand on it, ask it how it's feeling, and linger there. Reassure it that you won't hurt it. Wait for an answer. Trees move and communicate much more slowly than humans, so be patient. Use that time as quiet meditation, and let your mind clear. Pay attention to feelings or images that come drifting to you. When it's time to go, do you feel like you know this tree now? Can you sense its spirit?

When you return home, record your experience in your journal: "Today, a tree told me … "

Trees Are Great Listeners—and Healers

Besides listening to trees, you can also ask them for help. Renowned Pagan author and icon Silver RavenWolf shared via the magical realm of Facebook that in her own witchcraft tradition, which encompasses local Pennsylvania Dutch powwow witchcraft, one could go to a tree and ask for help. She advised people not to be distracted by whether or not this makes sense, but rather, to just try it to see what happens. So, I did.

I'd had shoulder surgery a couple months prior, and it wasn't healing as quickly as I wanted. The constant pain and stiffness were wearing me down. So, I went out to the mother tree in my own backyard—a huge albizia that creates a protective umbrella over the entire yard—and leaned against it, letting it support me completely. I greeted it, thanked it for its wonderful shade, and abundant nectar for so many bees and hummingbirds, and asked it for help in relieving my shoulder pain. I placed my hand on the trunk, parallel to my head, and leaned my body slightly forward, to trigger a stab of pain—just enough to show the tree, "This. It's *this*. Please help it heal. Please take the pain away."

I have a strong bond with this tree. I saved it from a nursery dump pile long ago, and that wimpy little sprig grew into the mightiest tree in the yard. It receives leftover ritual water and herbs, so we have a magical relationship as well as a long history. That tree knows me well. After asking the tree for healing, within a few days, my pain began slowly subsiding. No, I can't prove the tree aided me. But until someone can prove it didn't, that's my story and I'm stickin' to it, because prior to that, my shoulder was stalled in its healing process. Some might declare this a placebo effect. However, I once had a very wise and open-minded physician, and consulted him about glucosamine, which I wanted to take for joint pain. He studied the label, and said glucosamine was harmless; however, there was no scientific support for any medical benefit.

"It's sort of like eating hair to grow hair. It doesn't really make any biological sense. If anything, it's just a placebo."

"However," he added with a wry smile, "if a placebo has an effect, it's still an effect—even if it doesn't make any sense."

Humans have a horrible habit of believing only what they can explain, and when you start investigating wonders and mysteries, whether it's the tree in your backyard or the cosmos itself, you discover that there's an awful lot that humans can't explain. Maybe there's a spiritual mycelium between plants and humans that scientists can neither detect nor explain—yet. Maybe it's a vibratory field, which certainly exist, even for the most skeptical of scientists. You have an energetic vibration, I have an energetic vibration, and every living thing and even non-living things like rocks and crystals have an energetic vibration[16]. Can trees detect, and understand, the vibrations of non-plant life? We haven't yet discovered every single vibration, how it works, and what it does, so I'll echo what Silver said: ask a tree for help and see what happens. At the very least, just confiding your pain to a tree is comforting. They're excellent listeners, and they charge way less than doctors. A little tree and sympathy can work wonders!

16. Peter Genzer, "Scientists Pinpoint Energy Flowing Through Vibrations in Superconducting Crystals, "Phys.org, last updated April 30, 2018, https://phys.org/news/2018-04-scientists-energy-vibrations-superconducting-crystals.html.

Spirituality Began with Biocongruence

Our ancient ancestors didn't have explanations for the things they noticed in nature, but they surely did notice them. In the Paleolithic prehistoric era, there weren't yet stories of gods pulling the sun in chariots across the sky, or great arching mothers of the night, covering and protecting the land. There was only wonder, and taking comfort in the things and patterns that became familiar and predictable.

Your ancient ancestors noticed that the moon traveled in a certain direction, and became larger and larger, and then smaller and smaller, disappearing entirely, only to reappear again, all in a predictable pattern and span of time. They noticed other patterns around them too: seasons, tides, animal migrations, sexuality, birth, aging, and death. Wondering about how and why these things happen inspired explanations, which were the early stirrings of spirituality. And not just any spirituality—one that's entirely immersed in the natural world. The natural world was the template within which spirituality evolved.

The oldest known forms of human spiritual awareness have been traced back to burial rituals in the Middle Paleolithic Period, which spanned from 300,000 to 45,000 years ago,[17] long before any evidence of organized religion, which isn't documented until 5,000 BCE.[18] Hundreds of thousands of years have transpired since the birth of early human spiritual awareness. That's a very long human history of nature-based spirituality.

Those original spiritual beliefs and practices were prehistoric, occurring long before any form of written language. We can only glean what sparse information we have about ancient spirituality from cave wall paintings and burial sites. Without written language to explain them, we must do a lot of guesswork to try and understand. We can't go back in time and hear their stories and beliefs, but there are people amongst us who are a direct bloodline of those who told the ancient stories, and know those stories themselves: the indigenous people of our land—the First People. Today's indigenous people

---

17. Karl J. Narr, "Prehistoric Religion, the Beliefs and Practices of Stone Age Peoples," Encyclopaedia Britannica, accessed July 8, 2020, https://www.britannica.com/topic/prehistoric-religion.

18. Ancient History Encyclopedia, "Religion Timeline," accessed July 8, 2020, https://www.ancient.eu/timeline/religion/.

are an unbroken line from the First People to right now. Their insight, wisdom, and spirituality were passed on intact, orally, through lore and tribal stories. You may be able to find some who are willing to share their wisdom, history, and stories with you.

I am insatiably curious about the history, stories, and spiritual beliefs of our indigenous people because I feel deeply connected to *this* land. It's the only one I know, and I sense its spiritual energy. One day, I had a long chat with my friend Garry, who is Saginaw Chippewa (or Anishinaabe, the Ojibwe word for "the People") and has spent much of his life studying indigenous history. Before retiring, he was an educator at D-Q University (Deganawidah-Quetzalcoatl University), which was a tribal college in northern California with an exclusively Indigenous American focus and curriculum.

Garry told me that the sacredness of life and the land are at the heart of indigenous American spirituality. Connection to Spirit happens directly with individuals and not through a central authority figure (although there is the Native American Church, which encompasses widespread indigenous beliefs, some Christianity, and sacramental use of peyote), and isn't something practiced at a particular time on Sunday mornings, with an authority figure acting as middleman between Spirit and an individual. As Garry describes it, indigenous spirituality is interwoven with daily life and the natural environment. Nature is the template from which their spiritual biocongruence emerges.

If you are also curious about the spiritual biocongruence of First People of the land where you live, Native Land[19] is a website with a map of the indigenous nations of the United States (including Hawaii and Guam), as well as Canada, Mexico, South America, Australia, New Zealand, Greenland, the northern parts of Norway, Sweden, and Finland, and a tiny bit of Russia. When you identify which nation was there first, you can start researching to find the lore and stories of the spiritual biocongruence of your area.

---

19. Native Land, Territories, accessed July 17, 2020, https://native-land.ca.

Nature Just Is

Indigenous Americans weren't the only ancient humans with spiritual stir-rings and stories inspired by nature. All ancient humans worldwide tried to make sense of their environments by wondering how and why things happen in the natural world. Absent of any tangible explanation, their attention turned from the seen to the unseen: spirituality. They transitioned from observing *that* things happened to wondering *why* they happened. We've been very curious creatures from the beginning. Curiosity is also in our DNA.

But what about nature itself? Does it have spirituality? The wild geese aren't concerned with finding a church, the crocuses popping up through the snow aren't in search of a savior, and that red fox walking the edge of a field isn't seeking enlightenment. Nature isn't religious. It just *is*. Now, *that* is truly tantalizing. In the Book of Exodus in the Hebrew Torah (the Old Testament in the Christian Bible), when Moses asked God who he should tell his people that He was, He essentially replied that He just *is*: "I am who I am."[20]

God identified Herself as "I am." I interpret this as "I am existence itself. I *am*." God just *is*. He/She/They/It just *is*. They just exist. That's what every non-human living thing does: just exists. Every living thing just *is*. If you want to see God, look no further than a rosebud unfurling or the ladybug crawling up its stem—they exist. They *are*. Their tiny life force, by virtue of existing, *is* God.

Is and *am* are forms of the same verb: to *be*. Anything that is "am-ing" or "is-ing" is simply *be*-ing. When you see a living thing striving to be—a living *be*-ing—you're staring right at God (or the universe, or Spirit, or the All) Themself. You are looking at "I am." You don't need to find a guru on a mountaintop or study in a monastery for a decade or read every book on spirituality to find God. Just go outside and look. She's right there in front of your eyes, and always has been. Nature doesn't have spirituality. Nature *is* spirituality. Nature *is*. Human dissertation on spirituality or religion, in whatever facet, is merely an embellishment of the spiritual congruence that already exists in the natural world.

20. Bible Hub, Exodus 3:14, accessed July 8, 2020, https://biblehub.com/exodus/3-14.htm.

Activity: You Are

Take some time to be still, and let your mind go clear and calm. Breathe. Bubble your intrusive thoughts and release them. Imagine yourself in a quiet natural setting—a field or forest, or beside a stream. Relax and just be in that moment. Feel your surroundings with all your senses. Gently, slowly, say to yourself in your mind or whisper out loud like a heartbeat, "I *am*... I *am*... I *am*..." and spend time there. Rest for awhile in that state of simply *be*-ing. When you're ready to come back, ask yourself this: Were you alone? Or was there another presence, another consciousness, permeating your awareness? Can you identify it? Did it have a message for you? Were you congruent with it?

Write about that experience in your journal. It may trigger insights or memories. Just begin, and see where your mind meanders: "I know I *am* because..."

Gaia is Our Mother

Mother Earth, which many Pagans call Gaia, isn't merely a big, dead rock floating in space. She breathes and has lungs (forests turning carbon dioxide into oxygen), she has blood (oceans and rivers, ever churning and flowing), a body (the firmament), and a living spirit, the Goddess. All living things are connected to Gaia. Nothing can survive without her. We live because she lives.

Gaia is a rare miracle in this massive universe; there aren't many planets just like this one that can sustain life as we know it. Those we've discovered are too far away to reach in a thousand lifetimes with the technology we have now. Gaia is our one and only home, our one and only Mother, our only chance to live. Your biocongruence is the essence of your connection with her. Let's set aside some time to feel that connection.

Activity: Meditation with Gaia

Sit or lie in a comfortable position, where you have some quiet time alone, and breathe with Gaia. Feel her. Soak her energy in.

Inhale... and exhale.

Continue. More slowly, more gently. Gradually, let your breath become deeper. Feel your lungs filling up... reaching capacity... and releasing. Release thoughts from your mind, and let it become still. Should thoughts intrude, capture them in a bubble and let them float away. Return your focus to your breathing. Drop your shoulders...relax your jaw...feel the surface you're sitting or lying on completely supporting you. Feel the safety and security of this moment. Tell yourself, "I am safe."

As your breathing gets fuller and deeper, relax into it, go with it, and move the focus of your breathing further down your body to the center of your belly, just above your navel. If it helps you to connect to this spot, gently place a hand there. Now, imagine inhaling from that spot, as if pulling the air in from there, and then releasing it and allowing the air to flow back out effortlessly, like ocean waves rolling in and out. Continue breathing gently and easily like this for as long as you want.

Feel the connection to your own body, and extend it downward, outward, and upward to Gaia herself, and feel the connection with her. You are alive because of her. Without her, just like without breath itself, you'd perish within moments. Let gratitude well up within you and extend it outward to her.

When you feel ready, move your attention to that spot above your navel, and gradually back to your lungs. Open your eyes and return to the space around you. Soak in this serene feeling, bask in it, knowing that you can return to this safe place with Gaia any time you feel stressed, or the need to ground, center, focus, and reconnect to your own body, and your Mother's.

Remember that no matter where you are, Gaia is always with you. You literally can't go anywhere on this Earth without her being there too. It's easy to find her. Just breathe.

Cosmocongruence

Just as we can have biocongruence with the natural environment around us, and feel spiritual energy flowing back and forth, we can re-imagine our relationship with the cosmos and be congruent with that too: cosmocongruence. If we can view ourselves as spiritually connected with nature, we can view ourselves as spiritually connected with the cosmos. We just need a new paradigm for how we understand the cosmos.

Most people view the cosmos as a thing, and that thing isn't alive—pretty much the same way they view the planet we live on. Scientists don't call the cosmos "alive," mainly because they're unable to prove that it is. So, our understanding of the cosmos isn't defined by our knowledge, but rather, limited by our ignorance. Humans are like fruit flies, which live little more than a month, sitting on the branch of a redwood tree, which can live as long as two thousand years, declaring that the tree is "not alive" because for that entire fly's life, it hasn't seen the tree move or change once. In terms of the mysteries of the universe, we're nothing more than cocky little fruit flies without any useful perspective on the passage of time or the expanse of space.

Kaboom

The current scientific theory on the origins of the cosmos is the Big Bang, where the universe began with a single massive blast, propelling matter-filled galaxies out across the expanse of space. According to *National Geographic*, scientists theorize that before this cataclysmic explosion, the universe was extremely compact, a fraction of the size of a single atom.[21] Remember when I declared that you are literally made of the matter of the universe and time itself? Stardust? I wasn't being giddy or glib. You really are, and so is every single living thing you see, and every square inch of earth and sky on our wonderful planet, and everything beyond it. It's all made of the exact same stuff, contained in that original sub-atomic particle that exploded; it's just the proportions that change.

As for that initial Big Bang, which propelled its matter in 360 degrees, hurtling out through space, scientists once thought that the universe would reach the end of its expansion and collapse back in on itself (called the Big Bust), or maybe just slow down and stop like a fired bullet. Now, they're discovering neither may be correct: The rate of propulsion is actually speeding up, with no sign of slowing down.[22] Whirling galaxies are being flung farther and farther apart, and in time, the stars and constellations we see now will ultimately disappear.

Now, before the notion of a starless sky causes you anxiety, let me quell your fear with facts: Relative to the speed at which the universe moves, and the length of time at which it moves, our human lives are but a billionth of a billionth of a second. The stars won't disappear within in our lifetimes,

---

21. Michael Greshko and *National Geographic* staff, "Origins of the Universe, Explained," *National Geographic*, January 18, 2017, https://www.nationalgeographic.com/science/space/universe/origins-of-the-universe/.

22. Ethan Siegel, "The Universe Is Disappearing, and There's Nothing We Can Do To Stop It," *Forbes*, August 17, 2018, https://www.forbes.com/sites/startswithabang/2018/08/17/the-universe-is-disappearing-and-theres-nothing-we-can-do-to-stop-it/#19513908560e.

and not in our descendants' lifetimes either. You can relax. We have plenty of other things to worry about.

Which theory will be right: The Big Bang and infinite, endless expansion or the Big Bust and everything snapping back together like a rubber band? What if they're both wrong—and also right, at the same time? What if the universe itself inhales and exhales, rinse and repeat, for all of infinity? There are some hints of evidence for this possibility.

The stuff that humans identify as matter out in space only makes up about 5 percent of the universe's contents. Twenty-seven percent is dark matter, and 68 percent is dark energy.[23] And here's where it gets really interesting: Mark Strauss, writing for Mentalfloss.com, explains, "Dark matter and dark energy are the yin and yang of the cosmos. Dark matter produces an attractive force (gravity), while dark energy produces a repulsive force (antigravity)." Attraction, repulsion... attraction, repulsion... inhale, exhale... inhale, exhale. Could it be that the universe breathes? And is therefore... alive? Are we like that cocky little fruit fly, unable to perceive the cosmos as alive because our existence and knowledge are infinitely limited?

We only know that dark energy and dark matter exist, but not what they are or how they work. Now, prepare for your mind to be blown: Dark matter and dark energy don't only exist in outer space. They exist in inner space as well.

Within our bodies is a microscopic cosmos of atoms, 99 percent of which are hydrogen, oxygen, or nitrogen—the same chemical components found throughout the cosmos, originating at the Big Bang, from the same, single atomic-sized particle. Inside each atom in your body (and everywhere) are protons, neutrons, and electrons. And you know what's in between them? Space. Now scientists are discovering that like space in the cosmos, this sub-atomic space isn't empty either. It's very much like the dark energy and dark matter in the universe—we can detect it's there, but we don't really know much about what it actually is or what it does.

What if the vibrations inside the sub-atomic cosmos in our body can align with the vibrations of dark energy or dark matter of the cosmos itself? Have you ever heard someone tune a guitar and tweak it until the vibration of the note aligns with the vibration of the tuning mechanism? You can hear

---

23. Siegel, "The Universe Is Disappearing, and There's Nothing We Can Do To Stop It."

the vibrations align. This is how cosmocongruence feels to me: an aligned spiritual vibration. I can detect it when experiencing "un-aloneness" in a quiet moment. It's a connection and recognition of the "I am" that we feel and notice in those moments of simply *be*-ing. It's that vibration, connection, and awareness that I refer to when I talk about "the universe" as a spiritual, energetic entity as opposed to the actual natural universe, or cosmos. Some might call that entity God or Spirit. To me, they are all one and the same. When I refer to the Goddess, it's specific to our planet—that same cosmic spiritual energy contained right here on and around Earth. Just as you are a unique container for cosmic spiritual energy, so is this planet and its atmosphere.

We know that physically, everything in the natural universe came from the same origin. One Big Bang in one tiny spot. It seems logical to me, therefore, that our spirituality has a common spiritual origin too. We *are* God. And so is every living thing, across the entire cosmos. Being open to that possibility and embracing it is the conduit for cosmocongruence. It brings us back to "The Charge of the Goddess," doesn't it? "If that which thou seekest thou findest not within thee, thou wilt never find it without thee." Or, rather, in the case of the spiritual energy of the cosmos (or God or Spirit), you need not seekest without thee, because it is already within thee. In fact, it *is* thee.

It's All Connected, All Congruent

There is a spiritual energy vibrating throughout the cosmos and in every living thing within it. We aren't separate from our natural environment, nor are we separate from whatever it is that's out there when we stare up at the night sky. And, all of it, down here and out there, began as one entity. One subatomic particle—physically and spiritually. It's all connected. All part of one fabric. Whatever exists out there is part of you, and vice versa, and its ability and potential are far, far more expansive than the mere limits of the human mind—as are you.

We're but a speck on a speck on a speck in this cosmos, and the only thing as vast as our ignorance about the cosmos is the vastness of possibility it holds. That's a macrocosm of yourself: There's much more possibility within you than you ever imagined. Just as scientists have barely tapped into an understanding of the wonders, mysteries, and potential of the universe, you are yet to tap into the wonders, mysteries, and potential inside yourself. The universe's dark matter is as baffling as your own gray matter.

Wonder, mystery, potential, possibility—it's not just the cosmos! It's you! May your wonder always eclipse your doubt.

So mote it be.

Recommended Reading

Harrison, Paul. *Elements of Pantheism: A Spirituality of Nature and the Universe.* Shaftsbury, Dorset, UK: Element Books, 2013.

Hawking, Stephen. *A Brief History of Time—From the Big Bang to Black Holes.* New York, NY: Bantam Books, 1988.

Hawking, Stephen. *Black Holes and Baby Universes and Other Essays.* New York, NY: Bantam Books, 1993.

Recommended Viewing

Ancient Civilizations of North America (series). 2018. Chantilly, VA: The Great Courses. The Teaching Company, LLC.

CHAPTER 6

Plant Spirit

Investigating, understanding, and making use of plants in the surrounding environment is something indigenous people around the world have done for hundreds of thousands of years. Some of these early healers and shamans connected with plant life on a magical or spiritual plane, while others explored medicinal uses for plants. This knowledge was passed down from shaman to shaman, healer to healer, generation to generation. Healing with plants is one of humanity's oldest medical practices.

Besides having medicinal and magical value, plants are also infused with their own unique spiritual energy. They are living beings with a consciousness of their own. They're much more than decorations in your garden or greenery along the road.

There are thousands of medicinal and magical associations with plants. For our purposes, we'll lean mostly toward the magical, spiritual end of the spectrum.

Magical and spiritual associations with certain plants vary and even contradict each other from one culture or Pagan tradition to another, although there are several associations that cross boundaries. There's no right set of associations. There's just the one that resonates with you and provides magical significance in your own life and practices. If you decide to follow a particular Pagan path later on, you'll learn about the specific sacred plants for that tradition. It may differ from mine. Just a heads-up: as a freelancing Garden-Variety Pagan for the time being, you're free to create your own list of magical, sacred plants based upon your own experience and exploration. Be sure to record those in your journal.

Plants and Plant Energy

I've always been spiritually connected to plants, going back to early child-hood. I was always planting seeds and sticks in the backyard, and propagated so many coleus plants in high school that my bedroom looked like a leafy purple and red jungle. My yard now has something growing from every square inch. I just love plants, and they seem to love me back. Imagine my disappointment in my Pagan toddlerhood, while learning about the sacred trees of the ancient Celts and Druids, when I realized that the trees in my own environment weren't represented. I felt left out.

The Druids have thirteen sacred trees or plants linked to their calendar. In order, beginning in late December, they are birch, rowan, ash, alder, willow, hawthorn, oak, holly, hazel, vine, ivy, reed, and elder. Ancient Celts additionally held apple, blackthorn, broom, cedar, elm, fir, furze, juniper, mistletoe, pine, and yew as sacred. Each is associated with specific magical or symbolic meaning and uses. While a couple of these trees grow where I live, like oak and pine, most are native to the cool, foggy, moist hills and woods of the British Isles, and not the very hot, very dry northern California valley where I live. I've never seen a rowan or yew tree or furze. These plants don't resonate with me. And yet, as I explore Paganism, I'm supposed to hold them as sacred? That doesn't work for me. It feels like pretending.

These traditionally sacred trees and plants don't have intrinsically superior mystical powers. They're simply the trees and plants that were familiar to the ancient Celts and Druids because that's what grew in their environment. The sacredness of those trees and plants was determined by proximity. If the Druids had been located in Mexico, their sacred plants would be palm trees, cactus, and mesquite. Just as in real estate, declaring trees or plants sacred is all about location, location, location.

The traditional sacred Celtic plants and trees are situationally sacred, not intrinsically. Me, I'm in a different situation, and it doesn't include rowans or yews. However, on a purely historical level, I enjoy learning about traditional Celtic symbology, and it gives me a common vocabulary with those who follow ancient Celtic or Druid paths. As for myself, in my own Garden-Variety Pagan practices, I needed a list of sacred trees and plants that were actually part of my own environment. That's entirely more meaningful to me. I *know* the things that grow around me. I decided to learn about their medicinal, spiritual, and magical associations and symbology, and involve them in my practices rather than plants and trees I've never seen, and maybe never will.

Unless you live in the foggy, misty areas of northern Europe, where the traditional Celtic and Druid plants and trees are meaningful because they're all around you, you can do like me: find out what grows around you, what it does, and how its spirit affects you.

Which Plants Attract You?

Go out and really look at the trees and plants in your yard, town, and surrounding areas. Examine them closely. If a certain plant calls to you or gives you joy, pay attention. Just as we're drawn to certain people, we're drawn to certain plants too. It may be their beauty, their scent, their shape, or some reason we can't quite put our finger on. There's just *something* about that tree or that plant. (Spiritual energy!) Pay attention to shifts in your mood or energy when you're near those plants. It may be a clue about their magical properties.

Plants don't have to be growing wild to be sacred. The ones in your yard have medicine and magic of their own, whether you put them there or nature did. I have a particular fondness for dandelion greens, and let them grow wild in my yard. If you're pulling them up or using weed killer on them, stop! They are free food, and free medicine! Besides dandelions, my little yard is packed with trees, bushes, flowers, and vines, and most have medicinal and/or magical value. All of them vibrate with spiritual energy, and I have a relationship with each of them. They are my leafy friends, and I am their Garden Goddess. I created that little patch of paradise.

Plants and herbs that can be eaten, brewed as teas, or sprinkled onto salads and into soups all have kitchen magic potential. Pay attention to how you feel after consuming certain plants and herbs. Incorporate them into your diet and your magic. When I need some natural plant medicine or a particular plant or energy for magical work, I can simply walk out into the yard and get it. How handy is that?

That said, as mentioned earlier, I don't just go out and yank things off my plants. These trees, bushes, vines, and herbs are my plant spirit allies. They must be treated with care and respect. When you grow things to harvest for yourself, particularly for food or magical/medicinal use, be respectful and express gratitude. Whenever I need something from a plant in my yard,

I greet it, explain my need, and thank it after I've cut or picked something away. In exchange, I give my plants plenty of water, nutrition, and sunlight so they can thrive, I keep the bugs and critters from gnawing on them, and prune away dead branches so they can sprout new, healthy growth. It's a relationship. We support each other.

My Own Sacred Plants

Each of the following trees, bushes, flowers, and "weeds" has a spiritual, magical presence in my yard and in my life. I feel them and I know them. These are the sacred plants in my environment:

Albizia: Also known as mimosa or silk trees, these are the messiest damn trees on Earth, producing an astounding amount of litter, from thick layers of summer fluff to bushels of seed pods that sprout new trees all over the place, usually where you don't want them. Despite its messy nature, albizia bursts with magical energy. Albizia grows very tall, with an umbrella-like shape that creates an amazing spread of dark, cool shade. It stretches out overhead with protective energy, almost covering the entire yard. Its flowers make a cloud of pink fluff that attracts bees and hummingbirds, which themselves are animal spirit allies with magical energy of their own. The Mother Tree in my yard is a huge albizia, and is my own special plant familiar. If I need protective mother love for my magical work, a pink albizia puff represents that intention.

Almond: Vast almond orchards are part of the rural landscape surrounding my town. I have one growing on my front lawn. In February, almond trees produce gobs of delicate pinkish-white blossoms, perfect for making magically infused moon-blessed water, which we'll discuss further later on. Almonds are a superfood, and can be included for intentions of strength and good health in all sorts of things, from salads to cookies. Almond blossoms and nuts can be used to adorn a magical or seasonal altar.

Basil: If I could pick only one herb to have in my cabinet, it would be basil. I love the taste, the scent, its energy, and its traditional symbology of good luck and financial prosperity. There's nothing like the aroma of a fresh basil plant on the kitchen counter. If you want to freshen the air in your home, bring in a basil plant. Basil is traditionally associated with attracting money. Placing a basil leaf in your wallet to make it a little fatter. Sadly, basil is rather delicate and finicky, bushing out over the summer, but withering and turning brown when it starts getting cold. It will only grow year-round in tropical climates or indoors. You can buy plants or seeds at any nursery. What luck and prosperity would you like to attract? Let basil help you manifest it.

Bay: Some common species of bay are Bay Laurel, which are the dried bay leaves you use for cooking, and California Bay Laurel, which is about a thousand times more potent and will ruin a recipe in an instant. I have the California species, because I want the leaves for herbal medicine and magic. A crushed California Bay leaf will clear nasal congestion in a spicy snap, much like wasabi. Dried bay leaves are a favorite for magical purposes, such as writing an intention on the leaf and then burning it, releasing it to air to carry your intention away for manifestation. The leaves may also be used as incense by themselves or in combination with other things, like pine, cloves, or sage.

Buddleia: Also known as *butterfly bush*, buddleia is a magnet for those fluttering magical messengers of air. Its cone-shaped flower spikes emit a thick, honey-sweet scent that fills the yard. They can become quite big—taller than the fence—and must be pruned back each winter to allow for new growth and to keep them from getting so big that their branches split and crack off. Magically, a sprig of buddleia attracts butterfly energy: metamorphosis, rejuvenation, lightness, and joy; the ability to flutter here and there and collect all the "nectar" (ideas and creativity).

Cherry: In Eastern philosophy, the cherry tree is associated with love and femininity, as well as Venus, the Roman goddess of love. Both the fruit and the blossoms of cherry trees have magical value. The delicate pink blossoms are perfect for making moon-blessed water, and the blossoms and fruit will bring femininity and romance to magical work, especially love magic. A medieval Italian cherry liqueur called *visciolino* can be made from the leaves, creating a wonderful altar offering to a deity, as does cherry juice or the fruit itself. Cherry juice can substitute for blood in magical workings.

Citrus: I have limes, oranges, lemons, mandarins, and grapefruit in my yard, and they give bushels of fruit from December through April. Their fruit and evergreen leaves are wonderful for any seasonal altar, but they're at their fruitful glory in winter. Citrus fruit is full of vitamin C, which has a variety of health benefits. Some fresh lemon squeezed into water will refresh and energize your mind. As for magical properties, use lemon to clear or cleanse. A slice of lemon in a small dish of salt wards off negative energy. If better health is your magical intent, it's easy to incorporate most any citrus juice in salad dressings, marinades, or teas, or just drink fresh-squeezed. Mandarins are easily pulled apart and tossing into green salads along with the intention of good health for your amazing body. All citrus blossoms are lovely for making moon-blessed ritual water.

Dandelion: These hardy little "weeds" are a precious gift of good health. You can eat the leaves raw or cooked, or use or prepare like spinach. Some don't like the bitter taste. I happen to love it, drizzled in olive oil. Dandelion is a nutritional powerhouse. Dandelion roots are dried and used in tea for their liver-cleansing properties. For magical use, if the spell deals with strengthening, healing, or purification, dandelions are perfect, and available year-round. Bees also love the flowers, and anything that's good for bees is good for all of us. Putting a yellow dandelion flower on an altar attracts bee energy. And, whenever those whimsical little dandelion puffs spring up, it's an opportunity to make a wish or set an intention, and let air carry it off for manifestation—and also to let more magical dandelions spring up.

Fig: Figs are one of the oldest plant species on Earth, appearing even before mammals, and originating in Africa. In Greek mythology, fig is associated with love and fertility, and is honored in Buddhism as the tree under which the Buddha reached enlightenment. Fig leaves were also famously used by Adam and Eve to cover up their privates. We won't hold that against them. There is nothing more delectable than the taste of a perfectly ripe, fresh fig, and they can be used in so many recipes, from desserts to meat dishes. Figs are also just sexy. When you pick a nice, big, plump one, it feels like, well…a testicle. Just the right size and weight. If male or projective energy is desired in your magical work, or rituals or spells for a romantic evening, figs are perfect. Use them as an aphrodisiac, split in half and drizzled with honey, and see where the night leads you.

Jasmine: Nothing compares to the sweet, sensual scent of jasmine. Jasmine symbolizes love, healing, tenderness, and the heart chakra. Jasmine blossoms are yet another perfect ingredient for creating moon-blessed water, particularly when the intention involves matters of the heart or tender healing. Jasmine blossoms infuse green tea with their enticing, sensual scent. I drink jasmine tea whenever I need some self-care or a gentle emotional lift.

Lavender: Calming, soothing lavender is the go-to scent for massage oil. The flowers are on spear-shaped cones, and can be used fresh or cut, dried, and stored for future use in everything from infused oil to herbal tea. Lavender is anti-fungal, antiseptic, and anti-stress. Lavender eases insomnia, and is a common ingredient in sleep pillows, which are small satchels or pouches placed under or near your pillow at night. The scent can be reactivated each night by crushing the pouch between your fingers. Add dried lavender flowers into chamomile tea to help you relax in the evening. Any magic that seeks to calm, soothe, comfort, or heal can be enhanced with lavender. Lavender essential oil is perfect for anointing your pulse points and temples, and can be used as a magical oil.

Pomegranate: Femininity and fertility are traditionally associated with pomegranate, which is rich with magical lore. In Greek mythology, Persephone ate pomegranate seeds to cement her betrothal to Hades. Pomegranates were the signature symbol of Queen Catherine of Aragon. In the tarot, pomegranates are on the two cards most associated with feminine power and mystery—The High Priestess and The Empress—and lend themselves to magic needing some of that energy. Pomegranates are a superfood, high in antioxidants, and are wonderful to eat as is, to make jelly or mead, or sprinkle seeds into in salads. The trick to getting the seeds out is to hold the pomegranate over a large bowl or pot, and beat it with a wooden spoon. Then crack it open and the seeds will fall right out. However, your hands will be dripping in deep red juice and you'll look like you just walked away from a murder scene. Pomegranates are at peak near the end of October, and will keep for a long time at room temperature, so they're wonderful for seasonal altars or decor. You can place them there whole or crack them open, just as they are pictured on the tarot cards. Pomegranate juice can substitute for blood in magical workings, particularly those involving intense feminine energy.

Redwood: I have a lone California Coastal Redwood, also known as sequoia, that I planted as a tiny seedling long ago, and now it towers above my house. Redwood is a crossover of two species—amongst both my sacred trees and those of the ancient Druids and Celts: fir and pine. Fir trees, such as redwoods, are associated with protection and the ability to see a long way or into the future. Because it stands so tall, redwood can see what other trees cannot. Use fir or pine needles in protection or visionary magic, as well as for being able to see through difficult situations. You may not be able to "see the forest for the trees," but the tall redwood can.

Rose: Roses are the iconic flowers of love and romance, particularly red ones. The whole flower or just the petals can be used. When the flowers fade on the bush, if you don't prune them off, they'll form rosehips where the flower was. Rosehips are ripe when they've turned red, and are particularly high in vitamin C. They can be added to soups, teas, desserts, and jams. They can also be eaten fresh when ripe. Cut them in half horizontally, remove the seeds, rinse, and eat. Rose petals are perfect for making moon-blessed magical water. Besides flowers, roses famously have thorns, symbolizing the fact that love, like a rose, can be delightful or painful. Rose bushes will create a magical protective barrier around your home or under windows and deter negative energy and intruders. (More under Thorns.)

Rosemary: Traditionally associated with protection, particularly when planted near the front door, rosemary watches over your house and greets you when you come home. I love trailing my hand against it on the way in and releasing its spicy fresh scent. Rosemary is evergreen, and provides year-round fresh herbs for cooking, oil infusions, magic, kitchen witchery, and magical oil. It's a classic ingredient for protection magic.

Spider plant: Spider plants are joyful little beings. When they're feeling healthy, they reach up for the sunshine. When mature, they shoot out long stems with adorable little baby spider plants at the ends, which can be clipped off to easily grow a new plant. What would you like to grow? Your bank account? A new relationship or business? Infuse that intention while starting a baby spider plant off on its own. Write your intention on a small stone and place it over the drainage hole in a small pot. Continue to focus on your intention as you fill the pot with soil, and as you place the spider baby in the soil. Cover its tiny roots, pack the soil firmly, and water generously, breathing your intention into it. Place it in a spot with ample sunlight, and finish by infusing it with a hearty, "Grow!" Every time you water it, you're watering your intention too.

Sycamore: Sycamore is such a versatile magical tree. Their mottled grey and green bark peels at certain times of the year, and the large, thin peels can be used like bay leaves for magic—write an intention on it and burn, releasing that intention to air for manifestation. The seed balls are also excellent magical tools. When I have to deal with sharp, nasty, difficult, abusive people, I visualize them as a sharp, spikey sycamore ball. Who cares what a sycamore ball has to say? Not me. Keep a sycamore ball on your desk or nearby shelf to remind you that anything the "sycamore balls" in your life have to say is meaningless. Another tree with sharp, spikey balls that can be used for the same purpose is liquidamber, called *sweet gum* in some areas. Let those spikey balls help you erect a protective psychological shield against sharp words and harsh people.

Thorns: Thorns aren't plants per se, but they're present on many plants, from roses to cactus, and have intense magical value. Plants grow thorns and spikes to deter predators, which lends them to protection magic. My citrus trees grow tall, thick suckers lined with large spikes sharp enough to pierce your hand. The spikes can be used to scratch protective intention on a candle, or included in a protection spell or witch's bottle. Strategically planting thorny, spikey plants around your property, particularly under windows, deters negative energy intruders. Thorny or spikey plants are also self-protective, and that has magical use too. When you've had your heart broken, or are struggling with abuse or grief, adopt a cactus plant. Barrel cactus in particular is perfect for when you're feeling fragile, bruised, or broken, and need to protect your own aching heart. Those needles won't allow anything to touch the tender green plant underneath, helping you to set a magical intention to protect yourself as you heal and recover. Nobody gets close to you until you're ready.

Violet: Shy little violets are on the delicate side, preferring cool shade and plenty of water. The flower is deep purple, like the third eye chakra, lending itself to intuition, insight, and psychic abilities. The flowers can be included in a lavender sleep pillow, transforming it into a dream pillow, which welcomes intuition and insight from your dreams. Violet flowers are also edible. Float one in your tea and drink it down to heighten your psychic abilities and intuition. The flowers can also be sprinkled onto salad with the same intention.

Activity: Find Your Own Sacred Plants

I've made my own list of sacred plants and their magical energies—now it's your turn. With a pencil and notepad, head outdoors—your own yard, a nature park, or a wild space—and learn what's growing there. (That Picture-This app will be really helpful for this.)

What's growing in your own surroundings? What calls to you? Attracts you?

Make a list of these plants and find out more about them. Observe these plants, touch them and spend some time with them, and see what they communicate to you. Research their medicinal properties and magical associations. Pick those that speak to you or have properties or associations that resonate with you, and list them your journal, along with their information. Draw a picture of the plant next to each entry.

Goddess of Your Own Garden

If you don't have access to a wild place, you can transform your own yard into a magical plant paradise or grow plants indoors. Many houseplants and herbs thrive inside, particularly if you have good sunlight. You could select plants based upon their magical associations or medicinal uses or just go to a nursery and see which plants call to you: "Hello there! Take me home!" I can assure you that plants do this because if I go into a nursery for one little thing, I'll come out with several pots of plants that begged to come with me. I have trouble saying no to plants. And they know it.

Here are a couple considerations, however, because you don't want to bring home a plant that can't thrive where you live. Most people who insist they don't have a green thumb simply didn't pay attention to what the plant needs.

- Read the informational tag on the plant, and believe it. If it needs full sun and you plant it in the shade, it will become yellow and sickly. Conversely, if it needs shade and you plant it in a hot, sunny patch, it will wither and die. The tag will also indicate if the plant is drought-resistant, and the range of temperatures it can tolerate. Also, note how big this plant will get. My redwood tree began as a tiny sprig I got for free at the state fair. Now, it towers over my house and is still growing. Rapidly. When you plant something, don't just see it as it is. Imagine it full-grown and plant it away from anything it might get crushed against or destroy, like a roof or fence.

- Annual or perennial? Annuals are one and done. They live through a single season and then die back. However, some annuals, such as marigold, snapdragon, and hollyhock, drop seeds that will sprout new plants in the spring, or you can collect the seeds and plant them. Perennials are alive year-round, such as roses, geraniums, and jasmine, but may only bloom at certain times of year. Annuals are great for small spaces and container gardens and will do well in pots. Perennials will also do well in pots, but may need to be repotted into larger containers as they grow. Both annual and perennial flowers have all sorts of magical associations.

- Know your zone: If your plants are going to live outdoors, even on a balcony or patio, you need to know your hardiness zone, which can easily be found online by searching "hardiness zone" or "find my hardiness zone." If you have your heart set on a gorgeous crimson fuchsia, which thrives in moist, temperate coastal zones, it won't last long on your snowy, midwestern porch.

- Make sure any plant you buy isn't poisonous for pets or children that will have access to it. Check for the specific pet(s) you own. What isn't poisonous for a bunny might be lethal for a cat.

Activity: Make Your Plants Feel at Home

When you bring your new leafy friends home, get to know them before planting them. What do you sense from them? How do they make you feel? What are they telling you? Don't just start digging holes—move the pots around until they're situated in just the right spot. You can even leave them there for a day or two to be sure. Plants hate to be transplanted once they've taken root. It actually puts them in shock. So, find just the right spot for them.

The act of planting can be a loving ritual. Before starting, sit with your new plants or hold them. Close your eyes, touch them, and infuse them with magical intention and your Garden Goddess love. Communicate to them that you will take care of them. Keep conveying this message as you fill the pots or prepare the soil, visualizing that plant growing and thriving. A nice magical touch is to scratch or write "Thrive!" or "Green and Healthy" on a stone, and use it to cover the drainage hole in the pot or just place it into the hole where you'll be planting. Like the spider plants, you can infuse any plant with a magical intention as you place it in the soil, like success in your career or a flourishing relationship. *Will* it to be so, and watch your plants—and your magic—grow.

Once planted, you can adorn your little green being's space with decorations or pebbles or wind chimes—something that feels special and meaningful. You're creating a magical garden, whether it's an acre or a windowsill. You are the healer or shaman in who will assign meaning, magic, or medicine to these sacred plants. You will create their lore, your own plant magic, and your own sacred stories about them. You are the goddess of your garden! (And that's so whether you're male, female, both, or neither!)

Are You a Green Goddess?

How green is your thumb? Have you always had a knack for growing things or do you struggle with it? If you're sure your thumb is black, "not and gone" that belief and start fresh. As mentioned, your failures with plants are more likely because you didn't pay attention to their needs, not because you have some sort of nasty plant-murderer juju.

There's a physical reason when plants don't thrive. Most of the time, it's one of three things: not heeding the plant's needs (sunlight, temperature, and watering requirements), invasive insects, or fungus or mildew. A plant that's not getting enough sunlight fades and yellows. It will do the same when getting overwatered, and its base or roots may rot. When a plant gets too much sunlight, it will wilt, burn, and brown. It will do the same when underwatered and will ultimately dry up and die.

If insects are the issue, try using garden predators such as praying mantis or ladybugs to control aphids, or planting things nearby that destructive insects don't like, such as mint. If you must spray, make an environmentally friendly spray, such as mixing a cup of vegetable oil, a tablespoon of dish soap, and a quart of water in a spray bottle. Avoid poisons if at all possible, particularly systemic poisons, because they will kill both helpful and destructive insects indiscriminately, and each time you spray, you're contributing to the toxic load in your environment.

Fungus and mildew may look like brown spots or white powder on the leaves. A natural treatment for fungus or mildew is one teaspoon each of baking soda and dish soap, and one tablespoon vegetable oil to a gallon of water. Use a spray bottle to apply to affected areas.

Magical Gardening

You can grow your own magic by planting a vegetable or herb garden. Before planting, write your intentions in the soil with a stick or your finger, and chant magical rhymes, or a four-line stanza (called a quatrain) over the garden plot, such as "Blessed be this garden mine, strong and healthy all, growing stalks and winding vine, Goddess love will make you tall." Quatrains are common in magical work, and I prefer making up my own—they're easier to remember. You can use your quatrain as a loving chant when you're planting, tending, watering, and feeding. And, don't just rattle off your quatrain like a bored second grader reciting a poem in class—put some feeling into it! Draw up your Garden Goddess energy and let her speak through your words! Let your inner drama queen come out and play!

When you plant your own garden and harvest from it, remember to thank those plants when you harvest. Prepare that garden bounty with intention. Things you grow yourself are potent ingredients for kitchen witchery, which we'll discuss further in chapter 10. Whether it's a cup of tea or vegetable soup or grilled zucchini, it was nourished with your own Garden Goddess love, and prepared with magic and intention. Whatever you make with your home-grown bounty, the special ingredient is your own loving, magical energy.

Indoor Gardens

A living plant in any room generates soothing green earth energy. A room with a plant in it feels different than one that doesn't—softer, calmer. Alive. You'll have the best luck with houseplants indoors, although some outdoor plants will thrive there too if they have enough sunlight. As with outdoor plants, pay close attention to each plant's water and light needs.

When you bring plants indoors to live with you, you'll really notice their individual personalities because you're around them so much. I have a relationship with each of my houseplants. Yes, I talk to them. And sometimes wiggle the ends of their leaves to say good morning, and even kiss them. They like it. I'm sure of it.

If you're a houseplant beginner or haven't been successful with them in the past, choose easygoing ones. Spider plant, coleus, pothos, and Swedish ivy are hardy and very forgiving, and will delight you with many new plants you can easily propagate from cuttings. All you need are some jars, water, and sunlight, and soon you'll have new plants—maybe more than you know what to do with! Conversely, purple velvet plant, African violet, and Boston fern are fragile and picky, so if you're a first-time indoor gardener, follow the recommended care to the letter. I've had my heart broken more than once by Boston ferns, and my thumb is pretty green.

Herbs also grow well indoors or in small spaces like a patio or balcony, and have the additional bonus of being valuable for magic or kitchen witchery or just good old tasty cooking and good health. You can grow fresh basil, parsley, oregano, and thyme year-round, and once you've used fresh herbs in a recipe, dried herbs are so unimpressive. Just as you do outside, harvest your indoor sprouts and herbs with gratitude and respect. When consuming it, welcome that plant's gift into your body.

If you find yourself with an overabundance of herbs, even though fresh is better, your own magically grown and harvested dried herbs are better than store-bought because they were grown basking in your own energy. To dry herbs, lay them out in a single layer on a paper towel or collect bunches bound at the ends with a rubber band, run a string or piece of yarn through the band, and hang upside down. When the leaves are completely dry, hold them over a bowl or paper towel, strip off the leaves, and store in an airtight container, away from light. If you get in a rhythm of growing, harvesting, drying, and storing, you'll never run out of herbs for cooking or magical work.

Asking Plants for Magical Assistance

You can develop a relationship with plants that grow wild or don't belong to you, and magically petition them when you have a need. All you have to do is ask.

A gnarled old oak tree stands over my horse's paddock, and he loves napping under its shade. One lovely summer evening, I sat near that oak tree for a long while, studying its twisting limbs and rugged bark, connecting with its energy. I finally went up to it, placed my palm on it, and asked it to always watch over Penn, every moment we're apart. I stayed there for awhile, touching the tree, until I felt like I was heard—much like when I asked my Mother Tree to relieve my shoulder pain. Only days later, a lightning-sparked fire exploded into one of the biggest in California history, the LNU Lightning Complex Fire. It burned for nearly two months, destroying more than 363,000 acres in five counties, leaving nothing but blackened land and ash in its wake.

In the hills around the ranch where Penn lives, a windswept wall of flame hundreds of feet high devoured the hills in mere hours, leaving behind only bare, blackened skeletons of old oak trees reaching up from the charred, black hills. But not the ranch where Penn lives. The fire burned right up to the edges of the property—and stopped, as if a protective bubble was over the entire ranch. Not one tree burned there—in particular, not the one next to Penn's paddock. Did that oak tree protect the ranch? Did it survive the fire unscathed because it had a magical job to do? I choose to believe so.

Years earlier, I was dropping my daughter off at her dorm to start college. She was excited and thrilled, but I felt like my heart was being ripped from my chest. Besides the grief of not seeing her every day anymore, I was leaving my small-town baby bird in the big bad city and was gripped with anxiety. I wanted to scoop her up and make a run for it back to the nest, but it was time for her to fly off on her own wings.

I pasted a smile on my face, hugged her, kissed her, wished her luck, and then cried all the way back to my car. Along the way, I noticed a towering cypress tree growing next to her dorm, a protective energy emanating from it.

I stopped, connected with it, and asked it to watch over her always. With gratitude, I plucked a small, round seedpod from a branch, no bigger than a hazelnut, and put it in my pocket as a token of our agreement: that tree would always watch over her. Whenever I had anxiety over my daughter's safety, I'd visualize myself soaring high over my town and flying quickly over cities, fields, hills, and valleys, seeing the ground quickly passing by underneath me, and circle over the tree. I could see it perfectly in my mind, watching over her, and trusted that my intention was being manifested.

I placed that seedpod next to her photo. It began to dry out, and one day, burst open like a heart so full of love that it expands to twice its size—just like a mother's heart. My daughter is all grown up now, and lives in faraway Ohio, but that cypress tree has kept our agreement. I asked for always and it's still watching over her from afar.

Some things in life are out of your control, like raging fires or children growing up and moving away. Petitioning a solid, silent tree for support and protection can help you cope and get through times like these.

A Magical Relationships With Plants

Plants offer all sorts of medicinal and magical wonders. They aren't just decorations. Just like our wild ancient ancestors, we learn about what plants have to offer through our own experimentation and experiences with them. Learning about traditional spiritual and magical associations of plants is enriching, but it's your own experience and intuition about the green, growing things around you that will be the most meaningful and magical.

Recommended Reading

McBride, Kami. *The Herbal Kitchen*. Newburyport, MA: Conari Press/Red-Wheel/Weiser, LLC, 2019.

Murphy-Hiscock, Arin. *The Green Witch: Your Complete Guide to the Natural Magic of Herbs, Flowers, Essential Oils, and More*. Avon, MA: Adams Media, 2017.

Warren, Spring. *The Quarter-Acre Farm—How I Kept the Patio, Lost the Lawn, and Fed My Family for a Year*. Berkeley, CA: Seal Press, 2011.

CHAPTER 7
Animal Spirit

The term *spirit animal* has become a bit controversial lately, as some view it as appropriated from indigenous spiritual beliefs. However, the concept of certain animals possessing certain wisdom and symbolism, and communicating in spirit form, is not exclusive to indigenous people in America. It's universal, crossing many cultures and countries.

Spirit animals have qualities, energies, and behaviors that can inspire, educate, empower, and encourage us: lessons or teaching, in other words. Sometimes these lessons differ from one culture or tradition to the next, or even contradict each other. In indigenous American lore, Owl is a rather fearsome teacher, but in the Pagan world, Owl is a venerated spiritual ally, fearless in the dark and inspiring precision in evaluating our surroundings and the people in them. When I discover conflicting information, I go with the one that resonates with me.

The spirit animal lore of various cultures and traditions is a learning resource; however, you can also learn about a spirit animal's essence more organically by observing real, live animals and noting what their behavior inspires. You can embellish what you're learning with your own real-world discoveries, or create your own unique Garden-Variety Pagan lore.

In this chapter, I'll share my own perceptions and experiences with animal spirit allies and share some information about spirit animals commonly present in the Pagan community. When the name of the animal is capitalized, I'm talking about the spiritual essence of an animal, not the physical animal itself.

Getting to Know Spirit Animals

We're lucky. We can find an abundance of information about spirit animals. However, the ancient people who inspired that information didn't have that convenience. They couldn't just search online for "antelope" and find out what that spirit animal had to offer. Sometime, somewhere, an ancient human watched a lone wolf that refused to run with the pack and declared, "Wolf means freedom!" That observant human shared the story around the fire with the tribe, and the story was passed down through the generations, and so it began: opinion became legend. Every story of every spirit animal began somewhere, with one person who simply paid attention to natural animal behavior, and the feelings and insights it inspired.

You can create your own stories from your own inspirations, insight, and experiences, which will make your spirit animals much more meaningful to you. If they align with traditional spirit animal symbology, fine. If not, also fine. If you see a squirrel and it brightens your day with its chattering and antics, and reminds you to laugh, lighten up, and enjoy life, go with it. Don't get bogged down worrying that this is Dolphin's job, or that Squirrel is *supposed* to tell you to plan ahead, get busy, and collect what you need to prepare for hard times ahead. That's not *your* experience. Always embrace what's true and genuine to you.

Animals and wildlife pulsate with meaning, magic, and symbolism. Those in your own environment often hold the most meaning because you see them in your daily life, like woodpeckers, dragonflies, and jackrabbits. However, you may be drawn to animals that don't exist where you live, and are therefore almost impossible to see up close and personal, let alone be part of your own landscape. You can still bring the essence of that animal into your life through meditation, art, rituals, and altars, and connect to its magical, spiritual essence. An animal doesn't have to be exotic, or even wild, to possess spiritual inspiration and teaching. Your own local wildlife or domestic animals are just as magical as faraway flamingoes or gazelles. Whether near or far, common or exotic, a spirit animal's power is its ability to connect with and inspire you.

Activity: That Animal You've Always Loved

Think back. Which animal were you just crazy about as a child? Was there one you were just fascinated with? What particular animal wrapped around your young heart—the one you may not have thought about in a long while? It may be waiting for you to call it back into your life.

In your journal, let your memories, thoughts, feelings, and insights about that animal flow freely. Begin your entry like this: "I have always loved (this animal) because ... " When you're done, if a particular memory or comment impresses you, go back and circle it. Those things you circled can become writing prompts of their own. For example, maybe you circled, "I loved feeding grass to the sheep, and spending time alone with them." Pick that apart: How did you feel when you fed the sheep? Was it peaceful? Could you spend time alone with them? Did you get satisfaction from making the sheep happy? Did feeding the sheep distract you from your problems? What were those problems? Are they still there? Pull the threads from the fabric of that memory and see what you discover about yourself.

If that animal provided insight or support at the time, or still does, add this to your journal entry, and include details about how that animal touched your heart or your life. You may discover that you've had a spirit animal all along.

You Know It's a Spirit Animal When...

Just being totally crazy about a particular animal doesn't necessarily make it a spirit animal. I really, really, really adore goofy, fluffy, floppy alpacas, but as spirit animals, not so much. Horse spirit helps me move mountains. Owl spirit empowers me to be fierce. Alpaca spirit? What might its spiritual message be ... "Be whimsical and weird"? Well, okay, but I actually don't need any help with that.

Animals you love just make you happy. But spirit animals are much more than cute, cuddly companions, or cute little trinkets we collect. Spirit animals have a job to do or specific lessons to offer. They may prompt you to evaluate your choices and make changes, or they may empower you in whichever way you need.

As opposed to animals you simply love, a spirit animal that just starts appearing in your life or which you're inexplicably drawn to is carrying a message from Spirit itself. There's something Spirit wants you to look at, and a spirit animal shines a spotlight on that. A certain animal may suddenly start appearing in real life, artwork, songs, or photos. It may start popping up in the most random places—a billboard or someone's tattoo. It's tapping you on the shoulder and saying, "Hey! I have a message! Pay attention!" like a spiritual kick in the butt. When these animals appear in your life, there's something qualitatively different about it. I see wild animals frequently around here, but they don't trigger that "pay attention!" feeling. When you feel it, you feel it.

When you feel a particular animal tapping you on the shoulder, follow that trail and find out about the magical energy or symbolism of that animal. Learn about its natural behavior and what that behavior inspires. Try to discern a pattern or significance to its appearance. Do you always see a ladybug when you're missing someone? Does a certain birdcall affect you a certain way? When you're out walking or hiking, do you always come across a particular animal? Does a certain type of animal trigger a particular emotional response in you? Did a raccoon appear in your yard, when you've never, ever seen one there before? What's *that* about?

Describe your peculiar animal visits in as much detail as you can in your journal, and see if its significance emerges as you write. Invite it to visit you while meditating, or into your dreams as you're falling asleep—your subconscious may reveal that animal's message in dreams. Beckon that animal, invite it in, and connect with its spiritual essence. Let it inspire and enlighten you, and show you something about your life or yourself that you hadn't noticed before.

What is a Spirit Animal?

Spirit animal is sort of a catch-all term. Depending on who you're talking to or what tradition you're exploring, they're also called totems, power animals, guardians, and familiars. There's some disagreement between traditions about which is which, and the lines can become blurry. While you'll often hear those terms used interchangeably with *spirit animal*, although they're similar, there are a few subtle but key differences:

Totem: A physical representation of a spirit animal—often hand-carved or chiseled from wood or stone—intended to draw that animal's energy to an individual or group, often to protect it. They are similar to sports team or school mascots, which represent the spirit of the team and invoke that animal's energy for battle. Everyone in the group, or on the team, or attending that school, knows exactly what that mascot animal's energy is, and often refer to themselves as that animal: I'm a Wildcat. I'm a Tiger. I'm a Buffalo. I'm a fightin' Banana Slug. (Seriously. That's the UC Santa Cruz mascot. I don't know what banana slug says—"Be slippery," maybe?)

Totem poles are iconic amongst the indigenous tribes of the Pacific Northwest, often featuring several animal spirits or mythological creatures that are guardians of particular tribes.[24] Totems are also featured on some Native American jewelry, as small totem poles or of individual animals. On Zuni jewelry, an animal totem (usually made of carved stone) is called a *fetish*, and allows the wearer to keep their sacred iconic animals near them, often for protection.

Power Animals: These are animal energies you consciously invoke, on purpose, when you need a specific thing. A power animal is like an Allen wrench. You don't need it most of the time, but when you need it, that's the only thing that will do. For example, the cold, predator energy of Rattlesnake isn't something I typically need. However, there could be times when aggressive, lethal Rattlesnake energy would be appropriate. I might need protection from harmful people I want to steer away from me, or a situation or person that needs to be warned, and attacked if the warning is ignored. Most people, if they're smart, will back away when they hear Rattlesnake's warning rattle. If they're not so smart, they'll get bit.

Guardians: Animal guardians appear without being invoked or sought out. They just show up. A guardian has your back—like a guardian angel. It has a particular message or teaching for you, like a spirit animal, and may watch over you to make sure you've learned that lesson. Guardians may appear in your dreams, and/or representations of them may start popping up in your life. Some of my most transformative spirit animal experiences were guardians: horse, coyote, and lion. I didn't seek them out. They appeared at the precise times in my life when they were needed—when course corrections were desperately in order and I was clearly flailing.

---

24. "Totem Pole Facts," Native American Indian Facts, accessed January 19, 2021, https://native-american-indian-facts.com/Native-American-Indian-Art-Facts/Native-American-Indian-Totem-Pole-Facts.html.

Familiars: A familiar is a living animal—typically one you have a relationship with, often a pet. The spirit of a deceased pet *might* interact with you as a familiar, but that's not the usual scenario. People use the word *familiar* quite loosely about any animal they love, but a familiar is actually quite specific. In her charming book, *The Little Book of Cat Magic—Spells, Charms & Tales*, superb witchcraft author Deborah Blake describes a familiar as "any animal that has an affinity for magical work and lends their energy to those workings."[25] This has been my experience. I've had and loved many cats over the course of my life, but only one was my familiar: Minnie.

Minnie, my tiny classic witch's black cat, is peculiarly attracted to my writing, which *is* magic as far as I'm concerned. I type words, other people read them, and my thoughts appear in other people's heads! Magic! Whenever I'm writing, Minnie's right there beside me. At the monthly tarot gatherings I host, she perches on the back of a nearby recliner, her eyes sparkling and wide, overseeing everything. If I leave my whimsical glittery Halloween witch's hat within her reach, she'll curl around the brim like she's part of the decoration, and if I leave a pile of witchy books on the floor, she'll roll and twist around them and knead the air over them. When I set up an altar on a small folding table near my desk, I left the room for half a moment, and returned to find Minnie delicately perched on the altar, examining everything intently. Although she's very tiny—only 8 pounds—it's a light, wiggly table, yet she hopped up there without overturning anything. I suspect she levitated.

I've had many cats over the years, but none took any interest in my writing or magic, least of all Minnie's nemesis, Maxx, who, at 22 pounds and with all the grace of a lumbering three-legged buffalo on a whisky bender, has zero interest in anything other than reaffirming that he is the center of the universe. Maxx would have crushed my witch's hat flat, and knocked the entire altar over and sent everything flying. On tarot night, he plops right down on top of people's spreads—not because he's interested in tarot, but because the cards are distracting attention away from him. If he waddles in when I'm

---

25. Deborah Blake, *The Little Book of Cat Magic: Spells, Charms & Tales* (Woodbury, MN: Llewellyn Publications, 2018), 138.

writing, it's not to participate in my magic, it's to demand food. Loudly. And right *now*. Don't get me wrong—I love Maxx dearly. He's a character. But he's not my familiar.

Activity: Have You Met Them Before?

In your journal, record your animal interactions for each of the following categories. You can list one animal, or several. If they're just animals you really like, that's okay. You may learn of their magical significance later on, and discover why you've always been attracted to them. List the animals that really speak to you—that jump right out:

Spirit: What animal(s) have appeared in your life that seemed particularly significant or inspired you to consider something from a new angle or take a different course of action? Did it appear out of the blue, or was this animal always part of your life?

Totem: Is there an animal that represents your family, tribe, team, workplace, or community? What qualities does it inspire? If there isn't one, think of whichever of those groups is significant to you; what animal would be an appropriate totem?

Power: Have there been times when you needed a specific energy to get something done, work something out, or endure a difficult time? What animal represents that energy for you?

Guardian: Do you have a sense that something is metaphysically watching over you? What sort of energy does it have? Is it a particular animal, or does that energy make you think of a particular animal? When and where have you sensed its presence or image?

Familiar: Is there an animal that becomes particularly engaged or interested whenever you're pursuing your heart's work or hobby, or exploring your creative or magical side?

If you don't have answers for all those questions just yet, no worries. If you aren't sure which spirit animals are attracted to you, or vice versa, it will materialize at the right time.

Spirit Animals Are Transformative

For me, connecting to animals is effortless. If it grunts, purrs, barks, moos, or chirps, I get a full body squeegasm every time. I love them all. However, one animal stood out above all the others, capturing my heart and soul from the start: horses. I was a horsey girl when I was still in diapers and obsessed about pretty much nothing else for most of my young life. We had horses when I was young, and they were my best friends. I loved them more than people.

I left horses behind when I first got married, but they didn't leave me. Horse spirit was still watching over me, my unknown spiritual guardian. Thirty-five years passed without horses, and then they suddenly reappeared in my life, without me orchestrating it. I'd abandoned any hope of having a horse again. Just thinking about horses was too painful. Why torture yourself thinking about something you could never have? Out of nowhere, a horse was given to me. For free. Just when my twenty-six-year journalism career was speeding toward a dead end—no future, no possibility of satisfaction and, unfortunately, no off-ramp in sight. My future was to continue what I was doing until I was unable to do it anymore, and spend the remainder of my life reflecting on the poor life choices I'd made. Horse spirit wagged its finger at me and said, "I don't think so, missy."

My reconnection to horses, and Horse, went next-level. Not long after Penn was plopped into my life, I started facing the reality of my career. My entire life pivoted in a different direction, and then came the epiphany: I need to write a book about this.[26] Sure, I'd always wanted to write books— but not *that* one. Without Horse, I'd never have written that book, because it wouldn't have occurred to me. All the horse books had surely already been written. Had I not written that book, I wouldn't have written the one you're reading now either. Horses and Horse were transformational. Without them, I'd still be withering away as a bitter, miserable, unfulfilled newspaper editor with no hope, no future, and no joy. Horses and Horse changed the trajectory of my life.

---

26. Debra DeAngelo, *The Elements of Horse Spirit: The Magical Bond Between Humans and Horses* (Woodbury, MN: Llewellyn Publications, 2020).

Different Animals, Different Jobs

Horse spirit was the epicenter of a seismic change in my life. But Horse wasn't the first spirit animal to participate in my life. Long before that, other guardians tapped me on the shoulder. Some have stayed for the duration and became part of my life, while others were "one and done," message delivered, time to move on. My first experience with spirit animals came many years before Horse appeared, in what feels like a different lifetime. And, in fact, the reason it feels so different is because of those spirit animals.

Before my sashay into journalism, I worked in the social services field. This was during my calamitous first marriage and Adventures in Christianity. Both entanglements were toxic. A coworker brought medicine cards to the office and offered animal spirit divination sessions. I was sure those cards were the Devil, but was irresistibly drawn to them.

I met with her for a session, and drew a card: Coyote. My coworker furrowed her brow. Coyote is the Trickster. The one who causes his own disasters. Well, wasn't that a coinky-dink. My marriage was agony, and digging in at a Christian church made it exponentially worse because despite some combat-level emotional abuse at home, my Christian "friends" insisted it was my duty to be a good, obedient wife and pray for God to show me how better to please my husband.

I can scarcely type that without barfing.

Coyote shined a light on the fact that I'd created both of those messes myself: marrying the wrong person and hooking up with an evangelical church when I wasn't even Christian in the first place. Coyote additionally made me realize that I was the only one who could clean those messes up. Once I'd accepted responsibility to make corrections in my life, Coyote saw that his work was done, and moved on. He never came back to visit again. However, another spirit animal took the baton and moved me forward.

When I first met Coyote, I was grappling with chronic, crippling anxiety, which was wildly amplified by sinking into a fear-based religion. I was living life on a narrow balance beam, and that beam was a razor blade. I started having full-blown panic attacks if I had to drive alone farther than about twenty miles from home. A coworker told me I needed something to be in charge of, so that being afraid wouldn't be my job anymore. While out shopping one day, I noticed a yellow stuffed lion on the toy shelf. Yellow!

A cowardly lion! That's me! I bought him, and placed all my anxiety on him. I know it sounds nuts, but it worked. If little Lion is busy being afraid, I can relax. Whenever anxiety started boiling, I'd shoot it right over to Lion.

Lion imagery began appearing to me everywhere. Coyote made me take a hard look at my situation. Lion picked up where Coyote left off. Lion empowered me to do something about it. I gathered up lion imagery around me, particularly the fierce males. They inspired courage, power, and ferocity—things I wasn't experienced with. I learned to be lionhearted. I started standing up for myself and pushing back for the first time in my life. I learned to say no. I eventually managed to extract myself from the church and, a few years later, my marriage too. Lion remains with me, amongst my most powerful spirit animals.

Coyote, Lion, Horse. They demonstrate the difference between an animal you just love and a spirit animal: they inaugurate change.

Messengers from Other Realms

Sometimes a spirit animal's job is very subtle. That "change" may be comfort and support. It may be conveying a message from another realm. The distinct presence of a loved one may be sensed whenever that animal appears. So it was with my friend, David, whose mother had recently passed away, leaving him heartbroken. David knew she really loved hummingbirds, but that was pretty much the extent of his awareness of them.

"I never noticed them prior to my mother's passing," he says. "The year my mom passed, a female built a nest in our yard, and raised another. Whenever I feel a bit off—or particularly joyful—they appear. I notice the clicking first and then I see them."

Even before David noticed hummingbirds, they noticed him. As he was giving his mother's eulogy with friends in his yard, a hummingbird was in attendance too, flitting around and observing everyone there. Following his mother's death, David started noticing hummingbird imagery in random places. When he and his husband, Mike, went away for a weekend following the memorial, the room was decorated with hummingbird paintings.

David says hummingbirds convey a distinct connection to his mother.

"I always feel my mother's presence when they're around. There's always a sense of calm and well-being when I see a hummingbird. I wouldn't say they have changed my life, but it has confirmed for me that we do connect with spirit animals, and if we pay attention, they will speak to us. Even Mike has made the connection—and he's an engineer and does not readily see these kind of things."

Attracting Spirit Animals

Spirit may send an animal messenger to you, with guidance you didn't even know you needed, but you don't have to wait for one to materialize in your life. You may already know what you need, and can seek out a particular spirit animal to attract it. For example, if you want to be more assertive, you might seek out Tiger. Maybe you need to focus on physical or emotional healing, and you call upon Bear. If you have a creative project in mind and need a burst of color and energy, you could invite Hummingbird to flit in and inspire you. Whether you seek a particular spirit animal or the universe sends one to you, your relationship with that animal will be just as meaningful and inspirational.

One way to attract a spirit animal is to create an altar for exactly that purpose, with the animal's image, things it likes, and the energies it represents. (More on altars in section three.) You can also wear jewelry or clothing with that animal's image on it to keep its spiritual energy close to you. To enrich your relationship with that animal, find out everything you can about it, both in nature and magically or symbolically. Talk to that animal in meditation, and let it materialize in your mind. Allow yourself to become completely fascinated with that animal, and the energy it represents.

Activity: Meditation to Invite a Spirit Animal

In her book, Deborah Blake notes that you can't force an animal to be a familiar. It either is or isn't. And, the animal will be the one to decide. You can facilitate the universe's assistance in guiding a familiar to you by simply asking, and you can do the same to meet any special spirit animal with a lesson you need.

Find a quiet moment. Get comfortable. Relax. Feel the chair you're sitting in or the surface you're lying on supporting you completely. Breathe slowly from the center of your belly, and clear your mind of everything but one thought: I am open to a spirit animal entering my life (or familiar, if that's what you want specifically). Don't specify the animal, just slowly and gently repeat this mantra in your mind until it feels like enough. Then just be still and breathe. If intrusive thoughts drift in, capture them in a bubble and let them drift away. The image of an animal may appear to you—or not. If not, no worries. The universe has heard your request and is searching for just the right one. Be attentive over the next few days or weeks—that animal may appear to you. Trust the process, knowing absolutely that the universe will guide the right spirit animal to you at the right time, or even in a dream.

Pagan Spirit Animals

Despite a mosaic of spirit animal lore across cultures and traditions, we're going to meet some that are considered sacred, magical, or spiritually significant in the Pagan community. You'll see these animals on artwork, pendants, and fabrics, represented in statuary and trinkets, and as embellishments on everything from chalices to wands. They aren't merely decorations. Animal representations that you wear or place on an altar or include in ritual have a precise magical or spiritual purpose. They're part of a magical intention. Many Pagans gather images, figurines, or symbology of particular animals in their homes to feel closer to that animal's energy or draw it to them. You'll also see this spirit animal imagery on clothing, jewelry, and tattoos.

The following spirit animals are those you'll likely meet on your walk through the Big Pagan Garden. This isn't a comprehensive list—just a sampling.

Bat: Bat is quite comfortable at night, and contrary to popular belief, isn't blind at all. Bats have sharp vision in the dark, but also use echolocation to find food and navigate dark places. They are nocturnal, streaming from their caves at dusk, and lend themselves to shadow work, shamanic journeying, dreams, and astral travel. The spiritual attributes of bats include fearlessness in the dark, transformation, rebirth, and the underworld. Bat assures you that you needn't fear the dark. Bat can assist you when you need courage to travel through dark times or places, even the ones that exist in your own mind. Bats live in densely populated tight quarters in dark caves, which symbolizes family, tribe, and community. Bat reminds us that we're safest when we stick together.

Bear: A powerful earth energy animal, Bear symbolizes strength, rest, protection, and dreamwork. It hibernates inside the earth itself, in dens or caves, returning to its earthly womb and reemerging when it's rested, ready, and able to resume its life. Bear assertively protects its boundaries and its need to turn inward to rest and heal, for as long as necessary. If you have difficulty setting boundaries to take time to rest or heal, Bear can assist you. Bear is also fiercely protective, and represents that iconic mother-bear energy. Get in between a mother bear and her cubs and you may pay for that mistake with your life. Call upon Bear when you want protection for your own cubs. Bear says, "Rest, rejuvenate, and arise refreshed." And also, "Stay away from my cubs."

Bee: Bee is the tireless worker, representing productivity, teamwork, determination, organization, and the "hive": your group, clan, or family. An air element animal, call upon Bee when you need to stay focused and get a job done, particularly in a cooperative effort. Bees are crucial to life. Without them, pollination would collapse, and trigger a domino effect of environmental catastrophe. Our lives depend upon bees, but they can't do their work alone. They must work together. If you're faced with a very important or daunting task, employ the support of your "hive" to stay focused on the goal. Bees' lives are devoted to gathering pollen, which they transform into honey. Bee reminds us that the rewards of hard work, perseverance, and cooperation are sweet. Bee says, "If you want the honey, you must do the work."

Butterfly: Butterfly is all about metamorphosis and transformation. One must do time as a creeping, crawling caterpillar before becoming a soaring, fluttering creature of beauty and lightness. Butterfly also inspires patience for letting metamorphosis occur. You can't force metamorphosis, or transformation. It has a process it must complete in its own time, on its own schedule. If you cut a cocoon open, the butterfly will die. It takes time for the caterpillar to become what it was destined to be. Let Butterfly inspire you to be patient enough to transform from the mundane to the magnificent. The reward of patience is self-actualization. Butterfly's message is, "Believe in your magnificent, magical destiny."

Cat: Cat is the epitome of independence, magic, mystery, and pleasure. Cats are historically associated with witches, particularly black cats, which are iconic in Paganism. Cats are the cherished animal of Bastet, the Egyptian goddess of pleasure, femininity, fertility, childbirth, and protection, particularly of women, children, and cats. Cat spirit is aligned with psychic magical ability. When you wish to travel between worlds seen and unseen, Cat can assist you, inspiring you to embrace your magical nature. Cats are also survivalists. They can move stealthily and unseen through the dark to catch prey. Even domesticated cats retain their wild DNA, are able to hunt to survive, and can survive independently without humans if they need to. Cats, as opposed to dogs, do not have a hardwired biological desire to please humans in exchange for praise. They are unconcerned with pleasing us. Cats can be selfish, demanding, and sneaky, and will unashamedly bask in pleasure, purring and rolling when petted, and sleeping in whatever warm spot they wish, whether you like it or not—and we adore them anyway. Are there times when you need to shamelessly put your own needs first? Be fiercely independent? A little more demanding? Be a little selfish for a change? Call upon Cat, who reminds us by saying, "Pursue your needs and desires, with no apologies or regrets."

Coyote: Coyote is the trickster, the jokester—and sometimes the joke is on him. In the classic Warner Brothers' Roadrunner cartoon, Coyote makes big plans and schemes that consistently backfire on him. But he's never thwarted for long. He gets back up and tries again. Coyote is wily like Fox, but not as cunning and careful. He might figure out how to walk along a fence top to get to the chicken coop, and then slip and fall right into a pile of cow manure. He creates his own situations, sometimes hilarious, and reminds us that learning to laugh at our own mistakes can be a good thing. Coyote reminds us by saying, "Don't take yourself too seriously." He also inspires us to get right back up when we feel defeated, dust off our bruised egos, and try again: "This time, it'll work!"

Dog (or Hound): While dogs are typically associated with unconditional love and loyalty in the non-Pagan world, they have a fiercer persona in the Pagan world. They are associated with the Roman goddess Diana (Artemis in Greek mythology), the key goddess of Dianic witchcraft, as well as

Hecate, Greek goddess of magic, spells, nighttime, and the crossroad. The Egyptian god of the afterlife, Anubis, is portrayed with a hound's head, and guides the dead to their destination, and is associated with the dead, cemeteries, tombs, and mummification. Loyal Dog spirit will stick by your side whether you're hunting or approaching a magical crossroads or facing a journey into the dark shadows. When you need protection and an animal spirit that always has your back, no matter how formidable the situation, call upon Dog. Dog's message is "Whatever happens, I am with you."

Dolphin: Dolphin inspires water energy of playfulness, gracefulness, and friendliness. Dolphin's call sounds like chirpy, cheery laughter. Life is so damn serious, and we often forget we need to play too. Dolphin reminds us of that. Call upon happy, playful, carefree Dolphin when your life seems dull, heavy, or unhappy. Dolphin dives deep into the emotional waters and can leap up above them as well, spinning and playing, inspiring freedom of emotion (water) and thought (air), moving effortlessly between the two. When your feelings and thoughts are thick and troubled, Dolphin spirit can help you navigate them with joy, ease, and positive energy. Dolphin's message is, "It's okay to play."

Dragonfly: Dragonfly's iridescent wings and aerial acrobatics are a reminder that anything is possible. Like Butterfly, Dragonfly also represents transformation, but much longer and deeper. Upon hatching from eggs laid in water, dragonflies spend up to two years of their early lives underwater as nymphs. Once fully grown, they crawl out of the water, shed their skin, and emerge as a full-grown adult dragonfly. Evolving from a water creature to an air creature symbolizes our subconscious emotions and creativity emerging into conscious expression, and expressing our true nature and potential. Dragonfly prompts us to go inwards, reconnect with ourselves, make the changes we need to make, and when we're ready for that transformation, reemerge and take flight. Dragonfly tells you, "All the colors of your dreams are within reach." They may not come overnight, and may take some introspection, but they *will* come. Let Dragonfly inspire you to allow yourself the time you need to make your own transformation a reality.

Eagle: Eagle soars high into the sky and can see everything from above in great detail; the scope of the entire picture is clear—which inspires the familiar term, eagle-eyed. An iconic air element animal, Eagle is among the most sacred of animal spirits to many Native American tribes, and symbolizes connection to the Divine. Its feathers are also sacred, and should never be used for decorations by those who are not connected to those tribes. When you need to see the entire big picture clearly, and zero in on decisions, let Eagle embolden you. Eagle aligns you with divine energy, and helps your plans and ideas take flight. Chosen as the symbol of the United States, Eagle also embodies fearlessness, courage, and freedom. Eagle spirit will help you soar to new heights. Eagle inspires us to let divine inspiration help you see everything clearly.

Fox: Fox symbolizes cunning, stealth, adaptability, cleverness, and avoiding confrontation. The iconic sly fox is a clever little survivor, and will adapt to a situation to get what it needs, and slink away from confrontation whenever possible. Do you need to be intellectually nimble and creative? Are there people or situations who'd be better dealt with using mental strategy than by engaging in a full-frontal assault? Let Fox help you slink and skitter around your foes, or those who stand in your way or threaten you, and to use its cunning nature for positive outcomes, not deception. Fox's message is, "Choose clever, creative strategies for success."

Hawk: Hawk also soars high in the sky, and like Eagle, can see the entire scope of any situation. Hawk's piercing cry is a signal to pay attention, and also to make yourself be heard. There's nothing shy about Hawk. Another iconic symbol of air energy, Hawk helps you soar, dip, and dive, refreshing and enlivening your thoughts, speech, and writing. Hawks often perch on telephone poles in my area, patiently watching for prey. When they spot it, they dive swiftly and silently down, grabbing it in their talons. Call upon Hawk when you need to carefully evaluate your situation, recognize the correct decision, and act upon it immediately; falter, and you'll come up empty-taloned. Hawk inspires you to keep your mind clear, your eyes open, and to not merely trust your judgment, but act upon it. Hawk says, "Rise above your situation and you'll find what you seek."

Horse: Horses are associated with the Celtic goddesses Eiocha, Epona, Rhiannon, and Macha, as well as the ability to cross back and forth between this world and the underworld. However, they're more typically representative of masculine energy, movement, courage, freedom, and raw power. Horse is multifaceted and multitalented, like a spiritual Swiss Army knife. Horse is my working spirit animal—my go-to when I have a tough job that must get done. Other spirit animals reinforce and inspire me when I want to *be* a certain way. Horse reinforces and inspires me when I want to *do* a certain thing. Horse can empower us physically, emotionally, intellectually, psychologically, and spiritually. Just as horses have transformed human culture throughout history and across the globe, Horse can empower your own personal transformation. Horse *manifests*. Whatever you need to do, wherever you need to go, Horse will make it happen. Horse's message is, "Git 'er done."

Hummingbird: Hummingbird's energy is light, quick, and delicate. Do you need to lighten up and appreciate life's sweetness? Let Hummingbird guide you. Is your mind feeling slow and dull, and creativity and inspiration nowhere to be found? Hummingbird is of the air element, the realm of the mind, and is a perfect spirit animal for writers. Call upon Hummingbird when you need to freshen, brighten, and quicken your mind for any writing endeavors. Hummingbirds can zip about effortlessly and perform all sorts of aerial acrobatics, and even hover in place to suckle nectar or even stop to contemplate a big, strange human invading "their" garden. Quick as a snap, they can dart away and disappear. They're colorful and joyful to watch, and like Bee, work very hard to get their sweet rewards. Let Hummingbird remind you to be bright, quick, colorful, and joyful, and to "Let your ideas fly."

Lion: The lion is revered in Scotland, appearing on the Royal Banner as the "Lion Rampant," clawing, rearing, and roaring. Lion is known across many cultures as the king of beasts, and its spirit animal symbology includes strength, courage, assertiveness, and the ability to engage in battle when necessary. Lion is also the symbol of the astrological sign of Leo, whose traits include dominance, passion, gregariousness, and a love of adoration and attention—just like any king or queen might demand.

Like the astrological sign, Lion belongs to the element of fire, with its characteristics of boldness, fearlessness, and physical strength. Lion appeared in my life as a guardian, and is now one of my power animals. If I'm feeling intimidated, Lion reminds me to roar. Lion will do the same for you, and remind you that you are the king or queen of your realm: own your crown and rule your kingdom.

Owl: Owl is a major presence in Pagan symbology, its mythology extending back to ancient Greece, appearing on the shoulder of Athena, the Greek goddess of wisdom and war strategy. Owl was able to see the whole truth, and prevented Athena from being deceived by anyone. Owls are classic symbols of wisdom in both Pagan and non-Pagan mythology; the wise old owl image is iconic. Owls are fearlessness in the deep, dark night. That's when they hunt. Owls are fierce, deadly, and silent predators, and can be vicious foes when attacked. In some cultures, owls are associated with death itself. Yes, owls kill. But they also cull. This is a positive thing in nature. By removing the slow and weak, only the strong, smart, and fast survive. Owl is my "don't mess with me" power animal. When I'm feeling fearful, need things culled from my life, or need calm, calculating fierceness, I call upon Owl, who reminds me, "Be more fierce than the dark itself."

Raven: Dark prophecy, magic, mysticism, intellect, shape-shifting—these qualities are associated with Raven, which is closely associated with one of the original Celtic deities, the Morrigan, known for the same qualities. The Morrigan is the goddess of war, fate, and death, particularly on the battlefield, and could appear as a raven (or crow) on the battlefield. Like Owl, Raven is very common in Pagan symbology. Raven can bend and shape both time and physical appearance, and lends itself to magical work. Ravens and crows are related, but are not the same species. Both glossy, jet-black species perfectly complement the darker realms and energies, and both are highly intelligent, curious creatures. Like Coyote, they have some of that trickster energy. When you want to enhance magic, mysticism, and taking on other forms, call upon Raven to make magic happen.

Snake: By shedding its skin and emerging anew, Snake symbolizes transformation and resurrection. It sloughs off what is no longer necessary and reappears sleek and strong. In contrast to its sinful, evil reputation in the Christian Bible, in the Pagan world, Snake represents healing. The image of intertwined snakes appears on the caduceus, a symbol of the medical arts. The imagery of Greek god Asclepios, the god of healing and medicine, features a snake coiled around his staff. A snake is also central to the imagery of his daughter, Hygeia, Greek goddess of health and cleanliness, which shows her tenderly holding a snake and feeding it milk from a bowl. In Egyptian imagery, the striking cobra is a sacred icon, appearing on headdresses of pharaohs and gods, signifying sovereignty and absolute authority. When you need an infusion of good health, or are yearning for your own physical or psychological transformation, Snake will encourage you to slough off that which no longer serves you and to thrive. Snake spirit in cobra form can empower you to declare your own sovereignty and authority over your life or magical work. Cobra says, "Because I command it." In addition to their association with medicine, healing, transformation, and sovereignty, snakes are quick to protect themselves, and will coil and strike. They can be quite deadly. When you need some protection magic, Snake can be your ally, sending a clear message to stay away—or else.

Spider: Spider is nature's artist. Her spirit symbolizes feminine energy and creativity, particularly as it pertains to magic, spellcasting, and the shadow self. Spiders work diligently, and spin threaded works of art that look so very delicate but are strong enough to catch prey. What creative or magical endeavors would you like to weave in your own life? What dreams do you wish to weave into reality? Call upon Spider to inspire you in any creative endeavor, from needle arts to writing to painting. Spider tells us, "Imagination brings manifestation."

Wolf: Loyalty to "the pack," social connections, sharp instincts, and freedom are the energies associated with Wolf. Wolves are fierce and intelligent, and roam and hunt together cooperatively, letting their instincts and pack strategy assist them in bringing down prey. By contrast, the iconic lone wolf prefers a solitary existence. Whether in a pack or alone, Wolf is a wild, self-sufficient predator and survivalist. Wolves famously howl at the full moon, which is deeply connected to witchcraft and magic, which are often synchronized with phases of the moon. In tarot, the Moon card (which symbolizes the subconscious mind, fears, illusions, and the dream realm) features a howling dog and wolf, representing our inner, wild urges. Wolf reminds us to always trust our instincts.

Activity: Which Animal Says What

There are many more animals that inspire certain energies or teaching than the ones I've mentioned, both Pagan and otherwise. Let's invite them in.

In your journal, ask yourself the following questions, and jot down the first animal that comes to mind. If it's one from my list, that's just fine. If not, also fine. If something really random and unexpected pops up, go with it. If you draw a blank and struggle for an answer, don't force it. Move on. It may come to you later.

What animal embodies *joy* to you?

What animal embodies *power* to you?

What animal embodies *protection* to you?

What animal embodies *inspiration* to you?

What animal embodies *serenity* to you?

What animal embodies *safety* to you?

What animal embodies *adventure* to you?

What animal embodies *love* to you?

What animal embodies *earth* to you?

What animal embodies *air* to you?

What animal embodies *fire* to you?

What animal embodies *water* to you?

What animal embodies *Spirit* to you?

What animal embodies *magic* to you?

After identifying animals with these qualities, open yourself to their teachings, and invite them into your life. For each one, tell yourself, out loud, "I am open to the possibility that (Dolphin) will visit me and teach me about (joy)." And then, be attentive for that animal's appearance in your life, physically or symbolically. When it does appear, acknowledge it, and thank it. In your journal, record the circumstances of that animal's appearance. What message is it sending?

You can get insight into that message by learning everything you can about that animal's natural behavior and its cultural, magical, or spiritual symbology. Whatever the tradition or culture, the stories and symbology associated with spirit animals began with an observation of that animal's natural behavior. Their magic comes from nature.

Spirit Animals Can Prompt Positivity

Animals that appear in your natural surroundings can serve as prompts to remind you of something. Whenever you see them, you repeat a reinforcing affirmation. I learned this technique from a long-ago blog post by Silver RavenWolf, where she shared this meditative affirmation: "My life is filled with positive abundance. All my needs are met, and more." The next time we went outside, the first wild animal we saw would serve as a prompt to repeat that affirmation to ourselves—even if life wasn't feeling abundant, and maybe particularly so. Besides providing a simple way to inspire positivity, Silver was also teaching a very basic lesson in magic: believe in what you desire as if it you already have it.

The next time I set out to run some errands, there atop a telephone pole was a red-tailed hawk, which are very common in this area. I repeated the affirmation on the spot, and have done so ever since whenever I see a hawk—and that's been years and years. Hawk is my living, random reminder to stop and be grateful for what I *do* have, rather than focusing on what I don't. Hawk prompts me to focus on the half-full part of the glass, even on the days when the half-empty part is front and center in my mind. Hawk is a spiritual reset button, reminding me to remember that all in all, I'm doing okay, even on the crappy days, and to focus on my own abundance. Like Hawk spirit itself, the actual animal prompts me to rise above it and see all I have to be grateful for.

Activity: Give Silver's Affirmation a Try

Attaching a positive affirmation to an animal in your environment provides many opportunities to reinforce gratitude. Give Silver's "positive abundance" meditation and affirmation a try. Spend some quiet time focusing upon her affirmation: *My life is filled with positive abundance. All my needs are met, and more.* Say it out loud until it feels normal and natural; like it's yours. The next time you're out and about, see which animal shows up to represent that affirmation. Say the affirmation on the spot, whenever the animal prompts you.

Create the Animal Spirit Relationships You Want

Spirit animals offer us fresh perspectives on things we're dealing with in our lives. They represent qualities we wish to attract to ourselves, our work, or our magic. They may just pop up in your life, or you might go searching for them. Some animals may have been there all along, sending you a message you weren't hearing. Start listening with your spirit, not your ears.

There's a cornucopia of information available on animals and animal spirits. You shouldn't have any trouble finding more than enough on any animal you're attracted to. Pay attention to animals in your environment. Observe those animals' behavior, and notice how they make you feel or the thoughts they inspire. Craft a spiritual message from those experiences, and give the animal a mantra that summarizes its lesson, just as I did in my Pagan spirit animal list: "The wild geese tell me, 'Know when to stay and when to leave.'"

Somewhere out there, a spirit animal is ready to deliver the universe's message to you. Be open to that possibility.

Recommended Reading

Blake, Deborah. *The Little Book of Cat Magic: Spells, Charms & Tales*. Woodbury, MN: Llewellyn Publications, 2018.

MacKinnon, Danielle. *Animal Lessons: Discovering Your Spiritual Connection with Animals*. Woodbury, MN: Llewellyn Publications, 2017.

Sams, Jamie and David Carson. *Medicine Cards*. New York, NY: St. Martin's Press, 1988, 1999.

CHAPTER 8
The Wheel of the Year

The Wheel of the Year is amongst the most common and well-known Pagan concepts. It symbolizes the never-ending passage of the seasons, one into the next, divided by the solstices and equinoxes, with halfway points in between each.

There are eight points on the wheel, each signifying a Pagan holiday, or *sabbat*. There are four solar sabbats (solstices and equinoxes) and four agrarian or earth sabbats (everything else). In many Pagan traditions, such as Wicca, there are celebrations, rituals, and symbology associated with each of those eight sabbats.

Just like a day, the phases of the moon, and maybe the cosmos too, there is an entire breath on the Wheel of the Year, also aligning with the energies of inhaling (attracting) and exhaling (repelling).

An Eight-Spoked Wheel

You can imagine the Wheel of the Year as a pie chart. If you made a straight slice from twelve o'clock to six o'clock, you'd have the winter solstice on top, and the summer solstice on the bottom. Next, make a straight slice from three o'clock to nine o'clock. The spring equinox is on the right, and the fall equinox on the left. The plus-shaped figure in a circle is known as the *solar cross*, which symbolizes the solstices and equinoxes. These points are the *minor sabbats* or *solar sabbats*: Yule (winter solstice), Ostara (spring equinox), Litha (summer solstice), and Mabon (fall equinox).

Now, at the exact midpoints between the solstices and equinoxes, we'll cut a straight slice from one side of the pie to the other. These four points represent the *major sabbats* or *agrarian sabbats*: Imbolc, Beltane, Lughna-sadh, and Samhain.

The solar sabbats are directly linked to the amount of daylight and position of the sun, and are universally recognized across all cultures, even ancient ones, and aren't exclusively Pagan. The agrarian sabbats that fall halfway in between each are associated with agrarian activities and cycles, such as planting, tending, harvesting, and going fallow, and are traditionally celebrated as fire festivals in the Pagan community.

Although only the minor sabbats are linked with agrarian practices, all eight lend themselves to agrarian imagery if you happen to live in a place with four distinct seasons and a winter that includes snow. Just like those traditional names for the full moons, the agrarian symbology only resonates with those of us living in a similar environment and situation. If you're in rural Pennsylvania, perfect. In the northern California valley where I live, for example, the classic agrarian cycles fall flat. Crops are grown and harvested year-round here. We get sun, sun, and more sun, year-round. We don't have four seasons, where I live, only two: Fire Season and Not Fire Season, with a little spring and fall sprinkled in between them.

The Wheel's traditional agrarian symbology may not resonate with those living near the equator, or those in the southern hemisphere, who experience the seasons in opposition to the northern hemisphere. Those in the southern hemisphere have to flip the Wheel of the Year over, because their summer solstice is in December, and their winter solstice is in June. The southern-ers may feel a bit silly celebrating with holly, mistletoe, and snow at Yule when they're basking in the sun in shorts, sipping on a cool glass of iced tea. They'll need to adjust their sabbat symbology accordingly to align with their own environments.

While the literal seasonal agricultural symbolism on the classic Pagan Wheel of the Year may not resonate with everyone everywhere, the spirit behind those agricultural practices can still resonate metaphorically. Instead of planting, tending, and harvesting crops, you plant, tend, and harvest goals for the year, aligned with each sabbat's agricultural rhythms and practices. Instead of planting a crop, you can plant a goal for the upcoming year.

The Lore of the Wheel

In some Pagan traditions, the year is viewed in halves, symbolized by the lore of the Oak King and Holly King. The two kings battle each other in perpetuity, "winning" when each one's time begins, only to engage in the same battle again as the seasons turn, when the other "wins" and comes into power. Just like the Chinese mythology of the Dragon and Tiger, perpetually locked in battle, the Oak King and Holly King need each other in order to exist and remain in balance, like yin and yang. In Pagan lore, the Holly King rules the darker portion of the year and the Oak King rules the lighter. The Holly King's reign traditionally begins on the summer solstice, and the Oak King's on the winter solstice. However, the darker and lighter halves would more realistically align with the equinoxes, and some traditions adjust the kings' reigns accordingly, having their battles won and lost on the spring and fall equinoxes.[27]

In Wicca, the Wheel of the Year symbolizes the endless cycle of life and death, as represented by the Goddess and her consort God—a perpetual span of birth, life, and death, expressed over the course of each year, only to start anew as each new year begins. (Warning: Don't think about this story too hard, because it makes no logical sense. It's an allegory. Totally symbolic. Don't think it. Feel it.) Here we go:

---

27. Wicca Living, "The Oak King and the Holly King: Aspects of the God," accessed July 29, 2020, https://wiccaliving.com/wiccan-oak-king-holly-king/.

At Yule, the Goddess gives birth to a son—the God—who continues to mature through Imbolc, and extremely rapidly, because at Ostara, he becomes her consort, and they mate. By Beltane, the Goddess is pregnant, as the God approaches full maturity. The Goddess is gestating at Litha; however, the God has reached his full peak, and enters into midlife decline. At Lughnasadh, the God is rapidly aging, as the Goddess's belly grows round. At Mabon, the death of the God is imminent. At Samhain, the God dies, and the heavily pregnant Goddess goes into her dark phase to mourn her son/consort. At Yule, she gives birth to a son again and the cycle repeats, year after year.

As I said, don't think about this story too hard. It's good to be familiar with it, because you'll hear of it in your Pagan travels, and remember, for some Pagans, this story is sacred. So, no Oedipus jokes. You'll get some hard stares. Look at the story with one eye squinted, just let it blur and be, and you can see the revolving theme of birth, maturity, decline, and death, which is the very pattern of life, whether a human life or a field of corn. The meaning behind the story has substance.

The Sabbats

The Wheel of the Year has eight spokes, each representing a sabbat. The Wheel is a modern concept based upon ancient practices and festivals. Yule is customarily where the Wheel "begins." However, the starting point is rather arbitrary, as a wheel doesn't really have a beginning or end, just a perpetually turning circle. In the interest of everyone being able to talk about the same thing coherently, Yule will be our collective starting point, and its position on the wheel is twelve o'clock.

The Pagan sabbats predate our familiar modern identically-timed holidays. In the fourth century, the early Roman Catholic Church, which was aligned with the Roman Empire, embarked on an organized attempt to obliterate all things Pagan, including the Pagan sabbats. In addition to smashing Pagan temples and building Christian churches over them, the Church attempted to stamp Christian templates over Pagan celebrations.

Following are the eight Pagan sabbats and symbology, from a northern hemisphere perspective. The dates aren't always exact, as the time of the solstices and equinoxes fluctuate slightly from year to year.

Yule

Yule occurs on the winter solstice, the longest night and shortest day of the year, around December 21. This is the last night of darkening days, and the light of the sun will start returning on the next, which defines the spirit of Yule: hope. Yule traditions include burning a Yule log through the night to welcome back the sun, and decorations of evergreen, holly, and mistletoe, representing everlasting life through the cold, harsh winter. The Yule log and evergreens restore our hope that the sun—and life—will return. The traditions of feasting and giving gifts come from the pre-Christian Roman festival of Saturnalia, which included sacrificing the strongest, most handsome young man in the village for the guarantee of strength and victory for all. Over time, sacrificing a nice, strong evergreen replaced sacrificing a young man. And aren't you glad for that, because Christmas trees would look a lot different than the ones we're used to!

Obviously, the Christian holiday stamped over Yule is Christmas, even though Jesus wasn't even born in December. He was born during the Roman census, which occurs in the fall. However, there is parallel symbology: the birth of the Son, and the birth of the Sun (or the God, from the Wiccan lore). Some Pagan fundamentalists eschew all holidays associated with Christianity, but I'm not amongst them. If it's fun, I'm in. That said, I do Santa Christmas, not Jesus Christmas.

On the abstract level, using agrarian imagery, Yule is when farmers would imagine which crops they wanted to plant in the spring, so fiery Yule carries the spark for your goal for the upcoming year. Do a little brainstorming and wish-listing. Think big. What would you love to accomplish this year? What is something you always wanted to try? At Yule, start dreaming and imagining.

Imbolc

Imbolc occurs on or around February 1, and is the halfway point between Yule (winter solstice) and Ostara (spring equinox). The name comes from a Celtic word meaning "ewe's milk." At this time of year, lambs will soon be born, as evidenced by the ewes' teats filling with milk. The holiday is traditionally associated with the Celtic goddess Brigid, protectress of farm animals, and also goddess of fire, smith-crafting (ironwork, typically done on a forge), and fertility. Weaving a Brigid's Cross from straw—a four-armed star, with a square in the middle—is a traditional Imbolc activity and decoration, as is anything honoring Brigid.

In the non-Pagan secular world, this date is associated with Groundhog Day, which also proclaims that winter will be over in six weeks as long as that furry little feller doesn't see his shadow. In Christian circles, this day is Candlemas, a day to celebrate Jesus, the light of the world.

Imbolc is the time to make decisions about your Yule wish list. What exactly will you "plant"? It's time to pick one and put that seed into the ground. You might also create milestones for the remaining sabbats to measure your progress.

Ostara

Ostara occurs around March 21, the spring equinox, and got its name from Eostre, the Saxon goddess of spring. Ostara's traditional Pagan symbols represent fertility, particularly rabbits (hares) and eggs—sound familiar? Just like Yule and Christmas, I do both Ostara and Easter, but I do Easter Bunny Easter, not Horrific Public Execution and Subsequent Tomb Miracle Easter. (And also, Good Friday should be called "Really, Super, Awful, Colossally Horrid Friday." It's so *not* good.)

In agricultural areas, life is springing up everywhere at Ostara. Calves and foals are being born, the ground is being tilled, and greenery is appearing. That seed you planted at Imbolc should be sprouting. Ostara is a day of balance, so if you aren't seeing any growth, it's time to evaluate your progress and see if you need to tweak your plan.

Beltane

Beltane, occurring on May 1, is all about pleasure, rejoicing, and celebrating beauty and abundance. It's a very sexy sabbat. It's called May Day in many non-Pagan secular circles and elsewhere. An abundance of flowers symbolizes both. Dancing around a maypole is a familiar May Day theme, and has Pagan roots in Beltane. A large pole (representing the phallus), with a wreath at the top (representing the vagina), is adorned with colorful ribbons streaming from the top. Dancers each take a ribbon, and traditionally, men go one way, women the other, until they've woven the ribbons all the way down the pole in playful flirtation and sexual attraction.

In the Pagan world, sex is embraced as a normal and natural part of life, and is celebrated. Yes, sex is a good thing! In theory, dancing the maypole is a lovely, sensual weaving and intertwining of graceful, coordinated dancers. In practice, it's semi-organized pandemonium, but there's lots of joy and laughter. Also, those pretty pictures of finished maypoles don't look anything like the lumpy, sloppy messes I've helped create, but hey—sex can be lumpy and sloppy too. The main thing is that everyone involved has a good time!

Another Beltane tradition is handfasting, which is Pagan marriage, but with an escape clause: handfasting binds a couple together for a year and a day, after which time, either could opt for a "no fault" dissolution—sort of like taking the marriage for a year-long test drive. Handfasting is legally recognized as marriage in the United States. The term *handfasting* comes from a cord, often made of woven ribbons, which is used to tie—or fast—the couple's hands together. When removed, the cord stays tied in that loop for as long as the couple remains "fasted." Handfasting is a medieval Celtic tradition from the British Isles, with ranges of opinion about its beginnings, from the pre-Christian age to the Middle Ages.

By Beltane, your little Yule seed is a full-fledged plant, shooting up strong and healthy. Your goal should be completely formed and well underway. Visible, measurable progress should be evident. It's nowhere near done, but it's clearly taking shape.

Litha

Litha occurs on the summer solstice, usually on or around June 21. In some circles it's called Midsummer, the time when the fae folk are frolicking, sometimes right into our own world, as the veil between this world and the realm of the fae is at its thinnest at Litha. Time to get your faerie groove on! A bonfire to celebrate the beginning of the waning sun is amongst Litha's traditions.

Litha is also a very sexy sabbat, and also a popular time for handfastings. With so much in blossom, bees are very active at Litha, so honey is associated with this sabbat—in particular, honey in the form of mead, which is honey wine served to the newlyfasted to help get them in the mood to consummate that union—hence the term *honeymoon*, inspired by lusty honey-drunk nights just after saying, "I do."

Litha is delicious and luscious, but has a bittersweet aftertaste, because we know the days will now grow shorter. Litha marks the beginning of the seasonal "exhale."

In Christian circles, Litha is St. John's Day, devoted to honoring St. John the Baptist, and has various types of celebrations in different places, including bonfires, feasts, and fireworks. It's also a traditional time for Pagans and herbalists to collect St. John's Wort out in the wild for use in medicinal or magical tinctures and teas.

Litha is the rubber-meets-the-road stage for your Yule goal. Your "plant" should be growing steadily every day, getting taller and leafing out, and full of blossoms.

Lugnasadh

Lugnasadh (*loo-na-sod*) is the midpoint between Litha (summer solstice) and Mabon (fall equinox), occurring around August 1. Also known as Lammas, the sabbat is named after the Celtic god Lugh, god of light and the harvest. Lugnasadh is the first of the three contiguous harvest sabbats, and is particularly associated with the corn harvest. A traditional activity at this time of year is to make a corn dolly from corn shucks, which often adorn Lugnasadh altars. The wheat harvest is in full swing at this time of year, so grains and baking bread are associated with Lugnasadh.

Lughnasadh marks the beginning of the harvest season, and therefore canning and preserving to prepare for winter when food would be scarce. We have grocery stores now, so there's no pressing need to preserve for the winter. We have an abundance of food available year-round. However, with a bounty of fresh summer produce like peaches and tomatoes available, canning and preserving are a nice way to celebrate Lughnasadh. As an amusing old gnome once told me about this time of year, "Can what you can, and eat what you can't!"

By Lughnasadh, the seed you planted at Imbolc is fully mature. Ripe fruit is on the branches, ready for picking. Your goal is rounding the far turn and heading into the home stretch. It's time to pour it on and keep your eye on the prize. Success is in sight.

Mabon

Mabon occurs on the fall equinox, on or around September 22, and just like Ostara, there's equal daylight and nighttime. This is the second harvest sabbat, when classic autumn crops roll in: pumpkins, squash, corn, walnuts, and almonds, and making their annual big debut, apples. Here's a fun little witchy tidbit about apples: if you cut them in half sideways, the seeds form a five-pointed star—a pentacle—which is doubly perfect for a Mabon harvest altar, along with all those colorful leaves, nuts, and gourds.

Like Lughnasadh, baking, canning, and preserving continue into this sabbat, and in some areas, mornings start to turn chilly and frost may even appear in northern areas. At Mabon, you begin to detect waning daylight, which means winter isn't far away, so preparations must begin.

At equally-balanced Mabon, you must weigh out your progress. The fruit on your Yule plant should be ripe and ready for harvesting. Is that going to happen, or not? Will a big push carry you over the finish line, or is it obvious that you'll fall short? Mabon is the do-or-die stage for your goal. If it isn't coming to fruition and ready to harvest by Mabon, it probably ain't gonna happen.

Samhain

Samhain falls on October 31, which we all know and love as Halloween—the one time of the year when everybody's joyfully displaying witches, black cats, and cauldrons, Pagan and non-Pagan alike.

Samhain (pronounced sow-en—don't be a dork and say sam-hane) is the third and final harvest sabbat, as well as symbolic of the ultimate harvest: death. On Samhain, the veils between this world and the realm of the dead are thinnest. Messages from the other side may be heard, and messages from this side received. Altars featuring photos and remembrances of those who have passed through the veil honor our own beloved dead. Some have a feast called a "dumb supper," with one empty plate for those who have passed on, inviting their spirits to partake. The meal is eaten in silence to welcome the spirits of loved ones to the table.

Halloween is a contraction of All Hallows' Eve, a version of All Saints' Eve, which is the night before the Christian holiday of All Saints' Day on November 1. All Saints' Day coincides with the Day of the Dead—Día de los Muertos, a Mexican holiday, when deceased loved ones are celebrated with skeletons and sugar skulls, and their graves adorned with marigolds and ornate handmade miniature dioramas.

Of all the Pagan sabbats, Samhain feels the most "holy" to me. Juxtaposed with the wacky, wonderful fun of Halloween, it can also feel a little whiplash-y. But you learn to juggle this. I have my altars and rituals for my beloved dead, but I can spin right around and get my witchy on for the little trick-or-treaters or a costume party. I'm a Gemini. Doing two things at once is easy for me.

Samhain, the midway point between the fall equinox and the winter solstice, is the traditional end of the Pagan year, signifying a dark, still time of rest right up until Yule. The rest of the year was busy, and now it's time to slow down and cocoon, and let the fields—and your energy—go fallow. This is the polar opposite of October 31 in America, Hallothanksmasyear's Eve, when we launch into the nonstop stress and chaos of the holiday season. Rest? At *this* time of year? The true spirit of Samhain, a time of rest and stillness, could inspire you to keep things simple. Samhain can remind you that the holidays are only as stressful as you allow them to be.

As for that Yule goal from months ago, if it hasn't matured and produced fruit by Samhain … better luck next time. Just let the leaves fall. Put your goal on a shelf, let it rest, but don't wallow in self-defeat. There's still value in the attempt. During this dark, restful time of year, analyze what went wrong. What prevented you from succeeding? What can you learn from this? What could you do differently next time? Even when you don't meet a goal, or when you outright fail, there's something to be learned. Nobody ever learned to walk without falling flat on their butt first. A *lot*. Failure doesn't defeat you—only giving up does that. Use this still, darkening time of year to figure out how to make that project work next time. Maybe you can "replant" when Imbolc rolls around.

Conversely, if you met that goal, celebrate! Wow, how awesome does that feel? Congratulate yourself, give yourself a treat, pat yourself on the back, wrap your arms around yourself and squeeze. Relish those successes, and when the self-congratulatory *woot-woots* are over, make use of this dark and still time of year to analyze your success too. What obstacles did you overcome? What strategies did you use to get there? Can you make use of them for future goals? Employ those strategies for your next "planting." Whether you met with success or failure, introspection and analysis at this time of year will help make next year's goal succeed.

The Wheel Looks Different Here

One of my frustrations when learning about the Wheel was that the four-season imagery of life in the British Isles bore no resemblance to my own environment. Midsummer in June? Ha! In California, that would be the end of August. Nip of frost at Mabon? Ha again! It's still 105 degrees here in September, and half the state is likely on fire. We don't have a blanket of frost at Mabon, we have a blanket of wildfire smoke.

While the Wheel appealed to me metaphorically, in actuality, there was little about the Wheel's traditional symbology that resonated with me. It was some other culture's reality, not mine. For example, in northern Europe, pine and holly are symbolic of Yule, but those are the only green things surviving in the snow there. Where I live, citrus is at its full glory at Yule: mandarins, lemons, and oranges. Citrus is what grows in *my* yard at Yule—not holly. So, while I include traditional pine and holly on my Yule altar, I also include my own local glorious wintertime greenery: mandarin fruit and leaves. That feels much more genuine and honest, as opposed to cramming my foot into another culture's shoe, just because it's the "right" way to make a Yule altar.

The first time my Yule altar was adorned with sweet little orange mandarins, I realized that for all the other holidays, there's local plant life thriving at that time. I wanted genuine symbology for all the sabbats, so I decided to track the Wheel of the Year by documenting the Wheel of My Yard.

For one whole year, I followed the changes in the plants and trees in my own yard, as well as the plant life in the surrounding area. Using a weekly datebook, I jotted down everything I noticed—what was growing, dying back, flowering, bearing fruit, or dropping leaves, and noted which plants were most glorious at the sabbats, and designated them as my sacred plants for each sabbat. Now, I can tell exactly what time of year it is simply by looking at the plant life around me.

As I mentioned, ripe mandarins mean it's Yule. Almonds start blossoming at Imbolc. Ostara is heralded by orange California poppies dotting the hillsides, now lush and green. Beltane is the time of blossoms, both citrus and jasmine. Romantic roses and seas of sunflowers announce Litha's arrival. When the green hills fade to gold, the sunflowers' heavy heads turn brown and sag, and the field corn stands high over my head, Lughnasadh is arriving. An abundance of apples and nuts means Mabon, and when those bright orange persimmons and deep red pomegranates are ready for picking, it's time for Samhain.

Activity: Signify Your Sabbats

Signifying the sabbats by the annual changes in your own environment makes them more meaningful and real. It fosters a deeper biocongruent connection to nature as it rolls through its rhythmic changes over the course of the year.

Get a weekly calendar or datebook—one with space to write on for each day of the week, for the whole year. Llewellyn's Witches' Datebook is perfect for this activity, because it notes the Pagan sabbats, and has articles, stories, and information stashed throughout. It also charts daily astrological movement and phases of the moon, and will pull together so many things we're exploring.

As the year rolls along, note the changes in your own environment: weather, plants, flowers, animals, crops, and wildflowers that grow around you, and anything else that seems noteworthy. Be descriptive with your details, because it enriches your observations about the changing seasons, and also because it's easy to forget what you saw after several months go by.

When you have an entire year's worth of observations, select the sacred symbology for the sabbats relative to your own environment. You can include traditional sabbat symbology if you like, or switch to your own entirely. It's nice to have knowledge of the traditional sabbats and symbology so you have a common vocabulary with other Pagans, but in your own life, the seasons and their sacred symbology are what *you* say they are. They correspond to your reality, not someone else's.

When Seasons Were Calendars

Our ancient ancestors didn't track the changing seasons on calendars, or even the Wheel of the Year. However, they were very much aware of subtle seasonal changes in weather and plant life, as well as animal migrations—

it was a matter of life and death. Tarry too long in the mountains, and the snow may come before you can get to lower ground. The animals you hunt have moved on, and the berries you gather won't appear for many months. Even when humans took control of their food sources by becoming agrarian societies, tracking the changing seasons was still a matter of survival. Knowing when to plant, when to reap, and when to store food were key to surviving through the winter.

Nowadays, we can survive just fine regardless of the season, and not paying attention to the passage of time is little more than a disappointment, like missing out on fresh peaches and not being able to find them again until next summer. No big whoop. However, in the Pagan world, being in sync with the changing seasons and the Wheel is deeply meaningful, because it symbolically attunes us to Mother Earth's rhythmic energies, which align with many magical practices. When attending a sabbat celebration or ritual in the Big Pagan Garden, knowing the traditional meanings of those sabbats gives us a common language, no matter where we live or what our environments are like. We're all dancing to the same music.

Recommended Reading

Danaan, Clea. *Living Earth Devotional—365 Green Practices for Sacred Connection*. Woodbury, MN: Llewellyn Publications, 2013.

Dugan, Ellen. *Seasons of Witchery—Celebrating the Sabbats with the Garden Witch*. Woodbury, MN: Llewellyn Publications, 2019.

Mankey, Jason. *Witch's Wheel of the Year: Rituals for Circles, Solitaries & Covens*. Woodbury, MN: Llewellyn Publications, 2019.

CHAPTER 9
Sun, Moon, and Stars

When we look up into the night sky, or gaze at stars with binoculars, or just imagine what's out there, we're not seeing the bigger picture. Everything we see up in the sky isn't "out there," while we are "here." Our planet is part of that "out there," and moves in beautiful rhythm with all of it. The sun, moon, and stars aren't rotating *above* us, they're all *around* us, and further out, so is the galaxy, and beyond that, open space, and whatever is beyond *that* "beyond that." Everything moves, drifts, and spins together—an inconceivably massive sea of dark matter and dark energy in which a gazillion constellations, stars, planets, and asteroids float and swirl. That "out there" isn't a flat plane. It's perpetually expanding spherically, like a ball, from that original Big Bang pinpoint. That's the science of it. However, our *perception* of the cosmos, and how we make sense of it, is based upon our viewpoint here on Earth.

Going back to prehistoric times, human believed our planet was the center of the universe and everything in the heavens revolved around it. Greek astronomer Aristarchus of Samos is amongst the first to suggest that Earth revolves around the sun, not vice versa, in the third century BCE. His theories inspired Polish mathematician and astronomer Nicholas Copernicus to reiterate in 1543 that Earth revolved around the sun—not vice versa. He died before the Catholic Church could prosecute him for this heresy. Not so for Italian philosopher, astronomer, and mathematician Galileo Galilei, who advanced Copernicus' theory and was tried for heresy during the Inquisition.[28]

Since those early astronomers started shaking up humanity's notion of the heavens, we've learned that the sun doesn't really rise—the earth rotates, giving it the appearance of rising and setting. The sun is a constant flaming ball of gas, around which the planets in our solar system revolve. Our little solar system is but a tiny speck on the edge of the vast Milky Way galaxy, and our galaxy is only one of two trillion.[29]

As for the moon, just like the sun, it really doesn't rise or set, and it doesn't really have phases—that's just how it looks to us, here on Earth. In an article on the Sciencing website, science writer Ellie Maclin explains, "As the moon orbits Earth, the sun's light rays strike the moon. Depending on where the moon is positioned in relation to the earth and the sun, the illuminated portion of the moon that's visible to you on Earth changes."[30] Here on earth, we see a twenty-eight-day cycle of the moon appearing as a thin crescent, waxing to a full moon, when it's fully facing Earth, and then waning back to a thin crescent and disappearing into the new moon (the exact midpoint between the waxing and waning phases) and the dark moon, which is a span of one to three days surrounding that midpoint, when the moon isn't visible, prior to the next waxing crescent moon[31]. Regardless of phase, we always see the same side of the moon because it takes the same amount of time for the moon to rotate on its axis as it does to make one revolution around the earth.[32] The moon's rotation and revolution around the earth are perfectly synchronized.

28. Nicholas P. Leveilee, "Copernicus, Galileo, and the Church: Science in a Religious World," Inquiries Journal, 2011, http://www.inquiriesjournal.com/articles/1675/copernicus -galileo-and-the-church-science-in-a-religious-world.

29. Lindsay Brooke, "A Universe of Two Trillion Galaxies," Phys.org, last updated January 16, 2017, https://phys.org/news/2017-01-universe-trillion-galaxies.html.

30. Ellie Maclin, "Dark Moon vs. New Moon," Sciencing, last updated April 24, 2017, https:// sciencing.com/dark-moon-vs-new-moon-5082.html.

31. Althea Sebastiani, "Dark Moon vs. New Moon: What's the Difference?" Althea Sebastiani, last updated January 14, 2011, https://www.ladyalthaea.com/all-articles/dark-moon-vs -new-moon.

32. Adam Hadhazy, "Why Do We Always See the Same Side of the Moon?" Discover, last updated October 29, 2014, https://www.discovermagazine.com/the-sciences/why-do-we -always-see-the-same-side-of-the-moon.

As for those rotating constellations, they aren't constantly turning—Earth is. The sun and moon don't move through constellations—Earth's rotation and our orbital position around the sun, as well as the orbits of the other planets in our solar system, are what's actually moving. It's all perspective and perception.

Science fangirl that I am, going forward without mentioning the factual science of the cosmos would have made me feel intellectually... *dirty*. I find science even more jaw-dropping than magic itself. However, we Pagans sometimes have to *shuuush* science in order to connect to the magic. Science is pretty smart, but magic knows a thing or two that science doesn't. Science is the physical, and magic is the metaphysical. Going forward in this chapter, we'll speak the non-scientific magical vocabulary of all the stargazers that ever were and look to the heavens with wonder. For magic and astrology's sake, we'll imagine that we're still the center of the universe.

The Sun

The sun is one of the two major celestial entities that helped our ancient ancestors navigate their surroundings and interpret their lives. Imagine the sun's twenty-four-hour cycle as one long breath: The inhale begins at midnight, and the lungs continue to fill at dawn, reaching full capacity at noon, and then the exhale begins, continuing on through dusk, with lungs emptying just before midnight, only to inhale again, and so on, and so on. This breath has energy: Drawing in air (attracting) and releasing air (repelling). Being aligned with attracting and repelling energies is one of the basics of magic. If you want to attract something, do it during the inhale. If you want to repel, do it on the exhale.

If we organized our daily activities to align with that breath, and waxing and waning daylight, we'd align with our circadian rhythms, which are linked to daylight and are wildly disrupted by modern life. We wreak havoc with our circadian rhythms—which dictate our natural waking and sleeping cycles—with our work schedules, parties, and multiple screens we stare into all day long. In big cities, where life never stops, there's always something going on, something to do, something open. We don't want to miss out on anything! We defy our natural circadian rhythms with a little help from caffeine and/or alcohol, but our brains would really rather we didn't. We still have the same brain anatomy we had 10,000 years ago[33], and left to its own devices (chronic insomniacs notwithstanding) your brain would rather wind down at dusk and go to sleep, and wake back up when the birds start singing at dawn.

Tens of thousands of years ago, our circadian rhythms dictated our sleeping, waking, working, and resting cycle—not Netflix or Stephen Colbert or work schedules or alarm clocks. The invention of electricity and lightbulbs upended our alignment with our natural circadian rhythms and enticed us to ignore and override them[34]. Meanwhile, our ten-thousand-year-old brains are saying, "Hey! If you don't let me sleep when I want, I'm going to spank you with chronic fatigue!" Eh. Nothing another cup of coffee can't handle, right? However, you can only push your luck with that so far. If you keep outfoxing your sleepy brain (or think you are), it may spank you a little harder with something like a heart attack or stroke.[35]

Consider how differently you might feel if you aligned your circadian rhythms with the changing light from the sun, and let your brain—not the clock—decide when it's time for what. Be like the wild birds. They know when to roost and when to rest, and when to start singing in the morning. They're completely in sync with waxing and waning sunlight, regardless of the time of year. Let's play with that a little and see how it feels.

Activity: Experience Your Circadian Rhythms

Set aside a day to stop constantly battling your brain over when it should be time to eat, sleep, or wake up, and measure what you should be doing only by where the sun is in the sky, the amount of light, and the length of shadows. Don't look at any clocks, and that includes the television, your computer, and your cell phone. Put some non-transparent tape over all the clocks you can't turn off. Before clocks, before sundials, your ancient ancestors tracked the time of day by the sun. They didn't get back to camp because it said 6 p.m.

33. Simon Neubauer, Jean-Jacques Hublin, and Philipp Gunz, "The Evolution of Modern Human Brain Shape," Science Advances, last updated January 24, 2018, https://advances.sciencemag.org/content/4/1/eaao5961.

34. Ryan W. Logan and Colleen A. McClung, "Rhythms of Life: Circadian Disruption and Brain Disorders Across the Lifespan," Nature Reviews Neuroscience, last updated November 20, 2018, https://www.nature.com/articles/s41583-018-0088-y.

35. "Sleep and Chronic Disease," Centers for Disease Control and Prevention, accessed February 26, 2021, https://www.cdc.gov/sleep/about_sleep/chronic_disease.html.

on their Apple watch. They got back to camp if the sun touched the horizon, which meant that darkness was imminent. They went to sleep when it was dark, and woke up when the black of the eastern sky lightened to the gray of early morning.

This clock-free day will give you a little taste of living as your wild great-greats did, measuring time by waxing and waning daylight, and eating or taking a nap when their bodies needed it, not because it's time to do so. You'll may experience time as a perpetual flow rather than measured chunks and ticks on a clock. Your body and brain would love living like this, in alignment with your natural circadian rhythms—your boss, maybe not so much. However, letting sunlight and your body take charge from time to time can be an indulgence in stress reduction when you need it.

Sun Worship

Documentation of sun worship and symbology stretches back to the fourteenth century BCE in Egypt, but likely existed there and elsewhere before documentation even existed. The Egyptian god Ra (also Re) was the god of the sun and was depicted with a solar disc on his headdress, as well as those of goddesses Isis, Sekhmet, and Hathor. Ancient Egyptians believed that Ra traveled around the earth in a barge in the sky, lighting Earth by day, and disappearing at night to fight monsters before reappearing each morning. Most ancient cultures across the globe had their own versions of sun gods, such as the Aztecs (Tonatiuh), Greeks (Helios), the Incas (Inti or Apu-panchau), and Romans (Sol). Amongst the various forms of sun worship are the Sun Dance of the indigenous American Plains tribes, and ancient Celtic and Scandinavian celebrations of the summer and winter solstices, and the spring and fall equinoxes, all linked to the length of sunlight at those times, and still celebrated in today's Pagan community. The movement of the sun was one of the first ways ancient people were able to make sense of the days, months, years, and seasons.

The Moon

The moon is the other major celestial entity that helped our ancient ancestors track the passage of time and make sense of their lives. The sun "breathes" over the course of twenty-four hours. In the night sky, the moon "breathes" too, but it takes much longer—twenty-eight days—and appears to us in phases. At the new moon, the inhale begins, on up through the waxing crescent, half, and waxing gibbous, with full lungs on the full moon, and then the exhale begins, through waning gibbous, half, and waxing crescent, and so on.

Aligning spiritual and magical practices and rituals with phases of the moon is amongst the most familiar and universal of Pagan concepts, particularly Wicca, wherein witchcraft, rituals, and magic are timed with phases of the moon, and the energy associated with it: you attract things and energies toward you during the waxing moon, and repel them during the waning moon. In many Pagan traditions, the full moon is considered to be the most magically-saturated phase.

Gazing up at a full moon on a quiet dark night is universally mystical to most people. You sense something far, far more ancient than yourself. Every human being in all of time has gazed up at that exact same moon, ever since the very first ancient wild one looked up at the night sky and wondered, "What *is* that?" The moon is a thread connecting every person who ever lived on Earth. When I look up at that full moon, I feel connected to my ancient ancestors. I can feel their wonder whispering to me through the eons.

Under the Dark Moon

At the very beginning of our lunar breath, and also at the very end, is the new moon and its adjacent dark moon phases. Some Pagans say magic shouldn't be done during a new moon. Others disagree, myself included. I don't embrace the "new moon no-no" for magic or ritual. When I did that three-year Seasons of Avalon course, each new chapter began on the new moon. The new moon has its own energy, and it's part of that complete lunar breath cycle. You can't have an inhale without an exhale. Wouldn't it seem rather odd for someone to say, "Oh no, I only inhale." How would that even work?

When you exhale completely, and suck in your solar plexus to propel all the air out, it's a very internal sensation—everything propelled out of the body—your focus (and new moon energy) is completely within, completely internal; still and contemplative. New moon energy is conducive to meditating and simply being alone with oneself, particularly if you need to poke around in your own shadows and take an inventory of what's working in your life and what's not. The new moon is associated with the Greek goddess Hekate, and those who follow her use this phase of the moon to honor her. There are other goddesses, such as the Morrigan, Sekhmet, Santa Muerte, and Kali Ma, whose energies are more aligned with a dark "no nonsense" new moon, and there may be times in your life when that's the energy you seek.

Paganism has taught me not to fear the dark, whether the moon or within myself. The dark is only as terrifying as you let it be. Just as you can't have an inhale without an exhale, you can't have light without dark. Without dark, light has no context. Facing your own darkness, peering into your own shadows, can facilitate coming to terms with issues simmering inside you. Some call this getting in touch with your shadow or shadow-self.

Sometimes, magic or ritual isn't all about happy stuff. Sometimes, life can be very dark, and for those times, the new moon provides dark magical ambiance. To fear a new moon and avoid doing magic at that time leans a little too close to pointless superstition for my tastes. Just like Owl or Cat or Bat, sometimes the darkest nights are when we see and perceive best. Sometimes the thing we most need to find is in the darkest place.

About a million years ago, I attended a lecture given by alcoholism expert John Bradshaw, who told the allegory of a man who entered a cave and its entrance was suddenly covered by a rockslide. No way out. The man could see a crack of light in the ceiling, and desperately struggled to reach it, but could not. He refused to give up, and crawled and scratched to reach that light, and eventually died trying. When rescuers finally came and cleared away the rubble at the mouth of the cave, they found that just beyond the man's body, in the very darkest corner of the cave, was a tunnel to the outside. Had he been brave enough to go into the darkest place, he would have easily walked straight out to freedom and saved his own life. His fear of the dark—not the rockslide—was what killed him.

This allegory has inspired and encouraged me so many times. Sometimes you must go into the dark place to find freedom. Divorce comes to mind. Resigning from a job. Ending a relationship. Dealing with grief. These dark things are also part of life, and blowing sunshine and unicorn glitter all over them is exceedingly ineffective. There's a time and place for darkness. That's where the harsh truth is. It may not be pretty. It is what it is. But it's what you must come to terms with before you can advance to the next step on your path, or toward your own recovery, healing, or progress. So, remember that man in the cave when the new moon's energy calls to you. Don't be afraid to explore your own dark corners. The very thing you seek may be hidden there.

In the Light of the Full Moon

Magical energy is most saturated at the full moon, the full "breath," and for Wiccans, this is the time for drawing down the moon. In Wicca, the moon symbolizes the Goddess, and in ritual, a Wiccan high priestess may invite the essence of the Goddess to embody her, fill her with her divine light, and speak through her. That said, one need not be Wiccan to connect with and honor the Goddess on the full moon (as was mentioned in Doreen Valiente's "The Charge of the Goddess"), and this has leaked beyond strictly Wiccan circles. Anyone can draw down the moon and invite the Goddess inside if they choose.

In Wicca, each of the thirteen full moons is called an *esbat*, when gatherings are held for ritual and magic, and to honor the Goddess. Esbats are linked to the moon, as opposed to sabbats, which are linked to the sun and are the eight sacred days on the Wheel of the Year. This is why the number thirteen isn't considered unlucky amongst Pagans. Just the opposite: it's considered powerful and positive.

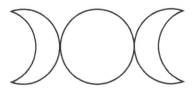

The symbol of a full moon with outer-facing crescents on either side is an iconic image in Wicca, representing the Triple Goddess in the form of Maiden (waxing crescent), Mother (full), and Crone (waning crescent). The full moon is a traditional time for blessing altar tools, crystals, and any other magical tool. That full-moon Goddess energy is abundant, and just soaks right in, cleansing and energizing an item, and soaks right into moon-blessed water. To saturate any magical item in moonlight, place it in the light of the full moon for an entire night.

Besides cleansing, moonlight energizes a magical item and strengthens your connection to it. When I get a new tarot deck or crystal, I'll set it out for a full moon blessing before engaging with it and putting it to magical use. This welcomes that item to my magical life. If wet weather is an issue, put the item in a Ziploc bag or on an indoor windowsill that sits in full moonlight.

Thirteen Moons

The Gregorian calendar has twelve months per year, each with twenty-eight to thirty-one days. However, there are actually thirteen full moons during the span of the year, with lunar cycles of twenty-eight days. A Blue Moon is a second full moon within one Gregorian calendar month. A lunar calendar is divided by the phases of the moon rather than months, which makes it easy to be more aware of that attract-and-repel energy.

Months on the twelve-month Gregorian calendar have the familiar names we all know. The full moons associated with each month have names as well, but they may differ between Pagan traditions, and between Pagan and non-Pagan circles. For example, in the *Farmers' Almanac*, it notes that its full moon names were inspired by American indigenous and colonial lore, so each full moon has several names.[36] The April full moon, for example, is called the Egg Moon, Sprouting Moon, Grass Moon, Budding Moon, and Moon When the Geese Lay Eggs. Take your pick.

Pagan traditions have their own names for each full moon, some of which overlap with non-Pagan moon names. Some Pagans don't use names at all, and refer to the full moon according to which astrological sign it appears in, such as "full moon in Aries" or "full moon in Libra."[37] Here are some common Pagan names for the full moons:

January: Wolf Moon; wolves, courage, hunting

February: Snow Moon; the heaviest snowfall of the year; bones, hunger

March: Worm Moon; softening earth, the reappearance of worms; robins

---

36. The Old Farmers' Almanac, "Full Moon Names," last updated April 27, 2020, https://www.almanac.com/content/full-moon-names.
37. Tetraktys, "The Thirteen Wiccan Esbats Explained: All You Need to Know," last updated May 12, 2019, https://www.thetetraktys.com/2019/wiccan-esbats-explained/.

April: Pink Moon: the first spring flowers, and the appearance of pink moss and birds' eggs, spring

May: Flower Moon; flowers, fertility, motherhood, planting, planting corn

June: Strawberry Moon; ripening strawberries, roses, honey, mead, summer solstice, the longest day

July: Buck Moon; bucks' antlers are growing; thunder, fruit, ripe corn

August: Sturgeon Moon; fishing season in full swing, for sturgeon and all fish; blueberries, green corn, wheat

September: Harvest Moon; harvest, fall equinox, corn, barley

October: Hunter's Moon; hunting season, falling leaves

November: Beaver Moon; time to set beaver traps; beavers, fur, frost

December: Cold Moon; winter solstice, the longest night, winter, darkness, ice

Unless you're living an agrarian life and/or dependent upon hunting and trapping to survive, and also live in an area with four distinct seasons, these moon names may not resonate with you. I mean, a Snow Moon where I live is preposterous. There's no snow here at all, ever, let alone the heaviest of the year. A more appropriate name for the February moon in my area would be the "Almond Blossom Moon" (isn't that pretty?), when the vast expanses of almond orchards covered in puffs of white blossoms glow with soft light under a full moon. And, from my perspective, it's never *ever* time to trap beaver. I'm not into sturgeon fishing, and there's only one known wolf pack in all of California in a remote area that's entirely too far away to hear them howling, on a full moon in January or any other night for that matter. So, most of those full moon names don't do much for me.

Activity: A Moon by Any Other Name Would Shine as Bright

Let's reexamine those full moons. Does the symbolism resonate with you? If you're all set to get your badass beaver trappin', sturgeon fishin' jam on, well, yay, you! But if not, let's look around our own environments, and give each full moon a name that means something precious and sacred *to us*.

This will be a long-term activity. In your journal, upon each full moon for the next year, look around your environment and note what is in full glory at that time—what's flourishing, blooming, or changing? What stands out as really significant or special? Choose a name for each full moon that captures the energy of your own surroundings. This will make those full moons and your connection to the Goddess much more meaningful to you than pretending that you're all about the reappearance of worms when you live on the tenth floor of a high-rise apartment and are surrounded by 20 square miles of concrete, through which no worms will ever appear. The Goddess doesn't want you babbling someone else's truth—she cherishes pure, perfect *you*, and your own truth.

The Stars

In many Pagan circles, astrology is a very serious course of study, and not just something you pluck off the internet for a daily horoscope reading. It's astoundingly complicated, and some focus on astrology exclusively. Astrology isn't my area of expertise, but my curiosity compels me to keep learning about it. There seem to be as many accomplished astrologers as there are stars, so I look to them to find out what's happening in the heavens. They're doing all the tough work for me. I don't feel compelled to create my own astrology charts. There are certain ones that resonate with me, and I just follow what they report. It's like tracking the weather. I don't need to be a meteorologist and chart the weather every day to find out if it's going to rain that day. The weather person on the morning news has already done the work for me. Is this lazy? Oh, absolutely. But one person's "lazy" is another person's "judicious use of time."

Astrology, Science, and Absence of Evidence

The rotation of the earth as it orbits around the sun creates the appearance of the cosmos rotating around us. From our perspective here on Earth, the sun and moon seem to travel through a rotating ring of twelve fixed constellations all year, moving from one to the next roughly every thirty days, creating our familiar signs of the zodiac. The planets in our solar system also appear to move through these constellations, which is a combined effect of the earth's rotation as it orbits the sun and our perspective of the other planets' independent orbits.

Although scientific evidence for astrology is flimsy, we have to *shooosh* that for a moment and hop into a metaphysical mindset to get into an astrology vibe. We humans are so arrogant—discounting the things we don't understand. And we don't understand *a lot*. Just because we haven't figured something out, or can't prove it scientifically, does that mean it doesn't exist? I say no. Remember our chat about dark energy? It's definitely there, and that's about the extent of our understanding. Could all the heavenly bodies be energetically or vibrationally connected, and therefore influence each other, and us? There's no proof of that. So far. However, we were once confident that Earth was the center of the universe, and that turned out to be completely inaccurate. Who knows what the next Copernicus will postulate about interplanetary and interstellar energetic, vibrational influences? So, although I can't provide scientific evidence to validate astrology, I also have no evidence for its invalidity either and—neither do scientists! You know the drill: absence of evidence isn't evidence of absence.

I Know What I Know

While there's a lot I don't know about astrology, there are a few things I do. Evidence or not, astrology has been spot-on more times in my own life than could be waved away as coincidence, and I've definitely noticed a few patterns that can't be categorized as coincidence:

- I get along best with other air signs, particularly Gemini women. We vibe. When there are multiple Gemini women in one place, there's a whole lotta energy goin' on. Truth in advertising: Other signs do not always appreciate effervescent Gemini energy. A little Gemini goes a long way. Other signs would like us to shut up for just one goddamn minute.

- I don't get along so great with earth signs—Virgo, Taurus, and Capricorn—unless I mute my Gemini-ness. We can coexist peacefully as long as I'm willing to stifle myself, but I have to level down to accommodate them, never vice-versa. Why can't they simmer *up* sometimes? Sheesh.

- I consistently have difficulties with Scorpios. Most every Scorpio I know suffers from an overabundance of personality. They're a little too *extra*—energetic tsunamis, stunningly, blissfully, and frustrat-ingly unaware that anything is amiss, blinded by their own wonder-fulness. Sometimes I have to leave the room so I don't drown in all that wonderfulness.

• Mercury retrograde is a thing. I have the interpersonal carnage to prove it.

Retrogrades

Retrograde in astrology means that from our perspective on Earth, a planet in our solar system appears to be going backwards in its orbit around the sun, due to a difference in speed of each planet's orbit. It isn't really going backwards, but it looks that way. During a retrograde, the energies associated with that planet get wonky.

Mercury retrograde has become a "thing," lately, even amongst non-Pagans. Mercury rules communication, particularly technology and between people. Some scoff at Mercury retrograde, but I detect a pattern. If a computer-oper-ated device is going to misbehave, it will do so during Mercury retrograde. If it has a microchip, beware. People don't have microchips, but they're constantly communicating, and Mercury retrograde plays havoc with that communica-tion, and sometimes scrambles it. If you're going to accidentally hit "reply all" on an email and distribute snarky comments that were intended for only one person to see, it'll be during Mercury retrograde. If you get into a big, stupid flaming war on social media, blame Mercury's pokey britches. If you and your partner suddenly can't say one word without getting on each other's nerves, thanks for nothing, Mercury.

While Mercury gets all the notoriety, and blame, for every single thing that goes wrong while it's in retrograde, the other planets also go retrograde at regular intervals, and just as Mercury's energies are thrown into reverse during retrograde, so are the energies of the other planets.[38]

Each planet is associated with certain energies and astrological signs—Mercury with communication (Gemini and Virgo), Venus with love and romance (Taurus and Libra), Mars with aggression and sexual drive (Aries),

---

38. Nina Kahn, "Your Guide to the Planets in Astrology and How They Affect You," *Bustle*, last updated July 23, 2020, https://www.bustle.com/life/how-each-planets-astrology-di-rectly-affects-every-zodiac-sign-13098560.

Jupiter with good luck and abundance (Sagittarius), Saturn with boundaries and discipline (Capricorn), Uranus with originality and change (Aquarius), Neptune with intuition and spirituality (Pisces), and Pluto with the subconscious, the underworld, and intensity (Scorpio). During a retrograde, the energies associated with those planets get funky—even more so for those whose astrological signs are associated with those retrograde planets. Being a Gemini, when Mercury goes retrograde, I should just put duct-tape over my mouth and around my fingers so I can't speak to anyone, send email, or post on social media, lest the verbal bloodshed begin.

Besides Mercury, I really feel Jupiter retrograde. Jupiter is the big daddy of the feel-good emotions and situations, big blessings, abundance, and good fortune, as well as overall peace and serenity. When Jupiter goes into its months-long retrograde, all of life seems difficult and contrary. Jupiter retrograde is four months long and it's such a big planet with big energies, when it shifts into reverse, it feels like one long stretch of "this is why we can't have nice things." All that said, it seems like one planet or another, or several, is in retrograde at any given point in time. Maybe it just makes us feel better to point our fingers to the sky and say, "Damn you, Mercury!" and believe that there's cosmic order to our troubles rather than accepting that the unfortunate things that happen to us are totally random.

Your Birth Chart

The very basics of astrology are the familiar sun signs, which are twelve constellations that appear to move in a ring around the earth over the course of a year. Our sun sign is the constellation the sun was in when we were born, from the perspective of Earth. The sun signs are the familiar signs of the zodiac: Aries, Taurus, Gemini, Cancer, etc. Your sun sign is your outer self, that everyone sees; the you that *others* might describe. Our sun signs are what we typically look for in daily horoscope readings, and our response when someone asks, "What's your sign?"

Your moon sign is the constellation the moon appeared in at the time of your birth. The moon moves through the constellations about every two and a half days, so you need to know the exact time and place of your birth to find your moon sign. Your moon sign is your inner self, your emotions, and true feelings and desires; the you that *you* might describe; your shadow self.

Sometimes this is all quite copacetic; however, if your sun and moon signs are at odds, you may have a very interesting blend of contradictory characteristics, say a gregarious and self-centered Leo sun, with a convoluted, mysterious, introspective Pisces moon.

Now, to really spice things up, you also have a rising sign, which is the constellation that was rising on the eastern horizon at the moment of your birth. Your rising sign reflects your outer persona—the person who interacts with the world, such as at work or in the community; the face you present.[39] So add to that imaginary Leo/Pisces mix a fastidious Virgo rising, for example, and there's a lot of fancy temperament-juggling going on: Leo preening in the spotlight, Pisces getting all moody about it, and Virgo thoroughly annoyed because those two are so unorganized. That's a lot to balance—but wait, there's more! Oh, so much more.

To create your complete birth (or natal) chart, you must also know where the planets, sun, and moon were at the moment of your birth in all twelve astrological houses, each of which deals with a certain aspect of our lives: 1) Aries, the self and consciousness, 2) Taurus, possessions and money, 3) Gemini, communication, 4) Cancer, home and family, 5) Leo, fun and pleasure, 6) Virgo, health, 7) Libra, one-on-one relationships and marriage, 8) Scorpio, sex and death/loss, 9) Sagittarius, religion and spirituality, 10) Capricorn, career and reputation, 11) Aquarius, friendships, and 12) Pisces, secrets and the unconscious. When all the planets' positions at the moment of your birth are plotted on your natal chart, it shows how each of them interacted at that moment. And, don't worry if that makes you dizzy—turn to an expert for now.

In addition to creating your birth chart, astrologers do daily readings and projections by charting the constant movement of these heavenly bodies through the houses and constellations, as well as their positional relationship to each other. The results are exceedingly detailed, up-to-the-minute astrological readings.

We could spend this entire book just on astrology, and thankfully many people have already done just that. If you want to dive deep, there are plenty of resources, both books and online.

---

39. Nina Kahn, "This is the Real Difference Between Your Sun, Moon, Rising Zodiac Signs," Bustle, last updated September 9, 2019, https://www.bustle.com/life/a-sun-moon-rising-zodiac-sign-explainer-that-will-help-astrology-make-so-much-more-sense-12222972.

Activity: What Do You See in the Stars?

Do you ever look at the stars in a constellation and wonder … how the heck does this box with sticks on the corners look like a flying horse (Pegasus)? Or that weird-shaped box hanging on a hook look like a lion (Leo)? What *were* those ancients smoking? Can I still get some?

Experiment with making the stars your own. On a clear night, as close to a new moon as possible when the stars are brightest, relax on a blanket and look up at the night sky. Forget the constellations you've been taught. Forget everything you've ever seen in the night sky. Look again with fresh new eyes. What do you see? What shapes appear to you? What would you name them? Imagine you're back with your own ancient great-greats. Point up and show them what you see, and give that constellation a name of your own. That sky, those stars—they're as much yours as anyone else's. Somebody else just named them first.

Our Celestial Nature

Learning about the energies, phases, and positions of the heavenly bodies can give meaning and symbolism to our Pagan paths and our magic. The naysayers who insist there's no connection between what happens in the cosmos and within our lives don't really have any hard evidence for that. The only thing they can truthfully say about the influence of the sun, moon, and stars on daily human life is that no scientific proof has been discovered *yet*. Until it's discovered, I choose to be open to the possibility that such a connection, and influence, exist, and proceed "as if."

Recommended Reading

Burk, Kevin. *Astrology: Understanding the Birth Chart—A Comprehensive Guide to Classical Interpretation.* Woodbury, MN: Llewellyn Publications, 2020.

Herring, Amy. *Essential Astrology: Everything You Need to Know to Interpret Your Natal Chart.* Woodbury, MN: Llewellyn Publications, 2021.

Section Three

The Magical Realm

CHAPTER 10
Exploring the Magical and Mystical

Magic isn't math. There isn't one correct answer for every situation. It's more like ceramics. You get a lump of clay, work it, and smooth and shape it into something of your own creation.

I'll show you how I throw clay onto the potter's wheel, but eventually, you'll do it your own way and make your own magical works of art. There's no one way, no right way, to do magic, unless you're following a particular path or tradition, which many have very precise steps, words, practices, and ingredients for magic, and may be quite different from what you're reading here. However, there are lots of magical common denominators between traditions and, thankfully, no Pagan Pope proclaiming who's right and who's wrong. In the Big Pagan Garden, nobody's in charge, and everybody's in charge.

What is Magic?

So, what *is* magic anyway? Waving a wand and presto, change-oh, mice turn into horses and pumpkins into carriages? Sorry, that's just a bunch of bibitty bobitty boo. Pagan magic isn't hokey "watch me pull a rabbit out of my hat" sleight-of-hand circus sideshow entertainment. Many Pagans spell magic with a *k—magick*—to differentiate it from hocus pocus and abracadabra magic. At its simplest, Pagan magic means doing a certain thing to produce a specific intended result. Magic is a metaphysical recipe that manifests the goal you've chosen. Magic isn't a trick. It's a skill. Like any other skill, such as woodworking, sewing, or stained glass, you must practice it to become proficient. In the beginning, you may feel clumsy and awkward, and that's okay. The more you practice, the better you'll get.

The structure of magic is simple. It has three parts: intention, implementation, and manifestation. To use a cooking analogy, my intention is to bake a cake; my implementation is mixing all the ingredients together, pouring them into a pan, and putting them in the oven; my manifestation is opening the oven 45 minutes later and pulling out a finished cake.

Intention and manifestation are part of every magical working. It's the middle part—the implementation—from something as simple as stacking stones into a little tower (called a *cairn*) to meticulously planned, elaborate, ornate, and precisely spoken ceremonial magic. I'm more of a stone-stacker. I like it clean and simple. For one thing, I suck at memorizing spells and quatrains, and precisely planned spellwork involves either memorizing other people's words or reading from a script, neither of which feels genuine and natural to me. I'd rather let my words and actions pour from my own heart and spirit, rather than someone else's.

Intention

Setting intention is simple: Define exactly what you want. A better job. A new home. A new car. A new love in your life. A million dollars. However, you have to think it through before setting an intention. Consider all the angles and be very specific. For example, a million dollars is fantastic, but if it comes from a settlement because your back surgery was botched, leaving you paralyzed—not fantastic. You might set an unspecified intention for a new home, and then it manifests as a tent under a freeway overpass. Yikes. Before implementing anything, consider your intention from every angle, and be very specific. I always like to add "with harm to none, and for the greater good of all" to my intentions as a magical insurance policy. If my intention will harm someone, I'd rather it not be manifested at all. If my magic doesn't work, I think, "Hmmm … stumped by the 'no harm' clause. Back to the magical drawing board."

Imagine that your intention is "I'm going to bake a chocolate cake." You can't stop right there and just imagine that cake, do nothing, and expect to have that rich, sweet, chocolatey goodness materialize on the plate in front of you. That's called a wish. A wish is granted—or not—at the whim of another entity. Magic is an action that you set in motion. If you want that cake to actually become reality, there are certain things you must do. That brings us to implementation.

Implementation

To make that cake a reality, you need a recipe (spell). You'll also need to gather together all the ingredients and utensils beforehand. When you bake, you don't just dive in and start mixing things up as you go, and then discover you're out of cocoa, or that you need a springform pan and don't have one. Likewise, when implementing your magic, you get all the necessary items together first, rather than getting halfway through and discovering you don't have matches to light the candle. Just like baking, read through the entire work or spell first and be prepared before beginning.

There is an unimaginably vast range of things you might need for your magical work, but there's one specific ingredient that's always necessary: confidence. When you implement your intention and set those wheels in motion, you aren't *asking* for something, as one might do in prayer, and hope that it's granted. No, you are *willing* something to happen. You are actively directing the course of the manifestation, like aiming an arrow in a particular direction and letting it fly.

"An' it harm none, do as ye will," comes from the beautiful Wiccan Rede[40], attributed to Doreen Valiente. "Harm none" is pretty straightforward, and sometimes a stand-alone Pagan phrase. I used to interpret "do as you will" as "do whatever you want." But there's another way to interpret it: "Do as you *command*." You don't beg or plead with magic. You command it. You *will* it. You propel your implementation assertively, powerfully. Magic isn't a being; it's not going to get its feelings hurt if you're too bold, or think you're cheeky and rude and get all butt-hurt and not call you for two months. Magic is an entity, and it responds to confidence. It parallels your own vibration. Be confident in your implementation, and magic will match that vibe and proceed. If you're hesitant or timid in setting your intention, magic will match that vibe too, and your results may be disappointing. If you act wimpy, you get wimpy.

When you're finishing your implementation, say the command, "So mote it be," the Pagan equivalent of "Amen." It's an affectionately archaic way of

---

40. Wicca Now, "The Wiccan Rede—The Complete Text Version," accessed January 27, 2020, https://wiccanow.com/the-wiccan-rede/.

saying, "Make it so." There's no "pretty please with sugar on top" in magic. No shyness or doubt. Just calm, controlled confidence. Will. *Will* your intention onto the metaphysical plane for manifestation.

Manifestation

Manifestation begins when you pop that cake into the oven. You release it to the oven spirits and let them start "moting it be." You can't tinker with it and make it happen faster. If you turn the heat up, your cake won't bake faster, it'll just turn into a burned black shell with an ooey, gooey mess inside. Leave it alone. It takes how long it takes. Unlike a cake, which takes an exact, predictable amount of time, manifestation happens on its own schedule. Once implemented, sometimes intentions manifest quickly. Other times, it takes a while, years even. It's like planting seeds. If you plant grass seed, it springs right up. But if you're planting an acorn, it will be many, many years before that oak tree matures. And, if you plant seeds and then dig them up every day to see if they're sprouting, they'll just die. Leave them alone, and trust that nature is natur-ing underground, without any assistance from you. Just like baking or planting, leave your magical implementation alone to develop on its own schedule, in its own time, or you'll ruin it.

Patience is part of magic, and patience comes from confidence. Manifestation requires both confidence and patience. Even if it seems like that manifestation is taking too long, don't contaminate it with worry and doubt. Cancel worry and doubt by saying, "Thank you, universe. I know my manifestation is happening." Don't let your magical confidence sag.

When waiting for your manifestation, be aware that it might not arrive in the form you're expecting. Expand your awareness and attention span, because sometimes manifestation comes in the form of directing you toward your intention. You notice things you previously hadn't. Say your magical intention is to find a place to rent. You passed by a certain house a million times, noting a sign in the window of your peripheral vision but not bothering to read it. But after setting that intention, you suddenly notice that sign reads, "For rent." Bingo. Sometimes, the universe directs you toward simple serendipity: You're in a grocery checkout line, and the person behind you is chatting on their phone about the great apartment they need to let go because they're moving away. Hello, there! Let's talk!

When Magic Doesn't Work

Sometimes your manifestation doesn't materialize, and it's obvious it won't. Maybe your intention was to get a certain job, and you get a rejection letter instead and someone else is hired. It could be because it wasn't for the greater good of all and unforeseen harm would have resulted—including to yourself. Maybe you thought your implementation through meticulously, but the universe recognized that an unpredictable catastrophe would have resulted: you got the job, and on your way to work one day, you were run down and killed crossing the street. That "with harm to none" clause saved your life. A manifestation failure might also occur because that ever-watchful universe may know that the job you thought you wanted might prevent you from applying for a much better position. The universe may be preventing you from settling for the Ford when you could have had the Mercedes.

Counter disappointments with the recognition that the universe is benevolent, and always has your back. It's always searching for your best outcome and, oddly enough, sometimes the best outcome is no outcome at all.

The Science of Magic

Nobody can really explain magic how magic works or prove that it exists in any tangible, scientific way. Science can't explain how dark energy works either, much beyond agreeing that it's there, and has attract-repel energy. Maybe we've just been looking for proof of magic in the wrong place. Maybe science holds the key—specifically, the field of quantum mechanics, which is an entire realm of *wow, Wow, WOW!* What seems utterly impossible becomes real—and scientifically provable—in quantum mechanics. A case in point is something called the observer effect.

An article from Science Daily recounts the existence of the observer effect: researchers demonstrated "how a beam of electrons is affected by the act of being observed"—the more closely the electrons were being observed, "the greater the observer's influence on what actually takes place."

The scientists discovered that unobserved electrons behaved like waves and could simultaneously pass through several openings in a barrier, rejoining on the other side of the barrier. However, when the electrons were being observed "the picture changes dramatically: If a particle can be seen going through one opening, then it's clear it didn't go through another. In other words, when under observation, electrons are being 'forced' to behave like particles and not like waves. Thus, the mere act of observation affects the experimental findings."[41]

Mull that over for a moment. The behavior of particles fired through openings in a barrier changes if they're being observed. In other words, human perception had an effect on the behavior of a subatomic particle. Let's transpose electrons with magic: what if human observation (magical intention) affects the behavior of particles elsewhere in the universe (manifestation)?

Another *wow* concept in quantum mechanics, "quantum entanglement," reveals that an action in one place can produce a tandem action in an entirely different place. Sounds a lot like magic, doesn't it? Is it then possible that the intention and visualization of an accomplished magical practitioner could produce a specific result elsewhere? That's essentially what magic is: an action—spell or ritual—performed by a magical practitioner in one place producing a specific result in another place. Seems to me it's entirely possible—just not provable. Yet. However, magical practitioners will tell you that based upon their experience, it's absolutely so.

Scientists like to scoff at magic. Once upon a time, they also scoffed at the notion that the world is round, not flat. Once upon a time, they thought space was empty. Far from it. We no more understand how magic works than we do how dark energy works—and the overwhelming majority of the universe consists of it. We know *that* it exists, but not what it is or what it does.

We know that everything—including the entire cosmos—has a vibration [42]. What if magical intention is the vibrations of our internal sub-atomic dark energy aligning with the external vibrations of dark energy in the cosmos and *directing it*, and manifestation is quantum entanglement—the desired intention being bounced back? What if quantum entanglement works exactly the same way with magic as it does in quantum physics? So far, the only quantum entanglement scientists have verified involves atoms

41. Weizmann Institute of Science, "Quantum Theory Demonstrated: Observation Affects Reality," Science Daily, last updated February 26, 1998, https://www.sciencedaily.com/releases/1998/02/980227055013.htm.

42. The Conversation, "Could Consciousness All Come Down to the Way Things Vibrate?" accessed February 25, 2021, https://theconversation.com/could-consciousness-all-come-down-to-the-way-things-vibrate-103070.

and particles. Proving it with human and cosmic vibration is a long way off. Science just isn't there. Yet. But that doesn't mean it doesn't exist, just as the earth was not flat even when people were sure it was. For all who scoff at magic, absence of evidence equals evidence, and you already know where I stand on that point: not.

I'm convinced that someday, scientists will discover what magical practitioners have known all along: magic exists. They'll find that magic and science are really two sides of the same metaphysical coin. Be open to the possibility of the existence of things that can't be proven, and open yourself to the possibility that magic exists, and works. It has order and function, just like dark energy, and does what it does, even *as* we're not understanding it, or able to prove it.

Types of Magic

Intention and manifestation are like magical bridge footings, and implementation is the magical bridge spanning between them. You have lots of options for materials to construct that span: concrete or wooden slats or rope or bamboo poles. I'm going to share my own favorite magical building materials, but this certainly isn't a comprehensive look at magic, in general or from tradition to tradition. I share some that are simple, comfortable, and great for beginners. There are no fancy tools required, and no complicated passages or quatrains to memorize. Any one of them is a good place to give magic a try.

Candle Magic

Candle magic is simple and straightforward. Small chime candles are perfect because they burn down within a couple hours and come in a variety of colors to supplement candle magic with color magic. Tea light candles also work well.

With a sharp object, like a pin or tack, scratch your intention on the candle. Candles can be dressed by rolling them in magical or ritual oil. You can additionally roll them in dried herbs or spices if you wish. For tea light candles, put a couple drops of magical oil onto them, and sprinkle a tiny bit of magical herbs onto the wax if you wish. Before lighting, focus on your intention and speak it into the candle. Light it, and let it burn out completely.

Hopefully it goes without saying, but just in case—never leave burning candles unattended.

Color Magic

Wearing or incorporating color for an intention or need is one of the simplest magical techniques, and one of my favorites. When I need to bump up my energy and focus for a particular purpose or event, I wear clothing, jewelry, scarves, and even undergarments in particular colors, setting an intention as I put them on. I also add items in certain colors to my altars to enhance my intention.

Imagine that you want a promotion, which hinges upon acing a presentation. You want to appear authoritative and powerful, so you employ color magic and wear a red blazer to the presentation. You stride into that meeting and nail that presentation to the wall. Your boss is very impressed—and you get that promotion. Does red cloth have metaphysical power, or did color magic inspire you to behave and speak with confidence? If it worked … does it really matter? Me, I will settle for *that* it worked over *why* it worked, every time.

The following magical color associations are fairly traditional, with a few twists of my own. The first six are the saturated colors of the rainbow, which are also the colors of the chakras—energy whorls in the body. In order, they are red/root chakra, orange/sacral chakra, yellow/solar plexus chakra, Green/ heart chakra, blue/throat chakra, purple/third eye chakra, and white/crown chakra (in some traditions, light violet).

Some colors share energetic associations, such as "protection" being listed for both black and brown. It's a matter of intensity or tone. Go with the one that feels right for your needs:

Red: Power, dominance, danger, willpower, romantic love, passion, seduction, fire energy; root chakra, the center of safety, security, stability, survival issues.

Orange: High energy, male energy, boldness, sexuality, creation, adventure, fun, celebration, fire energy; sacral chakra, the center of sexuality, pleasure, and procreation.

Yellow: Intelligence, learning, knowledge, all matters of the mind, including writing and investigating; morning, new growth, new energy, rejuvenation, happiness, the sun, air energy; solar plexus chakra, the center of courage, self-confidence, and self-esteem.

Green: Abundance, wealth, growth, good luck, healing, earth energy; heart chakra, the center of love, joy, inner peace, and compassion.

Blue: Communication, emotions, creativity, peacefulness, serenity, calm, water energy; throat chakra, the center of expressing emotions and the heart's truth.

Purple: Intuition, insight, psychic abilities, mysticism, divination, water energy; third eye chakra, the center of intuition and wisdom.

White/Clear: Purity, innocence, the moon, the Goddess, the sacred or divine feminine, Spirit; crown chakra. In some traditions, the crown chakra is violet or lavender. I prefer the alternate symbology of white or a clear prism. The crown chakra is spiritual connection to the divine. When light—regular or divine—passes through a clear prism, it emanates all the colors of the rainbow, and the chakras.

Pink: Friendship, tenderness, softness, self-love, motherly love, spiritual healing, female energy.

Hot Pink: Brightness, boldness, joy, parties, standing out in a crowd, fire energy.

Gray: Grounding, neutrality, calming, dulling, toning down, blending in.

Black: Indomitable spirit, force, power, protection, magic, the shadow, repelling, banishing, hexes, the new moon, invisibility.

Brown: Grounding, protection, safety, stability, calm, earth energy.

Neon (any color): Attracting attention; any color's magical energy brightened to full saturation.

Pastels (any color): Gentleness, toning down, lightness, delicateness, air energy.

Silver: Moon magic, the Goddess, spiritual protection, female energy, yin.

Gold: Sun magic, the God, power, money, wealth, male energy, yang.

Crystal, Stone Magic

I'm a freak for crystals and stones. I wear them as pendants and bracelets and put small stones in mojo bags to wear around my neck. Sometimes I carry them in my pocket and roll them around between my fingers when I want to keep the energy of my intention flowing. I have them on all my altars, and here and there around the house. Wherever I want to attract a particular energy, I place a crystal there. I'm particularly drawn to labradorite, fluorite, geodes, and clear quartz crystal.

Crystals and stones should be cleaned before engaging with them. Some crystals and stones may be washed with gentle soap and water, some not. Find out what your crystals and stones can withstand before washing them. Water will ruin selenite and lodestone, for example. Some crystals, such as amethyst and fluorite, will fade if exposed to sunlight. Clean crystals when they get dusty with a soft cloth or brush, or rinse with water and pat dry if they can tolerate water. After cleaning, indulge them in some incense smoke—after your shower, don't you like a nice scented spray or lotion too?

When you get a new crystal, magically cleanse it with a moon blessing—place it under the light of the full moon for an entire night— and pass it through incense smoke. After cleansing, hold the crystal in your palms, welcome it, and thank it for contributing its energy to your magical work.

When choosing a crystal, hold it in your hands. They don't all feel the same. You'll know which one is drawn to you. You'll feel it. Crystals can be used alone, or selected for elemental or color magic. Crystals and stones are often cut into animal shapes and fetishes, allowing you to combine spirit animal energy and crystal magic. You can place your crystals and stones on an altar, or keep them close to you by putting them in your pocket or in a small leather pouch to wear around your neck or tie to a belt loop. Stones and crystals can also be worn as a pendant, ring, or bracelet.

There is a vast landscape of stones and crystals to explore. Here are some of my favorites for magic or healing:

Agate: Grounding, soothing, physical health, survival, earth energy. Agate is a common stone, and comes in a variety of earthy colors. It's a "nothing fancy" stone; down-to-earth, keeping things simple and natural, and toning things down. Agates are "no drama, mama" stones.

Amethyst: Spirituality, divine connection, calm, serenity, healing, psychic energy, third eye chakra. An excellent stone for meditation and stress reduction.

Black Onyx: Protection, absorbs negative energy, protects against negative energy. Wear black onyx when you want to be invisible to negative energy or enemies or protected from them.

Carnelian: Concentration, courage, energy, vitality, fire energy, sacral chakra. When you need to spark up your charisma, carnelian provides that energy.

Celestite: Spiritual detox, spiritual and emotional release, relaxation, stress reduction, divine connection, divine healing, angels, crown chakra, peaceful sleep. This delicate powder-blue stone is calming and particularly helpful for emotional distress or anxiety.

Charoite: Intuition, cosmic connection, divine connection, psychic energy, increased attention span, mental focus, dreams, easing fear, protection away from home or when separated from loved ones, third eye chakra. Charoite reinforces your connection to the metaphysical plane, and gives confidence in trusting your intuition and divine guidance. Charoite crystals with clear quartz inclusions are particularly powerful—an eye into the beyond.

Citrine: Joy, sunshine, light, creativity, writing, air energy, solar plexus chakra. It is traditionally considered to be a money stone, although I prefer to use it for clearing the mental air and focusing on writing, and infusing it with joy and energy. I keep a citrine in front of my keyboard to attract the energies of air to my writing.

Clear Quartz: Clarity, focus, attracts divine light and energy, crown chakra, channeling energy. It can be used for any magical purpose in place of another crystal, and when placed next to another crystal, it will enhance that crystal's energy. Quartz crystal is excellent for receiving messages in divination or meditation, and can be used for the same purpose in the physical world. Quartz crystals are used in radio transmission, watches, and computers, and can produce electricity when put under physical stress, such as impact or heat. Keeping a quartz crystal nearby is like having a metaphysical radio receiver on an open channel all the time. If I could work with only one crystal, it would be clear quartz.

Fluorite: Calm, healing, stability, serenity, physical and mental health, physical and mental recovery. If lavender in color, third eye chakra. Fluorite comes in a variety of colors, most commonly translucent greens, whites, and purples, and often a combination of all three, with ribbons of each running through the stone. Fluorite is very cooperative and agreeable. It will enhance the "only good vibes" energy when placed next to another crystal or stone.

Geode: Protection, Mother Earth, earth energy, hidden mysteries, intuition, psychic energy, going within, the womb. Geodes contain a spray of crystals inside, often quartz or amethyst. Geode energy gives comforting support for those who feel broken or hopeless, or who are grieving the death a loved one. Their healing is going to take a while, and there's no immediate solution. Geodes are the crystal equivalent of holding someone for as long as need be, when quick, easy solutions aren't possible. You can represent yourself or someone else who is hurting with a piece of rose quartz, and place it in a geode half for emotional healing and protection.

Jade: Money, luck, wealth, heart chakra. Jade is a hard stone, which makes it easy to carve into trinkets and figurines. It is highly prized in China as an auspicious stone, attracting financial gain and good fortune. Its connection to the heart chakra also makes it a stone for balancing or calming troubled emotions.

Labradorite: Intuition, the subconscious, imagination, divination, stress reduction, warding off confrontation and stress, peace, calm. Wear this beautiful blue-gray stone with flashes of green and gold when dealing with difficult people. It eases conflict and if drama breaks out, serves as a prompt to disengage while everyone else melts down.

Lodestone: Attraction energy, particularly financial gain and wealth. Lodestone, also called *magnetite*, is a naturally magnetic rock made of iron. It has an actual magnetic force, and needs to be "fed" iron filings or magnetic sand weekly to keep it activated. Lodestone prefers to be left alone, unbothered. Master magician and money magic expert Clifford Hartleigh Low says that before using lodestone, it should be "baptized"—wetted with a few drops of whiskey—and given a name. Re-wet it annually, like on New Year's Day or your birthday. Use lodestone to pull something toward you, whether wealth, love, or luck.

Moonstone: The moon, the Goddess, the goddess Selene, yin, feminine energy, feminine healing and health, the female body, intuition. Moonstone is supportive for female or menstrual issues, and simultaneously soothes and enhances goddess energy. It aligns feminine energy and the moon's. Yin energy is dark, cool, and receptive, and moonstone amplifies this internal energy.

Red Jasper: Family, ancestors, grounding, earth energy, root chakra. Like the root chakra, red jasper is reaffirming and reassuring when you feel unsafe. It is supportive for those caring for an unwell or elderly parent, or caretaking for a loved one while dealing with end-of-life issues. Red is the color of blood, and this stone reinforces family bonds and the bloodline of ancestors, which continue on even after separation on this physical plane.

Rose Quartz: Self-healing, self-love, motherly love and protection, kindness, emotional recovery, grief recovery. Nothing emits gentle, tender, healing love like rose quartz. It goes right to the heart to calm and lighten painful emotions. Rose quartz offers a loving motherly embrace. Use rose quartz to heal someone else's heart, or your own.

Tiger's Eye: Physical strength and healing, stamina, courage, self-confidence, solar plexus chakra, fire energy. Tiger's eye empowers you when you're feeling emotionally or physically weak or unwell. The "Eye of the Tiger" theme song from the *Rocky* movies captures tiger's eye energy, and the gold, brown, and black stripes resemble the eye of a big cat. When you need to feel powerful or fearless, wear or carry some tiger's eye.

Turquoise: Physical healing, luck, protection, travel, youthfulness, renewal, long life, throat chakra. Turquoise is sacred to several indigenous American tribes, particularly the Navajo, who associate it with the goddess Estsanatlehi (Changing Woman), associated with the changing seasons. When Estsanatlehi appeared to be aging, she would walk to the east until she found her younger self, and would merge with her and become young again. Turquoise lore includes protection for warriors in battle or on horseback, and uniting Heaven and Earth.

Unakite: Balancing emotional and spiritual energies, healing past issues, moving forward, transitions, overcoming emotional or self-imposed blocks, communicating one's own truth, heart chakra. A unakite pendant was given to me when I changed careers, going from social work to journalism. This stone is an affirmation of moving forward in life without emotional baggage. When the time has come to move onward and live your life genuinely, wear or carry unakite, or place on an altar. Its pink and green color captures both the traditional and New Age colors associated with the heart chakra. Its message is "to thine own self be true."

Elemental Magic

Elemental magic employs the four earthly elements—earth, air, fire, water—and their energies. You can focus on one, more than one, or all at once. Use the magic of earth to ground and protect, air to clear and strategize, fire to charge courageously forward, and water to soothe and create. Sometimes you need more forceful elemental energy: earth smothers and crushes (landslides, earthquakes); air blows away and apart (hurricanes, tornadoes); fire consumes and incinerates (wildfires, lava); water drowns and inundates (floods). An element can be represented by any of its symbology or its associated color. Wear a representative item, put it on an altar, or keep it in your pocket.

Elemental magic can be used as a correction—when you're stuck in one elemental mode and you need to compensate with another. You may be overwhelmed with emotion, and need cool, calm, logical air. Maybe you're feeling intimidated and need to fire up some courage. Maybe you're raging and out of control—earth smothers fire, water puts it out. Be careful using air to compensate for fire—it might blow it out, or it might give it more oxygen. To attract the element you need, use actual items—such as a pebble for earth, a feather for air, a matchstick for fire, or a shell for water—or any item, color, crystal, or spirit animal that represents the energy of that element.

Spirit animals are wonderful enhancements for elemental magic because there are so many choices to represent each element. You can choose the perfect combination for your needs. For example, maybe you need earth to accomplish a dig-in and complete a difficult task. Horse will get that job done. Maybe you need air to clear your mind and plan a course of action. Eagle would do nicely. If you're seeking fire to give you courage to get through a daunting situation, roaring Lion would capture that energy. Or, maybe water could inspire your creativity. Dolphin can bring lighthearted, playful energy to that project. You can also find animals cut from stone or as fetishes, and choose a stone representing the element you need in the animal you want, combining elemental and crystal magic, with a dash of animal spirit. Three times the energy!

Fire Magic

Fire is both transformative and destructive and serves both magical purposes. Fire transforms an intention into smoke, where it can be carried off to the universe for manifestation. Fire can assist when something in your life needs to be "burned down" and turned to ash—ended once and for all. This is aligned with banishing magic, which jettisons a person out of your life, for good and forever. It isn't done with malice, it just means that whatever they'll be doing, they won't be doing it in your life anymore. Banish carefully. It's considered permanent.

Fire can also be cleansing and sterilizing and used for releasing or purifying as well. For example, you may wish to free yourself from an addiction or to recover from a toxic relationship—to be sterilized from that "contamination."

Fire magic can be helpful or destructive. For either, focus on your intention as you write a word or phrase on a piece of paper, or a dried leaf or piece of thin bark. Focus upon your intention. Meditate on it. Envision the result you want until it's clear in your mind. Speak your intention into the paper, leaf, or bark, light it, saying the words, then burn it in a cauldron, fireplace, or fire pit. Watch it ignite and turn into smoke. When it is ash, your intention has been transmitted to the metaphysical realm. Once completely cold, sprinkle leftover ash in the garden or bury it while focusing on your manifestation. If you don't have a yard, release the ash to the water element in the sink. If it was from a banishing spell, flush it.

Freezing Magic

Freezing magic is a form of binding magic, which neutralizes or makes something or someone inert. You can "freeze" annoying people, without harm. They can move on elsewhere, but they're frozen out of your life. You have the option of thawing that person out if you wish. Unlike banishing magic, binding magic gives you some wiggle room for second thoughts, reconciliation, or forgiveness, should that person mend their ways.

To bind with freezing, take their photograph, a piece of paper with their handwriting, an item belonging to that person, or write the person's name on a piece of paper. Wrap it in aluminum foil and bury it deep in the freezer. Done. Aluminum foil is reflective and "traps" that person there.

Kitchen Magic and Kitchen Witchery

Any time you prepare food or beverages for yourself or someone else is an opportunity for kitchen magic by including certain herbs, spices, or roots, and the most important ingredient: intention. Infuse your intention right into the food or beverage as you prepare it, while stirring clockwise (deosil), which is associated with creating or building up. Stirring counterclockwise (widdershins) is associated with undoing or tearing down. Breathe, speak, or chant your intention right into whatever you're preparing. Something as simple as cup of tea can be infused with intention, steeped with visualization, and drunk while focusing on manifestation. There's a kitchen witchery strategy for every need or situation. If you love to cook, this is the magic for you.

A simple way to get started with kitchen magic is by using herbs, spices, and sweeteners. You can purchase the herbs or grow them yourself and use in recipes as ingredients or brew as tea. Several have similar associations and can be combined as a magical blend in a recipe, like rose and jasmine petals for love and romance. Herbs can also be infused in oil, dried and placed in a sachet, sprinkled onto a charcoal tablet as incense, placed on an altar to represent a magical need, or used for dressing candles. Here are some of my favorite magical herbs:

Basil: Divine protection, peace, attracting wealth. It's a mandatory ingredient for Italian red sauce, which itself is a magical potion. Speak your intention as you sprinkle an ample amount into your sauce.

Bay Leaf: Protection, healing, purification, strength. Bay leaf is magical writing paper. Write intentions on dried bay leaves with a toothpick dipped in olive oil, wine, or most any edible liquid, and crumble into your recipe.

Chamomile: Calm, soothing. Soothes and reduces stress, alleviates insomnia. Put soothing intention into pure chamomile tea to calm the stomach, your stress, or a situation.

Cinnamon: Love, lust, sex, passion, heat. Cinnamon is a warming scent, with a touch of spicy sweetness that entices the senses. Magically, it heats things up, whether it's a romantic evening, creativity, or excitement. Cinnamon says, "Pay attention!" It will not be ignored. Sprinkle into hot chocolate or Godiva liqueur, or stir into a recipe as you whisper your sexy desires.

Clove: Energy, interest, productivity, heat. Like cinnamon, clove is a warming scent. Any magic that needs "heating up" could include clove. Speak your intention while adding to a recipe. Beyond the kitchen, rub clove oil on a candle, or burn cloves on a charcoal tablet as incense.

Garlic: Protection, healing, exorcism, repelling. Garlic is both antiseptic and antibiotic and believed to repel vampires. I'm more worried about the microscopic "vampires" that make you sick, and garlic repels those too. When you want to drive something away, use garlic. Chop it up and add to a recipe while cooking, infusing it with intention for good health and to repel whatever ails you.

Ginger: Healing, protection, soothing, calming. Ginger can be a dried powder or fresh root. Unless I'm baking, I always choose the latter. You can add slices of fresh ginger to tea or a smoothie. It's soothing to the stomach and reduces inflammation. Use it magically to improve the health of anyone or anything, and to reduce inflammatory conditions or situations.

Jasmine: Love, serenity, calm. Use dried or fresh blossoms alone or in green tea to create a feeling of calm and serenity, or in moon-blessed water. Inhale jasmine's intoxicating scent as you savor that tea or sprinkle moon-blessed jasmine water over yourself or your magical tools or altar.

Lavender: Love, sleep, bliss, peace. Use as a tea by itself or in combination with other herbs, and instantly relax as you inhale its soothing aroma. Lavender can be added to recipes, like roast chicken, but use very sparingly. It can overwhelm a dish and ruin it.

Lemon: Mental energy, purification, protection. The scent of lemon awakens and refreshes the mind—squeeze some fresh juice into tea or a glass of water first thing in the morning, and visualize your whole system being refreshed and cleansed as you drink. Use lemon juice or fresh grated rind in recipes as you speak your magical intentions.

Mint: Mental alertness, money, healing, travel, protection. The scent of fresh mint rubbed between the fingers clears and brightens the mind and alleviates headaches, and will do the same brewed as tea or in combination with other herbs. Drop some fresh sprigs into water to refresh and awaken your mind.

Oregano: Power, protection, purification. Oregano has antibacterial and antiviral properties and is very intense. When your intention needs to pack a punch, include oregano. Like garlic, it can be used magically for promoting health, fighting illness, or repelling. Breathe those intentions into your soup or sauce as you stir in oregano.

Rose: Love, romance, relationships, marriage. Rose petals or hips may be added to tea to infuse it with that wonderful, heady scent and to attract love into your life or into your own heart when you need some self-care and self-appreciation. You are enough. Rose also softens and sweetens a relationship.

Rosemary: Protection, health, vigor, purification, healing. Plant a rosemary bush near your front door for protection, as it provides an evergreen source of fresh rosemary. Rosemary is wonderful in savory recipes, like roast chicken, vegetables, or potatoes. Speak your intention into it as you chop it and sprinkle it on.

Sage: Wisdom, protection, cleansing, blessing, purification. Bless your recipes with these intentions as you sprinkle in some sage, particularly savory dishes like soups, stews, and meat.

Salt: Protection, purification. Salt defines boundaries, whether a ritual circle, your home, or your property. It absorbs and neutralizes negative energy. It repels. If you need to keep something out, particularly negative or harmful energy, focus upon that while shaking some salt into a recipe. Set aside a special container of salt that's only for magical work, in the kitchen or out.

Thyme: Health, healing, purification, courage. If you don't have any rosemary handy, thyme is a great second choice. It's a very bold spice, and you can easily ruin a dish with too much. Use thyme when you need strength or courage, or to repel or defeat something.

Vanilla: Love, lust, sweetness, sweet sex. Put a vanilla bean in a sealed jar of sugar to infuse it with sweet love, and use that sugar—and your sweet intention—in recipes, tea, or coffee. You can also use vanilla extract in beverages, but it's highly concentrated. Use sparingly—except when baking. I always use a sloppy measure with vanilla when baking. A little extra never hurts. Sweeten a harsh or strife-filled environment with the scent of vanilla.

Moon-Blessed Water Magic

Moon-blessed water is just what it sounds like: water infused with the magical energy of the full moon. Put some clear spring water into a jar, and drop in flower petals, blossoms, herbs, or leaves that represent your intention. Seal, and leave out under the full moon for a night. It will keep in the refrigerator for a couple weeks.

If you're using edible ingredients, you can drink the finished moon-blessed water using herbs or flowers that support your intention. You can also sprinkle the water over yourself or your magical items before doing a ritual or magic, or sprinkle it on paper or dried leaves, where you've written magical intentions.

Oil Magic

Ritual or magical oils have a broad spectrum of magical uses, and a long history in non-Pagan practices, such as mummification in ancient Egypt. Oils can be used for ritual and magical work by anointing your body at the third eye, wrists, neck, or pulse points, or dropped onto the felt in an oil diffuser locket or bracelet. The scent of the oil reinforces your intention all day long. Be aware that not all ritual oils are intended for use on the skin—only those specified for anointing or perfume are safe. Those intended for magical use only may irritate the skin.

Magical tools, altars, photos, crystals, or candles can be anointed with oil for magical purpose. Oil can also be spread over doorways or across the backs of chairs at home or at work, or dabbed onto personal items or possessions as an intention is spoken or chanted.

A ritual oil usually consists of a carrier oil, such as olive or jojoba, infused with herbs, spices, and perfumes for specific magical purposes, everything from protection to power to good luck to attractiveness. You can make magical oils yourself or purchase them already made from a variety of magical artisans with online shops. Another source for ritual oils is massage suppliers, which carry single-note essential oils and blends, like lavender, rosemary, or basil.

I prefer either single-note oils or premixed blends purchased from magical suppliers because the work has already been done for you. You can also infuse your own magical oil using olive or jojoba oil and whatever herbs or essences you wish.

Protection Magic

Protection magic, obviously, protects. When a situation seems potentially harmful, dangerous, or threatening, protection magic can be your shield or barrier. Protection magic repels harmful people, evil intent, and negative energy.

Brooms: A broom (also called a besom) is one of the most iconic witch symbols, and, hung horizontally over the front door, is protective, keeping unwanted people or energies away. Place one brush-side up next to the front door to deter unwanted visitors. (Placed brush-side down, it invites visitors.) Brooms are a traditional magical tool used to clear a space before doing a ritual, cleansing it of harmful or negative energy.

Salting and Sweeping: Combining a broom and salt expels negative energy from your home and creates a protective barrier. To begin, place a container of salt near your front door, within handy reach. Leave the door open. Go to the back of the house, and using a real broom or one you visualize, "sweep" all negative or harmful energy out of the house, room by room, moving it all toward the front door. Imagine it piling up there like a big nasty dust bunny. When it's all swept up to the front door, sweep it forcefully out the door while saying, "Be gone!" or "Gone for good!" All negative energy has been expelled. Brush your hands together and be done with it. Flick it away with your fingers for extra flourish. Pour a thin line of salt across the threshold outside the door, and when you go back inside, slam that door shut vigorously. For added protection, pour salt across the threshold of every external door and window. Finish by cleansing the area with sage smoke or protective incense like Dragon's Blood.

The use of sage smoke—particularly white sage—to cleanse an area, magical items, or people before a ritual has become very controversial. White sage is sacred to indigenous Americans, who use it in rituals. Because of sage's popularity and commercial value, it is often over-harvested in unethical ways. This robs indigenous Americans of a necessity for their spiritual practices and makes a mockery of something they hold sacred. If you really want to use sage, buy sustainably grown sage, preferably from indigenous American suppliers, rather than from commercial suppliers that strip the natural sage from the environment. If you live in a hot, arid area, you can grow your own sage. You can also substitute an herbal smoke for sage, such as cedar or dried bay leaf, lavender flowers, or rose petals.

Talismans and Amulets: A talisman or amulet is a piece of jewelry or symbol—often a pendant or ring—that protects you. It can be something as simple as an onyx pendant or protective animal like Owl, Snake, or Lion, or an elaborate sigil carved onto a piece of wood or bone or stamped into metal. My own protection preference is a pentacle pendant, as the symbol itself represents protection of the entire body and spirit, incorporating the four elemental energies and Spirit. Stones or crystals can be placed around your home in strategic spots as protective talismans. When you place them, draw a pentacle over them in the air with your finger.

A very ancient, well-known talisman is the Evil Eye protection symbol resembling a blue eye in the center of blue and white circles, usually made of glass and worn as a bracelet or pendant. It does what it says: Protects you from the "evil eye," which is a hostile gaze or spell aimed at you with the intention of causing illness or harm. The symbol's true name is *Nazar*. It dates back to fifth-century Greece and Rome, and appears in many Mediterranean and Middle Eastern cultures.[43]

Visualization: For mental protection imagery, settle into some quiet, undisturbed meditation time. Relax, breathe, ground. Feel your body supported

---

43. Forte Academy, "5 Things You Should Know About the 'Evil Eye' (and How to Protect Yourself), Medium, accessed January 28, 2020, https://medium.com/forte-academy/5-things-you-should-know-about-the-evil-eye-and-how-to-protect-yourself-3a01605cc303.

by the surface upon which you sit or lie, and feel its safety. Breathe into the earth, then turn your attention to the universe. Imagine a blue beam of light streaming down from the universe, funneling around you in a cone. See yourself in that cone, perfectly safe, perfectly protected. Next, imagine the exterior of that cone transforming into a mirrored surface, deflecting all negative or harmful energy. Seal that image in your mind and carry it with you. This protective cone is a mobile shield that can move with you all day. You can also do this visualization for another person, creating a cone of blue light and mirrors around them for protection.

Wards: Post wards above every door and window to repel negative or harmful energy, and also over or onto mirrors because they are metaphysical entry points. Wards can be symbols, such as dragons or gargoyles, or sigils, which are designs with a specific magical purpose. You can use premade images of symbols or sigils, or draw or paint them yourself on paper. I have a metal dragon above the outside of my front door and another facing the door on the inside, ready to barbecue any danger that comes calling. Wards are particularly effective for repelling negative magical or metaphysical energy being directed at you.

Witch's Bottle: A witch's bottle is a small bottle or jar filled with sharp protection magic, such as pins, thorns, teeth, claws, or needles, and other items with protective or repelling energy, such as black salt, garlic, and protective herbs or stones. A traditional witch's bottle also contains your urine or blood, which links the bottle to you, its creator. After putting what you want into the bottle, do a ritual to dedicate it to protection, and bury it. There is a difference of opinion about where to bury it. Some say near your front door, others say at the farthest corner of your property or at a crossroads. You can also bury it in a large a pot, plant a thorny rose or spiny cactus over it, and place outside the front door.

Satchel Magic

A small, magically charged satchel or pouch can carry a variety of intentions and is best kept near you. These are also called *mojo bags*, which comes from the Hoodoo tradition. In Hoodoo, very specific items are placed in the bag and blessed to enact your intention. They can also be purchased premade from a Hoodoo vendor.

A magical satchel is usually the size of your palm or less, and can be made of fabric, leather, or suede. It has a drawstring pull, often a leather lace or silk cord. They are quite simple to make yourself. In the bag, place things that represent your intention: stones, crystals, herbs, incense, coins, dirt, roots, or shells, and small images or handwritten magical intentions, if you wish. It can be any combination of things that reinforce your intention.

Once assembled, anoint the bag with magical oil or moon-blessed water and pass it through incense or herbal smoke to bless and activate the bag. Wear it around your neck, tied to your belt, or tuck into your pocket—keep it as close to you as possible, as much as possible. At night, tuck it under your pillow or keep it next to you on your nightstand. Keep it with you for as long as you feel the need.

Magical Ethics

Because magic is powerful, there are ethics involved. Remember that Wiccan phrase, "An' it harm none, do as ye will." "Harm none" is central to many Pagans, which is why you don't assume what someone else needs or wants and just launch magic in their direction. That's so arrogant. You might think you know what's best for someone, but you could be horribly wrong. When doing magic for someone else, get their permission first.

When you create your magical intention, create it with change for yourself only. Don't say, "Make Alex fall in love with me." Say, "Help me to be the kind of person Alex would love," and then leave it up to Alex to give it a thumbs-up or thumbs-down. In my opinion, magic shouldn't be done to control or manipulate others, and never to harm. Aside from being unethical, it brings us to the Rule of Three, which means that directing negative or harmful magic at someone will be reflected back onto you threefold. Some might call it karma. Don't create your own bad karma by commissioning the universe to harm to others.

The Real Magic Is You

Whether it's crystals or oils, wards or amulets, the common denominator in all magic is you. You infuse these methods and items with your confidence and magical intention and set that magic in motion. The magic is already in you, just waiting for an outlet.

Did a particular type of magic tickle your curiosity? Find out more about it. There are entire books and websites devoted to each of them. Give some things a try, and see what resonates with you. Record your discoveries and successes in your journal.

Recommended Reading

Blake, Deborah. *Everyday Witchcraft: Making Time for Spirit in a Too-Busy World*. Woodbury, MN: Llewellyn Publications, 2015.

K, Amber and Azrael Arynn K. *How to Become a Witch: The Path of Nature, Spirit & Magick*. Woodbury, MN: Llewellyn Publications, 2018.

RavenWolf, Silver. *HedgeWitch: Spells, Crafts & Rituals For Natural Magick*. Woodbury, MN: Llewellyn Publications, 2008.

Recommended Viewing

How the Universe Works (series). 2010-2020. Discovery Channel (2010). Science Channel (2012-2020). Stephen Marsh, producer.

Inner Worlds, Outer Worlds. 2012. Daniel Schmidt, producer.

CHAPTER 11

Divination

Divination is an ancient magical practice, stretching back to shamans, magicians, prophets, psychics, seers, and medicine men and women in practically every culture that ever was. Kings and queens often wanted to know in advance whether they'd be successful in battle or if someone was plotting against them. Should the prophet turn out to be incorrect, it could be a fatal error. Divination is also associated with "fortune telling," the kind seen at circus sideshows, and the quite racist image of the gypsy fortune-teller who always needs you to cross her palm with more coin if you want to know your future. While many do use divination to predict the future, I see it more as a map of what lies ahead. If I don't like where that map leads, I can change my course.

Here are some of the common forms of divination in the Pagan world.

Cards and Spreads

Reading intuitively from cards is a staple of divination. Each card has a meaning, the interaction between cards has meaning, and each position in a spread has meaning. Relying on your intuition, you interpret all these clues as a whole for insight into a situation, an upcoming challenge or choice, personal guidance, inspiration, and healing. "Cartomancy" means divination using a standard playing card deck, and there are many parallels between a standard deck and a tarot deck. The big three in cards and spreads in the Pagan world are tarot, the Lenormand oracle, and oracle decks.

Tarot

I love, love, *love* tarot, for insight, magic, inspiration, and endless learning.

I resonated with tarot the first time I picked up a deck. Tarot says "home" to me. It was familiar, even before I knew what it was.

You can never learn everything about tarot. The more you learn about tarot, the more you discover something new and enticing. As you work with your cards, you develop a relationship with them. You *know* each card like you'd know a relative or friend. They speak to you. And, like people, some of them show up all the time, while others are rarely seen.

Tarot began as a medieval Italian card game in the 1400s, called *tarocchi*. Many decks evolved from there, up to the classic Rider-Waite deck (also called the Rider-Waite-Smith, Universal Waite, or Smith-Waite deck), which features Pamela Colman Smith's iconic artwork, inspired by Arthur Waite's Golden Dawn influence. The imagery and meanings of many modern decks were inspired by the Rider-Waite deck, which was first published in 1909.

A modern tarot deck has four suits that align with regular playing cards: Diamonds are Pentacles, Spades are Swords, Clubs are Wands (or Rods), and Hearts are Cups. Tarot cards have the same ace-through-ten pip cards as a regular playing deck, as well as court cards: Kings and Queens, and Knights for Jacks. However, they have an additional court card that regular playing cards do not: the Page. In addition to these fifty-six cards, which are collectively called the minor arcana, there are twenty-two cards called the major arcana, that represent the human journey, from beginning to end, and everything in between, and starting back at the beginning once each journey is completed. Our lives have many journeys, like chapters in a story.

Most tarot decks come with a book or booklet of brief meanings for each card, which often have insight about how the symbolism points back to the Rider-Waite, which is the master language of tarot. Everything else is a translation. I highly recommend beginning with the Rider-Waite deck and developing some tarot fluency before giving in to the temptation of the hundreds of whimsical, fancy, and fascinating decks available. If there's something you love, there's probably a tarot deck for it: fairies, goddesses, magical cats, Gummi Bears, and ever so much more. Resist the temptation until you're familiar with the Rider-Waite. It will make learning tarot much cleaner and simpler.

When you do start expanding your collection, just so you know, "too many tarot decks" is not a thing.

Activity: Getting to Know Your New Deck

Treat your new tarot deck like any magical tool: Cleanse it with full moonlight or pass it through incense or herbal smoke. Greet your new deck and welcome it into your magical life. It's an intuitive partner that will reveal all sorts of amazing things bubbling in your subconscious.

If it's your first deck and you've never even held one before, set it on a dresser top or shelf where you'll see it every morning. You'll need guidance to get started, and there are a ton of tarot books out there. I strongly recommend Rachel Pollock's *Seventy-Eight Degrees of Wisdom: A Tarot Journey to Self-Awareness* for initial learning. You'll refer to it as you open the deck and go through it one card per day. Learntarot.com is an alternate quickie free resource. When you open the deck, the cards will be in order, which is perfect for the first lesson. Turn over one card per day, in order, and read the meaning from your resource.

Let that card sink in for the rest of the day. Take note when it "talks" to you or you see imagery or situations that point back to that card. When you've gone through the whole deck seventy-eight days later, shuffle them really well, until it feels like enough. Repeat this activity, drawing one card per day in random order, rereading its meaning, and watching for its message appearing in your life that day. You can repeat this exercise as many times as you like.

Even when you know the cards well, it's inspiring and challenging to draw one card each day and see what it reveals. It keeps your intuition fresh and flowing. Shuffle your cards and ask them what you need to know or be aware of that day.

A Couple Tarot Tips

Before you set off to explore tarot, a few quick notes: the Death card doesn't mean that you or anyone else is going to die. The card represents a finite ending to something, with no chance of going back. We have many "deaths" in our lives. Being born is the "death" of life in the womb. Graduating from high school is the "death" of adolescence. Getting married is the "death" of single life. The Death card means that whatever is ending, there's no going back. There's only a one-way exit. The Ten of Swords, with a figure facedown in the dirt with ten swords in his back, has a similar message: it's over. However, an ending to something painful, like a breakup or divorce, can be a huge relief. You can't get much deader than dead—you've bottomed out, there's no dropping any further. The suffering is over, and everything from now on will be an improvement.

Several cards have disturbing images, particularly in the Swords suit, but remember: The images are symbolic and archetypal. For example, Swords represent the mind, thoughts, and communication—not actual swords—which means those sharp edges are harsh thoughts or verbal exchanges. Also, the Devil doesn't mean that Satan's gonna getcha. This card represents addictions and enslavements, and the loose chains on the human figures imply that it's within their ability to leave this situation and free themselves.

Activity: Ready to Read

When you're ready to try a reading, I recommend skipping reversals. A reversal is a card that appears upside down, reversing the usual meaning of that card. Inform your cards as you're shuffling that you won't be reading reversals, and turn any upside-down card that you draw right-side up. When your cards feel familiar to you and you feel ready to read reversals, go for it. Reversal meanings are included in Rachel Pollock's book.

Before doing any spread, shuffle your cards until it feels like enough. Sit quietly and hold your cards in your hands or near your heart or third eye—whatever feels comfortable and natural. Clear your mind, slow your breath, and welcome whatever messages the universe wishes to send you. If you have a specific question or issue, ask your cards for insight. I prefer to ask my cards for a snapshot rather than asking specific questions. A snapshot is something the universe would like to shine a spotlight on—something you might not have considered or a new angle on a situation or relationship.

You can draw cards from the top of the deck, middle, or bottom, or spread them in front of you, pass your palm a couple inches over them, and pick the ones that pull you. I've had cards literally rise up toward my palm when spread out in front of me. Some cards *really* want your attention. A three-card spread is a good starting point: The card in the middle is your current situation. The card to the left represents diminishing influences. The card to the right represents increasing influences.

In the beginning, keep your resource book handy as you get to know the cards, but be sensitive to your intuition too. Trust it. If a card seems to be telling you something else, explore that. The traditional interpretations of tarot cards aren't the only interpretations.

Some Tarot Spreads

Tarot cards are read in spreads, where each position represents a certain thing. The cards can also interact with each other in a spread. Pay attention when a figure looks at another card, or faces away from it, and if the figure is holding a sword, it may be pointing to another card that needs scrutiny. The entire spread can also reveal an overall theme or overarching story. Other things to pay attention to are abundances of certain colors, numbers, or types of figures. The minor arcana represent the more average issues of daily life, but the major arcana cards are big energy. When you get a major arcana card in a spread, its message is in all caps: PAY ATTENTION! If a particular card mystifies, concerns, or confuses you, you can draw another card (up to three—more than that is confusing) and ask for more information.

Celtic Cross

The most familiar and widely known spread is the Celtic Cross, which has a circle of six cards on the left and a vertical line of four cards.

Although I like to create my own spreads, I do love the Celtic Cross. It's where my tarot journey began, it's comfortable and familiar, and it connects me spiritually to all those tarot readers across the centuries. It taps into a mystical communal realm. Each spot on the Celtic Cross means something:

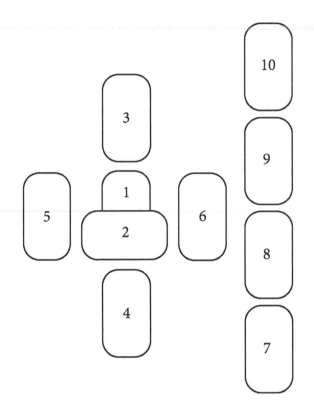

1. Your current situation; a snapshot of this particular moment in time.
2. This blocks you from fully experiencing your current situation.
3. What you're really aware of and paying attention to.
4. What's working beneath the surface; your subconscious or things at play that you may not be aware of.
5. Diminishing in importance.
6. Increasing in importance.
7. The role you're playing in your current situation.
8. The role others are playing in your current situation.
9. Your hopes and fears; what motivates or repels you in this situation.
10. The most likely outcome of your situation or question. This will most likely occur if you do nothing and just passively let all the factors at play proceed. If you don't want that outcome, look to the other cards for clues about making changes.

New Year or Birthday Spread

Do this spread on or near New Year's Day or on or near your birthday. Draw a card and place it face up. This will be the theme for the upcoming year, and the center of the circle of cards you're about to create. Next, draw a card and place it at one o'clock, then at two o'clock, three o'clock, and so on until you have a card for every position on the clock up to twelve o'clock. The reading begins at one o'clock, representing January or the month of your birth, and the months continue sequentially for each position, ending at twelve o'clock for December, or the month before your birthday.

This spread gives you an overarching theme for the year and monthly themes that point back to the annual theme. Do you see something problematic in the upcoming year? Now you have time to make a plan for dealing with that rather than being caught off guard; make adjustments now. Take a photo of this spread so you can track it as the months progress.

Sabbat Spreads

For any sabbat, you can create a spread surrounding its energy. For Beltane, maybe a love and romance theme, with all the prompts pointing to that: "What will improve my love life?" "Where will I find true love?" "How does my lover perceive me?" For Samhain, you might pick three cards to represent what you need to let fall, what you need to honor, and what needs to be still for awhile. Create whatever questions you wish, but keep it to five cards or less so you don't get overwhelmed.

You can also assign a meaning of your choosing to each letter in the sabbat's name, such as: I = Insight, M = Money, B = Breakthroughs, O = Overlooked, L = Love, C = Creativity; you've spelled out "Imbolc," which is a time for choosing a goal, or for new beginnings. Draw a card for each letter to see what it's saying about what that letter represents. It may offer insight in planning your goal or setting it in motion. After reading the cards for each letter, read them in a line, left to right. Do they tell a story? Are there common or complementary messages or imagery?

Nine-Card Spread

A nine-card spread is essentially an embellished center of the Celtic Cross. This spread is so rich with information, it has become my favorite spread. The first card goes in the center. The second goes faceup to its left, the third faceup to its right: a line of three cards. Next, draw three cards in a row, placing them above the first row, left to right, and then another three cards in a row, placing them below the first row, left to right. They should resemble a tic-tac-toe grid—three orderly rows of three cards each.

The center card is a snapshot of your situation at this moment in time. The vertical row on the left is "things diminishing in importance or moving out of the picture." The vertical row on the right is "things increasing in importance or moving into the picture." The top row is "things you're aware of or concerned about." The bottom row is "things you're unaware of or are repressing." The center vertical line is a triple snapshot of your situation at this moment in time.

Look at the entire spread as one tapestry. Are there repetitive numbers, colors, images, or suits? Is there a theme or overarching message? A bonus in a nine-card spread is a tic-tac-toe: there's an extra issue or influence for you to consider.

Lenormand Oracle

Learning traditional tarot won't help you with the Lenormand oracle deck one bit—it's an entirely different system, as are all oracle decks. The Lenormand oracle is sometimes called "the petite Lenormand," as the cards are a bit smaller than traditional tarot cards. The deck is named after late eighteenth-century Parisian fortuneteller Mlle. Marie Anne Lenormand. According to the Tarot Conservancy, "it is unclear whether or not she indeed used this particular oracle in her practice, however, after her death, Mlle. Le Normand's name was soon attached to published decks." The earliest version of today's decks dates back to the 1799 German publication of "The Game of Hope," in which the cards were laid out into four rows of nine cards, creating a board. Dice were then used to determine the players' movements.[44]

---

44. Mary Merton, "What is Lenormand?" The Tarot Conservatory, last updated August 31, 2017, https://www.thetarotconservatory.com.au/what-is-lenormand/.

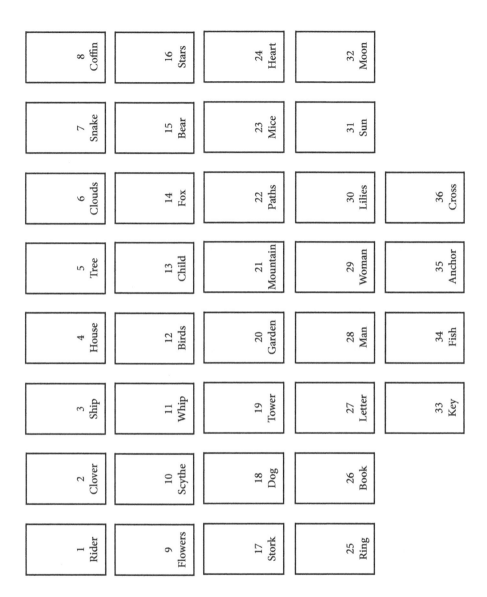

The thirty-six images on the cards are simple symbols: house, clover, dog, key, and so on. Unlike the mysterious archetypal imagery of the Rider-Waite, Lenormand cards mean what they say. What you see is what you get. Mice *always* mean poverty. Rider *always* means good news. Ship *always* means travel. There's no fudging and fumbling with intuition, like "Mice are cute— maybe a tiny gift is coming." No. Mice eat your food and leave you hungry.

As far as Lenormand is concerned, there's nothing cute about them. Tarot is a fluid reading, relying on intuition and insight, while Lenormand is more like math. The numbers don't lie, they are what they are, and they add up to a specific sum.

Just as with regular tarot, there are many Lenormand spreads, including three-card and five-card spreads. Just as the Celtic Cross is the go-to spread in tarot, the Grand Tableau or Grand Tableau of Nines is the go-to for Lenormand. Like the Game of Hope, there are four rows of nine cards, all placed faced up. A variation on this is four rows of eight cards, and a fifth bottom row of four cards. Each position in this spread is called a "house," and corresponds to the sequential number on the cards. For example, clouds is number six, and is the sixth card in the top row of the Grand Tableau.

To create this spread, lay out your cards in rows, then locate the significator card, which represents you: man for a man, or woman for a woman. This is a trouble spot with Lenormand: If you're non-binary, there's no gender-neutral card to use as a significator. Some use the child card, but I find that demeaning, and besides, the child card has its own meaning. Adding a gender-neutral "person" card to every Lenormand oracle would modernize it, but until then, we're stuck with a binary system. Pick whichever significator card feels best, or maybe, "least worst."

Once the significator card has been located, the vertical line of cards above the querent represents the conscious mind, and the line below, the subconscious mind. What is to the left of the significator card is the past, and to the right, the future. The four cards in the middle of the spread are the heart of the matter—similar to the first card in the Celtic Cross, as are the cards to the left and right of the significator. The card in each house has meaning, as do certain positions in the spread, such as the corners of the whole spread. The cards can also be read in small "sentences" of two and three or diagonally.

Caitlin Matthews' book *The Complete Lenormand Oracle Handbook: Reading the Language and Symbols of the Cards* is a great reference for learning Lenormand. It's packed with full-color images of the cards and spreads, and thorough explanations on the meaning of each, plus how certain combinations of cards create sentences or equations with a specific meaning, like "Dog + Fox = frenemy" and "Book + Bear = Mastering Wisdom" and "Rod +

Ship = Sex Between Strangers." Yes, there's a "one-night stand" combo in the Lenormand!

You may like the no-nonsense "what you see is what you get" approach of the Lenormand as opposed to the deep thought and intuition needed for reading a tarot spread. Unlike the Rider-Waite deck in tarot, there's not really a "master" Lenormand deck, and there are many to choose from. Pick the one that calls to you. Or a couple. They're so little. Just one more couldn't hurt. And, just like tarot, "too many decks" is not a thing.

Oracle Decks

An oracle deck is a tiny universe unto itself, with their own unique symbology and reading methods. They don't have suits, court cards, or major or minor arcana cards. Typically, they have a theme, such as animals, plants, crystals, mermaids, unicorns—pretty much anything you can think of. Oracle decks are a gentle, low-key approach to divination or inspiration, and are particularly comforting if you're struggling with difficult emotions, like depression or grief. You may not have the energy to invest in reading a tarot spread. Sometimes, you just need a friendly little prompt to help you get through that day.

Oracle decks usually have accompanying books or booklets, with meanings for the cards and spreads. You can get to know an oracle deck just like a tarot deck—draw a card each day for inspiration or insight. If you're intimidated by tarot or the Lenormand, an oracle deck is an easy gateway into intuitive cartomancy.

Divination Comes in Many Forms

Reading cards is only one form of divination. There are many others, some with long and interesting cultural histories. For me, tarot said "home." For you, it may be something else. Here are some other methods for learning to see what can't be seen.

Pendulums

A classic pendulum is a pointed clear quartz crystal hanging from a string or chain, held between the thumb and forefinger of one hand, over the palm of the other. They are made of many other crystals and can also simply be a needle hanging from a thread, a pendant, or anything that swings easily on a string or chain. I cannot explain why pendulums work, I can only attest to the fact they do consistently swing yes or no or no response. I have held them stone-still, asked a question, and witnessed them swinging on their own.

To consult with a pendulum, hold it by one end with the pointed end hanging over the center of your palm until you feel a slight tickly, tingly sensation. Breathe, still your mind, and focus on the pendulum. Before asking a question, tell it, "Show me *yes*" and note which way it swings. Stop and bring it to center and tell it, "Show me *no*," and note which way it swings. Usually, yes and no swing at perpendicular angles. If it's unable to answer a question, it may make tiny circles, quiver, or remain still. Once you've established yes and no, ask it a yes-or-no question and see how it answers.

Tea Leaf Reading

Reading tea leaves is as old as reading palms. And you get the bonus of a nice cup of tea before getting started. You must use loose-leaf tea and a classic teacup, or cup of similar shape rather than a straight-sided coffee mug. You'll also need a napkin or paper towel.

To begin, brew your tea, enjoy it, and focus on your issue, situation, or question. Drink all but about a teaspoon. Sit at a table and place the napkin in front of you. Swirl the tea gently deosil, and when you're ready, quickly invert it all at once and let the napkin catch the spill. Turn it back over and look at it from all angles to see if you notice images in the leaves. The position of the image pertains to the reading too. Near the rim of the cup represents the present or immediate future. The middle means a few days away. The bottom means weeks or months into the future.

There are hundreds of tea leaf images, but here are some easy ones:

Arrow: A message is coming your way. If pointing up, good news. If pointing down, bad.

Circle: Money, gifts, commitment, marriage.

Clover: Good luck, good fortune.

Cross: Difficulties, obstacles, misfortune.

Dashes: Thrills and excitement.

Dots: Money and security.

Heart: Love, romance, and pleasure.

Lines: If wavy, difficulties. If straight, progress.

Question Mark: An uncertain outcome.

Square: Difficulties, challenges.

Triangle: Unexpected good luck, good fortune.

Keep a resource book handy while you're reading. There are some amazingly esoteric images for tea reading, like rolling pins, lighthouses, and grasshoppers, and just about anything you can imagine.

Runes

Runes are Norse and Germanic alphabet symbols, dating to the second century, BCE, before the adoption of the familiar Latin alphabet. There are twenty-four letters in this runic alphabet, and in Lisa Peschel's book, *A Practical Guide to the Runes: Their Uses in Divination and Magick*, she emphasizes that these images were sacred to ancient people, and only a select few were entrusted with them. Their meanings were passed down through the generations orally.

"It must be remembered that the runes were mysteries to these people, in every sense of the word. They were forces, secret allies that the knowledgeable could use for many purposes," says Peschel.[45]

While the runes were possessed only by the spiritually worthy in ancient times, they now are available to anyone with an internet connection, and are often sold at festivals and conventions. The best ones are those you make yourself by carving or painting the symbols onto stones or squares of wood. As with any magical tool, anything you make yourself has your energy attached to it, and is unique, and more energetically enriched.

Runes are traditionally kept in a leather pouch, which you can also make. To read them, hold the pouch, concentrate on your question, and choose a rune from the bag to get your answer or gently toss the runes onto a flat surface. Whichever stands out to you is your answer. You can also draw three runes at a time, and put them in a line, reading them like a three-card tarot spread. The one to the left is your past, the one in the middle is your present, and the one on the right is your future.

---

45. Lisa Peschel, *A Practical Guide to the Runes: Their Uses in Divination and Magick* (St. Paul, MN: Llewellyn Worldwide, 1989), 3.

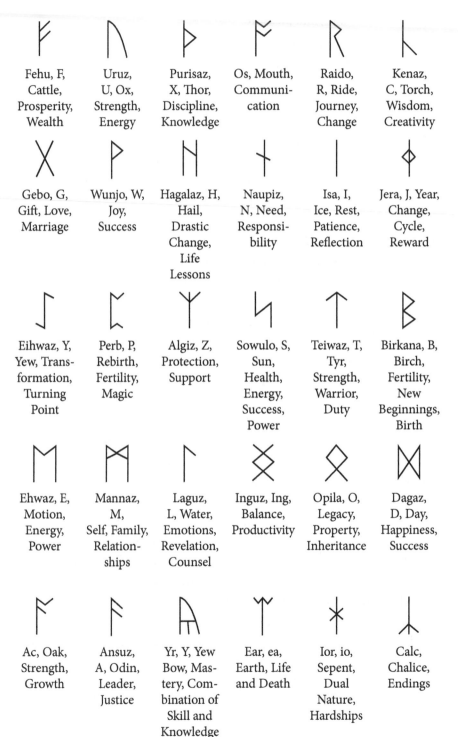

Fehu, F, Cattle, Prosperity, Wealth

Uruz, U, Ox, Strength, Energy

Purisaz, X, Thor, Discipline, Knowledge

Os, Mouth, Communication

Raido, R, Ride, Journey, Change

Kenaz, C, Torch, Wisdom, Creativity

Gebo, G, Gift, Love, Marriage

Wunjo, W, Joy, Success

Hagalaz, H, Hail, Drastic Change, Life Lessons

Naupiz, N, Need, Responsibility

Isa, I, Ice, Rest, Patience, Reflection

Jera, J, Year, Change, Cycle, Reward

Eihwaz, Y, Yew, Transformation, Turning Point

Perb, P, Rebirth, Fertility, Magic

Algiz, Z, Protection, Support

Sowulo, S, Sun, Health, Energy, Success, Power

Teiwaz, T, Tyr, Strength, Warrior, Duty

Birkana, B, Birch, Fertility, New Beginnings, Birth

Ehwaz, E, Motion, Energy, Power

Mannaz, M, Self, Family, Relationships

Laguz, L, Water, Emotions, Revelation, Counsel

Inguz, Ing, Balance, Productivity

Opila, O, Legacy, Property, Inheritance

Dagaz, D, Day, Happiness, Success

Ac, Oak, Strength, Growth

Ansuz, A, Odin, Leader, Justice

Yr, Y, Yew Bow, Mastery, Combination of Skill and Knowledge

Ear, ea, Earth, Life and Death

Ior, io, Sepent, Dual Nature, Hardships

Calc, Chalice, Endings

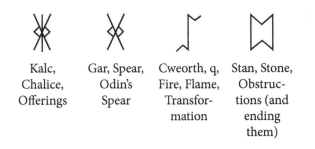

| Kalc, Chalice, Offerings | Gar, Spear, Odin's Spear | Cweorth, q, Fire, Flame, Transformation | Stan, Stone, Obstructions (and ending them) |

Haruspicy

Okay, just to be saucy, I've included the ancient art of Etruscan sheep liver divination because yes, I *did* attend a workshop on this—illustrating that the topics you can explore in the Big Pagan Garden are truly unlimited. If you can imagine it, it's there, and even if you can't, it's still there.

Haruspicy is linked to ancient Etruria, which has little documented history other than art and pottery. The language was lost. However, information on the practice of haruspicy—reading the livers of sacrificed sheep—survived. Etruscan priests used a bronze model of a sheep's liver, which was divided into forty sections with twenty-four gods named in the inscriptions. One who was trained in the finer art of sheep liver divination was called a *haruspex*. The liver was inspected for shape, color, condition, and signs of disease to divine the future, according to the bronze model. A clay model was then made of that liver as a record.

It may sound bizarre and grotesque but reading animal entrails was a common ancient divination practice in many cultures. Reading entrails is one of many things in nature used for divination, from birdcalls to cloud formations to piles of poop. Me, I'll stick to tarot.

Scrying

One method of scrying is to hold a bowl of water, mirror, or other reflective surface in your hands under a full moon, relax, and focus on the moon's reflection in it. Keep gazing, remaining in your still and quiet space, and see if visions or inspirations come to you, whether in the reflection or in your mind. If you relax your mind, and your eyes, a picture may emerge. Scrying can also be done with a crystal ball, flames of a fire, or a candle, using the same method: A calm and still mind, open to the possibility of inspiration, grounding and centering, and gazing into the ball to await messages, images, or information. Let your gaze go soft, like staring at one of those Magic Eye drawings. If you try too hard, you'll only see colored dots. Relax your vision to see through what you're seeing and let the image emerge.

Dowsing

Dowsing comes from that old farmer's trick of using a forked stick to find water. Using a Y-shaped stick, the ends are held in each hand, the long end pointing parallel to the ground. When the tip dropped, a water source was believed to be underground. Dowsers also search for missing objects or energy pockets in a room.

Palmistry

Also known as *chiromancy*, palmistry involves reading lines on the palm, including the life line, fate line, head line, and heart line. There are also other minor lines on some hands, as well as bracelet lines, and mounts, which are the mounds or bumps immediately below each finger on the palm and at the heel of the hand, correlating to the planets: seven bumps, associated with the sun, moon, Mars, Mercury, Jupiter, Venus, and Saturn. Line markings are also read, such as breaks in the lines, chains, crosses, dots, grills, squares, stars, tassels, triangles, and islands. Both right and left hand are included in a reading. In addition to the lines, the shape of the palm, fingers, and fingernails are also considered.

I-Ching

The *I-Ching* is one of the oldest forms of divination and is called an oracle. It dates back more than 3,000 years to the Zhou Dynasty in China. This form of divination comes from centuries of Chinese wisdom, recorded in the *I-Ching*, which means *The Book of Changes*. The book explains sixty-four hexagrams or archetypes. In this form of divination, with a question in mind, three coins (they can be Chinese, or not) are tossed six times, and their patterns and combinations of heads and tails noted. The patterns are compared to the hexagrams, each of which has a meaning, such as "The Creative," "The Receptive," "Initial Difficulty," and "Innocence." The *I-Ching* provides answers and insights for a particular question or your upcoming day.

Activity: Which One Attracts You?

Choose a form of divination from this chapter that you're drawn to, and find out more about it, using books, blogs, the internet. Get that divination system for yourself or make one. Play with it. Make friends with it. Read some more. Google it. See if a relationship forms with it—a feeling of familiarity and energy exchange. When you pick it up, do you *know* it? Does it seem to know you?

Take note of patterns that emerge and symbology that pops up in real life after you've seen them in your cards, pendulum, palm, or teacup. Document your discoveries and insights in your journal.

It's All About Intuition

Intuition is the heart of divination. Whatever method you choose, you must relax into your own insight and intuition, and be open to ideas, inspirations, and thoughts that come to you. When something stumps you, don't despair—go find out more. No matter how proficient you become at any form of divination, there's always something new to discover. Whichever divination system appeals to you, there's a website for that, a stack of books, and a Facebook group too. Maybe three or four. Well, maybe not for reading sheep livers, but for the other stuff, absolutely.

Recommended Reading

Dow, Caroline. *Tea Leaf Reading for Beginners: Your Fortune in a Tea Cup.* Woodbury, MN: Llewellyn Publications, 2011.

Greer, Mary. *Tarot for Your Self: A Workbook for the Inward Journey (35th Anniversary Edition).* Newburyport, MA: Weiser Books, 2019.

Matthews, Caitlyn. *The Complete Lenormand Oracle Handbook: Reading the Language and Symbols of the Cards.* Rochester, VT: Destiny Books, 2014.

Peschel, Lisa. *A Practical Guide to the Runes: Their Uses in Divination and Magick.* St. Paul, MN: Llewellyn Worldwide, 1989.

CHAPTER 12
Altars, Tools, and Ritual

Theoretically, you could do any magic or ritual you wanted with no tools at all—nothing but your own body and will. In fact, you've already done this in the elemental ritual at the end of chapter 4. However, creating altars and using magical tools can set a focused, mystical tone and put you in a more magical mindset. The thing to remember is that the stuff doesn't make the magic. You do.

The layout of an altar, and the tools and items included on it, vary from tradition to tradition and person to person. The same goes for ritual. That said, there are many common threads running through many traditions. My own solitary eclectic Garden-Variety Pagan approach leans Wiccan, because that's what I first learned and it's comfortable.

In this chapter, we'll explore altars, tools, and ritual, enabling you to create your own rituals and to be familiar with them enough to participate in a public or group ritual. Specific paths and traditions may do things differently and have practices that don't resemble mine. As always, in the Big Pagan Garden, there's no right tradition or right way to do things—only what's right for you.

Altars

An altar is a special, spiritual space with a collection of special, spiritual items, with a specific spiritual focus or goal. It's a spot for magic, ritual, inspiration, prayer, meditation, contemplation, celebration, remembrance, or worship, alone or in a group. An altar typically has one of three purposes: attraction, doing magical work, or honoring deity. It can be a stand-alone entity or included as part of a ritual. Sometimes creating the altar is part of the ritual; sometimes it's set up in advance as the focal point of a ritual.

Regardless of purpose, an altar is a deeply personal spiritual creation. Whether minimalistic and simple or elaborate and ornate, your altar should be meaningful to you and reinforce your intention. An altar isn't just a bunch of items you gather. It has a job to do, as opposed to a collection of cool witchy stuff. There's nothing wrong with collections of cool witchy stuff—you just need to recognize the difference: worktable versus decoration. It's not just an arrangement, it's a unique, working energetic unit—a magical aggregate, with a specific purpose.

An altar can be very large, like tabletop size, or very small. I have one on my dresser that's quite petite. Upon a large agate slice a bit smaller than my hand, are miniature altar tools and items. This little altar has big energy even though it's small. Magical energy isn't determined by the size of the altar, it's determined by your intention. Another altar in my living room spans an entire cabinet top, and is the magical heart of our house. There are other altars throughout the house of varying size and purpose—you can have as many as you want. Regardless of size or location, an altar should swirl with magical energy that you set in motion.

Creating an altar is itself a magical activity. You don't just set things there, brush your hands, and walk away. Take your time, sink into your imaginative, creative space and *feel* your way through it. Trust your intuition. Arrange it in a way that feels meaningful to you, not because a book said to do it a particular way. Also, don't make it too cluttered. Leave some breathing room for energy to move freely.

An altar may be left up for as long as you wish, or created for a specific purpose and taken down when your magical work is finished. If you'll be leaving it up for awhile, keep it clean and free of dust. Cleaning and refreshing your altars on the sabbats is a great way to keep your altar spiritually sparkling clean as part of celebrating that sabbat. If your altar's energy starts to feel stagnant, take it all down, clean everything, and start fresh. You don't have to put every single thing back. Some things may feel like they need to rest for awhile, so store them for awhile and try new items that seem to be asking for some altar time. Change up your altar whenever you feel that urge, just like you might to rearrange or redecorate a room.

When everything's in place, welcome your altar and activate it. Place your hands on the altar and do a quiet meditation on your intention. Cleanse and purify your altar by swirling incense or herbal smoke over and throughout it, and with sound, like a singing bowl, bell, rattle, or sistrum. Finish by saying, "Welcome."

Attraction Altars

An attraction altar does just that: it attracts a specific energy, like a magical magnet. Unlike a working altar, your creativity can wander far and wide for an attraction altar, and include all sorts of novel items. An attraction altar might not even have traditional altar tools on it at all. It could be designed to attract anything, from money to love to elemental energies, and everything on the altar would support that intention. A money altar might include actual money (paper or coins), lodestone, jade, gold, and silver, a piggy bank, and a wallet with a basil leaf inside. A love altar might include rose quartz, a bowl of rose and jasmine petals, fresh figs, chocolate and two glasses of wine, heart imagery, pink and red items, and the Lovers tarot card. Your intention doesn't have to be big and grand like money or love. It could be to adopt a new dog or bring a fabulous carpenter to build some new shelves. Whatever is important enough for you to want is important enough to design an altar to make it a reality.

Elemental Altars

An elemental altar includes imagery and items associated with that element, as well as items in the colors of that element, such as crystals, candles, cloth, and decor. Here are some examples:

Earth Altar

The earth element represents things that fall into the categories of health, wealth, and stuff: improving your own health, increasing your wealth, or finding a new home, for example. Earth is a grounding, growing energy, and possible earth altar items might include heavy stones, living plants, rocks, geodes, wood, pinecones, seeds, a bowl of soil, and items in earth's colors, browns and greens. Animals that burrow or dwell in caves, such as bears or squirrels, would suit an earth altar, as would forest animals, which are also associated with earth, particularly stags. Crystals form inside the earth, so crystals are perfect for an earth altar. Add the Ten of Pentacles tarot card to set a tone for a healthy, happy life.

Air Altar

Air is the element of the mind, and when air is directed, it provides focus and movement. If you're feeling scattered around, and your thoughts are swirling around like leaves on an unruly breeze, include things that inspire air-driven direction on your air altar, like a sailboat, hot-air balloon, airplane, or kite. An air altar would include items carried by air, like scent or sound. Include incense, sachets of potpourri, and bells, chimes, or rattles. Animals that fly will suit any air altar: feathers, bird imagery, or even a Pegasus. Air colors are light: yellows and pastels. If you have an intellectual, educational, or employment goal, include something that represents it, like a medallion, diploma, or contract, placed near the Ace of Swords for fresh, powerful air energy.

Fire Altar

A fire altar aims to heat things up: courage, energy, power, sexuality. Attract the fire energies you need by including imagery in red and orange, and things that burn like candles, matches, kindling, the sun, or volcanoes. If you're facing a difficult challenge or fear, the King, Queen, or Knight of Wands tarot cards will inspire bravery, while the Six of Wands would usher in victory. If your sex life needs some spicing up, include cinnamon sticks or oil, red satin, phallus and/or yoni imagery in whatever combination is appropriate for your relationship, and definitely a red candle. Fire's energy is symbolized by a rearing red stallion, dragon, striking snake, or roaring lion.

Water Altar

When you want to get your creative energies flowing, a water alter will attract what you need. Water might also attract energies for emotional healing, serenity, or stress reduction. Include water symbology, such as shells, fish, or plants associated with water such as water lilies or cattails. Mermaids are perfect for a water altar. Water's colors are blues, teals, and purples, which makes fluorite an excellent crystal for a water altar. Include some actual water on the altar, in a bowl or small fountain, or even a fishbowl with live fish.

In the tarot, the Page of Cups would inspire fresh creativity, while the Star would promote serenity and self-acceptance.

Sabbat Altars

Altars are a great place to celebrate the sabbats. Sabbat altars attract the joy and energy of that sabbat to your home. They don't have to include any magical tools unless you want them there. Anything that symbolizes a sabbat could be placed there, from colors associated with that sabbat to items. You might use eggs, bunnies, and pastel ribbons and candles for Ostara, flowery pinks and reds for Beltane, or autumn leaves, apples, and nuts for Mabon, splashed with bright oranges, yellows, and browns.

Samhain's colors are orange and black, however a Samhain altar is a special case. You could go full-on Halloween if you want to, but the actual spirit of the sabbat is the "final harvest." Include photos of your beloved deceased, and items that belonged to them or items they would appreciate. A Samhain altar attracts the spirits of your loved ones, and gives you a time and space to remember, honor, and appreciate them.

A traditional Yule altar would be trimmed in red and green decor, with pine, holly, and mistletoe, as well as a Yule log or candles to welcome the return of the sun. You can blend Christmas right in if you wish to travel in both lanes, and add whatever holiday decor you want. Santa and a bunch of cheerful snowmen come to visit Gaia and her goddess friends on my altar at Yule, and the white fairy lights get swapped out for colored ones, and everything gets strewn in sparkly garlands.

Activity: Create an Attraction Altar

What would you really like to attract into your life right now? Don't be shy— imagine the ultimate: money or good fortune; love or romance; new career opportunities; travel and adventure; new friends and fun times. Whatever you desire, let's attract it. If nothing springs to mind, you can create an altar for whichever sabbat is coming up.

Find just the right spot in your house for your altar. It may be a table, shelf, mantle, bookshelf, dresser top, or any place that feels like "right here" in your gut. It should be a place you'll see every day, and not a dark corner you rarely notice—unless you're going to enliven that corner and transform it with mirrors, candles, lights, and sparkly things.

Next, it's time to collect your altar adornments. You've got a lot of magical knowledge for this already: the elements; animal and plant spirits; color, candle, crystal, herb, and oil magic. Using any combination of those things, start gathering items for your attraction altar. Some items right there in your house may call to you to be included. Trust your intuition. If you'd like a natural feel, add fresh flowers, greenery, and stones or rocks. Maybe you want to get your sparkly on and include some magical glitter and glimmer, like ribbons, garlands, or fairy lights. A nice touch is to use a fancy piece of cloth for the base, like velvet or satin, in a color that complements what you're attracting. There's no right or wrong way to make an attraction altar. It's all about what you feel would attract that energy you seek.

When you've gathered everything up, play with it a bit. Move things around until it feels like "that's the spot." Let your intuition be your magical decorator. An attraction altar is joyful, so play some music, burn some incense, sing or dance as you create. Have fun with it! Should you pause and get a feeling that says, "It's done," trust it. You're ready to activate your magical magnet.

Activate your altar by cleansing it with incense or herbal smoke. You could also sprinkle it with moon-blessed water, recite a poem or quatrain, or sing a song. Place your hands on your altar, focus on the energy you wish to attract or the sabbat you wish to celebrate, and release it to the universe. In the meantime, enjoy your beautiful altar—a locus of attraction, inspiration, and affirmation.

Working Altars

A working altar is a magical worktable. It's a reverse energetic funnel, siphoning your focused intention up and out to the universe. Working altars are used by solitaries, who practice magic alone, and also in groups and covens, often as a centerpiece for a ritual or magical work. In some rituals, everyone is invited to add something to that altar and contribute their own energy.

Unlike attraction altars, which are a wide beam for broad-spectrum things, like money or career opportunities, a working altar is a place for magical work, with a specific, targeted intention: "a big profit on my house sale" or "a nursing job at Community Hospital." A working altar usually includes specific traditional magical tools for implementing that intention at your altar. Although I'm a huge fan of eclectic creativity, using traditional tools feels like tapping into the larger magical currents and going with that flow. It also provides a sense of connection to the larger Pagan community, past and present, who used or use the same magical tools. This is comforting and reinforcing when you're a coven of one.

Altar Tools and Items

A traditional working altar has representations of the four elements (colored candles or elemental items, like shells or stones), placed in the actual direction of those elements: north for earth, east for air, south for fire, and west for water. There is a representation of the God and Goddess, frequently with an athame (pronounced *ATHA-may*) and chalice (*CHA-liss*), respectively, or separate items in addition to those.

An athame is a ritual knife, used only for magical work, and represents hot, projective masculine energy—the God. With an athame, you direct energy directly at something, and command it. An athame can also be used to cast a circle before beginning a ritual or working at your altar. The chalice, being womb-like in design, represents cool, receptive feminine energy—the Goddess. In a symbolic motion to unite the energies of both the God and Goddess in perfect balance, the athame in your right hand is placed point-down into the chalice in your left. If you aren't comfortable with deity, you can replace God and Goddess with the projective and receptive energies of the universe, or just honor the earth.

An athame can be something as simple as a paring knife, and a chalice could be a wine glass. However, once you choose those items to represent the God and Goddess on your altar, use them for that purpose only thereafter. They're not kitchen tools anymore. They're magical tools.

Wands are another traditional altar tool, and are also used to direct energy, particularly for casting a circle before beginning a ritual. A wand can stand in for an athame in a pinch, and vice versa. You can make a wand with a straight, slender branch, about the length of your forearm. Sharpen the end to a point or attach a small pointed quartz crystal. Make a handle by wrapping flat leather or suede laces at the other end, and adorn however you wish or carve magical symbols or phrases into the wood.

Other common traditional altar items include bells, crystals, incense and incense burner, bowls of salt, a pentacle, white candles, tarot cards, God or Goddess statuary, and plant or animal spirit representations. An offering plate and smaller chalice (a small teacup and saucer will do) is also typically on an altar, and offerings to the God and Goddess (sometimes also addressed as the Lord and Lady) are placed there. The classic offering is cakes and ale, which is a bit of bread, cake, or cookie, and wine, mead, or a special liqueur. Unless your altar space is large and these items are small, it can get cluttered. Leave space for energy to flow freely.

You could spend a small fortune on altar tools, or nothing. Although the sparkly stuff is enticing and fun, you don't actually *need* it. A $49.99 price tag doesn't make that pewter wand any more magical than one you created from a stick you found. Having a fancy altar tool might create a mystical, magical tone for your altar, but they aren't actually necessary. The item isn't the magical tool. You are. Whether ornate, mundane, or handmade, when you dedicate something to magical work, it's infused with your own magical energy. The universe responds to the content, not the container.

Personalizing a Working Altar

Besides traditional tools on a working altar, you can be creative and embellish your arrangement with other things that will serve a purpose in your magical work. In other words, not decorations—tools. My working altar is a small wooden folding table, covered with a purple velvet cloth trimmed in silver brocade. The centerpiece is four horseshoes, welded together at the heels like a big four-leaf clover, invoking the energy of Horse, because Horse brings its powerful "git 'er done" energy to my work.

The space within each horseshoe holds representations of the elements: a crystal for Earth, feathers for air, a candle for fire, a shell for water. At the center is a silver pentacle about the size of my palm, which serves as a mini worktable for my magical worktable. There, I place magical work, such as a piece of paper with my written intention, and on top of that, an anointed chime candle that I've breathed a quatrain, spell, or intention into. There's also incense and an incense burner, candles, and large crystals. Because it's a smallish space, the God and Goddess are represented by my athame and chalice.

This is my basic working altar template. Depending on my intention, I might add other things, like bells, a small cast-iron cauldron, a mirror, figurines, photos—the list could go on and on. I add anything that supports my intention.

I keep a handy-dandy little magical toolbox under the altar. It contains anything I might need and easily forget, like pins, matches, pens, paper, salt, sand, and charcoal tablets. There's nothing more frustrating than getting your altar all ready, casting your circle, and then discovering you forgot to bring matches to light the candles and incense. I've learned this frustration the hard way. Keeping a magical toolbox under your altar comes in handy more often than you'd think.

Activity: Create a Working Altar

Let's create a very basic working altar with traditional magical tools. You don't have to go and buy anything, unless you want to. You can improvise with things you already have in the house.

First, pick the perfect spot for your altar. If creating an altar where others can see it feels uncomfortable to you, choose a drawer, shelf, desktop, or other personal space. Choose a place where kids and cats can't play with it, because they will. Spread a cloth or scarf there in a color that supports your intention, and on it place the following items:

God and Goddess/Athame and Chalice

If you're working with a small space, your athame and chalice can represent the God and Goddess. An athame should be a sharp, pointed item, like a paring knife or letter opener, and the chalice can be a stemmed glass, like a goblet or wine glass. If you want a separate representation for the God and Goddess, items that represent masculine/projective energy and feminine/receptive energy will work, such as a hand-drawn yin and yang symbol; something gold and something silver; cat and dog; Ken and Barbie.

Representation of the elements

Choose something to represent each element—an item, photo, or color— and place them in their corresponding directions.

Candle

A candle in a color corresponding with your intention would be great, but if not, a white candle can stand in for any color. A tea light candle will do just fine.

Offering plate and glass

When you actually do ritual or magical work at your altar, you'll put an offering on the plate and a special beverage in the glass, hold them up one at a time, and present them to the God and Goddess: "To the Goddess" and "To the God." If you're working deity-free, "To the universe" or "To Mother Earth" with each. After your ritual, pour your offerings out at the base of a special tree or bush if possible. If it's not, release them respectfully to the energies of water as they go down the drain.

When everything's assembled, spend some time with your altar. Just *be* with it. You might play some mystical music or burn some incense. Get a feel for its energy. You don't have to actually work with it yet, unless you want to. If you feel the urge to go further, cleanse it with some incense or herbal smoke, place your hands on it, and concentrate on a connection with the universe. You don't have to do anything fancy; just feel the energy, and say thank you to the universe.

You can leave your altar up for as long as you wish, add to it, change it, or take it all down and start over. As you become sensitive to its energy, different items may call to you to be placed there too.

Altars that Honor Deity

A deity altar is a visual expression of your desire to include a certain deity—god or goddess—in your spiritual life or magical work, or to worship or devote your service to that deity. If you are uncomfortable honoring specific deities, or even the God and Goddess for that matter, you can simply skip this section. Deity worship isn't required in the Pagan world. Many Pagan traditions honor deities and many Pagans devote themselves to certain deities, but there are also those who don't. Do what is comfortable for you.

When you find a deity that resonates with you or represents the energies you need in your life, your altar becomes a sacred mini-temple where you express appreciation and gratitude to that deity. It's a special, spiritual place to share your concerns and the secrets of your heart. It should feel spiritually energized and alive.

A deity altar features a representation of that deity—statuary, a figurine, or artwork—and that deity's sacred symbols, or representations of their lore, stories, qualities, activities, and responsibilities. This symbology can be embellished with items and offerings that deity would appreciate: fruit, flowers, crystals, gems, incense, candles—the possibilities are endless, as the realm of gods and goddesses is endless. Whatever you choose, place it there with pure love and devotion.

We'll hold off on an activity to create an altar to honor deity until the next chapter, when you'll meet some gods and goddesses from several paths and cultures. You may discover one that really speaks to your heart and spirit— one you need in your life.

Ritual

Ritual simply means "doing a particular thing a particular way for a particular reason at a particular time." A ritual is a time and space, public or private, set apart from regular daily life, wherein you align your energy with that of the universe, and present your goals, feelings, or desires, or do magical work. An altar is often the focal point or activity center for a ritual.

A ritual might also be a time to honor something or someone—a new home or a deceased beloved—or a celebration of a sabbat, or an official acknowledgment of a life passage, like the birth of a child or retirement. We have all been to rituals, whether we call them that or not: weddings, funerals, and graduations, for example.

A ritual can be something as simple as closing your eyes and meditating on certain words, phrases, or images before performing or giving a presentation, or a very elaborate, prescribed set of actions and words. Rituals can be done alone or with another person, with a group of people, or on a larger public scale with many people. A group ritual is usually led by one person, sometimes assisted by others with certain roles, like welcoming the elements or directions, reading poetry, or singing a song.

In their all-encompassing book of rituals *Life Ritualized—A Witch's Guide to Life's Most Important Moments,* Pagan authors Phoenix LeFae and Gwion Raven expand the concept of ritual beyond mere magical practice and suggest that many pivotal moments happen in our lives that often go by with little more than a shrug, like getting a driver's license, a first menstrual period, or getting a new car, and these milestones are important. They deserve acknowledgment. They deserve a ritual.

"Rituals and ceremonies create space to honor change, transition, growth, success, and loss," say LaFae and Raven. "Rituals and ceremonies create places where we can give ourselves over to grief, joy, love, and pain. And not just feel these emotions on a surface level, but really revel in them, fully immerse ourselves in them, and potentially begin to process and move through them. Rituals and ceremonies, by their very design, encourage us to slow down and experience the moment we are in."[46]

Beautiful.

---

46. Phoenix LeFae and Gwion Raven, *Life Ritualized: A Witch's Guide to Life's Most Important Moments* (Woodbury, MN: Llewellyn Publications, 2021), 2.

You Make the Magic

Although working altars and magical tools are commonly used in ritual, and add dramatic and artistic flair, let me reiterate: stuff doesn't make magic. *You* make magic. You could do an entire ritual without any tools or ornamentation at all. In fact, you've already done this in the combined elemental ritual in chapter 4: All of the elements were represented by the arm and hand signals you learned: earth is arms straight down, hands parallel to the ground; air is upper arms parallel to the ground, arms bent upwards at right angles, fingers spread wide; fire is upper arms parallel to the ground, arms bent upwards at right angles, hands in tight fists; water is arms held gently in front of you, against your body, one hand cradled in the other. You can use these same postures in a ritual as you welcome the elements and directions.

There are also hand signals to represent the God and Goddess: index and pinky finger of the right hand straight out, middle two fingers bent and covered by the thumb, creating horns, for the God, and on the left hand, the tips of the index finger and thumb pressed together, thumb flexing inward toward that finger, remaining fingers curled, so the thumb and index finger form a crescent moon shape for the Goddess. With your hands in these positions, swing them up high over your head and touch index finger to index finger: union of the God and Goddess.

In a tool-free ritual, your right index finger becomes your athame, and your cupped left hand is your chalice. The union of the God and Goddess or the projective/receptive energy of the universe, can also be represented by pointing the index finger of your right hand into your cupped left hand.

Your right index finger can also serve as a wand or athame to cast and uncast a magical circle, or to direct energy. Cleansing and clearing can be done with sound: singing, humming, clapping, snapping, or chanting, as can raising energy—only louder and more boisterously. For grounding and centering, all you need to do is close your eyes and breathe in the energy of the earth and the universe, exhaling any stress or distraction. As for special clothing, you don't even need that. Bare skin works just fine.

You already have everything within you to do an entire ritual and all your magical work without any altar or tools. Stuff doesn't channel magical energy. You do. That said, stuff is fun, and if it puts you in a magical, mystical mindset, use whatever stuff makes you happy.

Tradition Is Connection

Although I prefer doing things my own Garden-Variety-Pagan way, the traditional flow of a ritual and certain traditional phrases connect you to other Pagans, past and present, through time and across distance. When you do a ritual at traditional times, such as on a full moon, you know that there are magical siblings out there in the world, under the same full moon, doing and saying similar things, at the same time. It creates a calming, comforting, connective tone. It's metaphysical community.

Here are some traditional ritual phrases, known to most every Pagan:

- Finishing the greeting of each element and direction, as well as the energies above and below, with "Hail and welcome," and bidding farewell with "Go if you must, stay if you will—hail and farewell."
- "Blessed be," which means "blessings upon you" or "be blessed."
- "So mote it be," which means, "May it be so," spoken like "Amen" at the end of a prayer.
- "The circle is cast" upon finishing the casting of the circle.
- "The circle is open" upon finishing the uncasting of the circle.
- "Merry meet, merry part, and merry meet again," which is a joyful, enthusiastic exit from the magical realm and reentrance to the mundane, with hopes of being together again one day.

Group Ritual Basics

Just like a church service, wedding, or graduation ceremony, rituals have a structure, particularly group and public rituals. The specific components may differ from group to group or from tradition to tradition, but usually share a common template. Following is a typical ritual template you might encounter in your journey through the Big Pagan Garden, particularly at festivals or conventions.

Here are some ritual basics:

Cleansing/Purifying: Those entering the circle are cleansed with incense or sage/herbal smoke, or with sound: bells, tuning forks, or singing bowls. The ritual leader or a designated participant may swirl smoke or sound around people as they enter or after they've formed a circle.

Grounding/Centering: Grounding and centering means letting go of bothersome thoughts or feelings, being fully present in that moment, in that space, connected to the earth beneath you. Some common grounding and centering approaches are breathing together, humming or singing a tone together, or visualizing a connective cord between your tailbone and the earth.

Circle Casting: Casting a circle creates a magical container, where only helpful energies are welcome, and negative or harmful energies are kept out. The circle isn't flat on the ground. It's a protective bubble, sacred to this particular ritual, and treated as an energetic field. A circle is cast deosil (clockwise). Some begin the circle facing or gesturing toward north.

Calling Energies: Beginning with north, the elements are individually called or welcomed with a greeting and "Hail and welcome." Some traditions instead call energies, wards, towers, or directions. The energies of above and below are welcomed next, sometimes followed by deities or the God and Goddess. Cakes and ale may be consecrated to them on the altar. These energies watch over and/or participate in the ritual and magical work.

Raising Energy: Energy is raised within and between everyone present. Raising energy may involve physical movement, dancing, singing, chanting, or clapping. Sometimes, the ritual leader will direct the group to gather the energy and sweep it upwards together, creating a "cone of energy."

Magical Work: Magical work is the heart of a ritual. It's like attending a symphony: Excitement simmers as you enter; you're ushered to your seat, and anticipation builds as you wait for the curtains to open; there's a hush of mounting energy as the conductor in his tuxedo walks on stage and stands in the spotlight; he raises his wand, and the music begins—*that's* what you're there for! You become enraptured in the performance, which concludes with thunderous applause. Energy recedes as the house lights come on and the audience streams out, still savoring the joy and wonder of those magical, musical moments. The entire concert is the ritual, but the music is the magic.

Ritual magic could be anything from calling upon a certain deity for assistance to focusing healing energy toward a certain person or channeling it to someone not present. The intention may be broad and wide, like "increasing social justice," or precise and focused, like "finding a new ritual space." Magical work can be accomplished in a thousand different ways: the leader might work at an altar inside the circle or there may be a dramatic performance or a special reading, music, or guided meditation, and participation with some or all people present. There's no limit to the possibilities.

A magical working or spell often ends with a confident "So mote it be!" from the leader, which is usually echoed by the group, signifying that the focused, collective energy of that group's magical intention has been dispatched to the universe for manifestation.

Releasing the Energies: Gratitude will be expressed to all of the invited elements individually, who will be bid farewell: "Hail and farewell."

Uncasting the Circle: The circle will be unspun or released in a widdershins (counterclockwise) direction, ending where casting began. The magical bubble evaporates, and all are returned to the mundane energies.

Farewell: A traditional Pagan song may be sung together. People may or may not join hands, but there's usually a joyful collective shout of, "Merry meet, merry part, and merry meet again!"

Celebration: In a large public ritual, people may just filter out, just like that symphony hall. In a smaller group, there's usually some socializing afterwards, and often refreshments and nibblies. It's a time for bonding, enjoying the company of others, chatting, and celebrating.

Ritual Etiquette

Every tradition has its own twists and turns on ritual, and even within a tradition, each group or coven may have their own special practices. If you have questions or concerns about what will be happening, simply talk to someone. If the group leader is available, great. But if they're busy or focusing their energy on what they're about to do, ask someone else instead.

If a question pops up during a ritual, don't hold your hand up or blurt things out unless invited to do so by the leader. Save it for afterwards. No one should be speaking during a ritual except the leader or their designated assistants, unless prompted to do so. So, no talking, and that includes whispering. Mouth closed, ears and eyes open in ritual.

It's astounding that this even needs to be mentioned, but experience has shown me that it does: Always turn your cell phone *off* before entering the ritual space. Always. Not on silent—completely off. There's nothing more maddening than a magical group vibe building, and then someone's cell phone shattering the moment. It's a huge Pagan party foul for cell phones to ring during a ritual. Huge. Besides it being incredibly rude to disrupt a ritual with electronic racket, or worse yet, taking the call and yakking into your phone, you're supposed to be focused on what's happening and contributing your energy to that ritual, not watching for incoming calls or texts. Cell phones are energy siphons.

Once the circle is cast, should you suddenly need to leave, don't just walk away. If you just leave a magical bubble, you pop it. A symbolic doorway must be cut and then resealed after you leave. If a helper can be quietly cued that you must leave, they will cut the doorway for you. If there's no assistance available, using an index finger, cut yourself a doorway, step through, and then seal it before leaving.

Another Pagan party foul is touching the altar. Never touch an altar in a ritual or shared space without asking first. Additionally, don't touch any magical tools or items someone is carrying or wearing without asking first.

Rituals of One

A ritual done by yourself (solitary) can follow the same ritual template, with the same phrases and activities. However, in solitary ritual, you are your own leader, so you have to consider all the factors:

What do you want to accomplish? What tools or items would enhance your intention? Would you like to include poetry or quatrains? Do you want to use traditional phrases or chants, or write your own? Do you need to write them down so you won't forget?

Which phase of the moon best suits your ritual—the "inhale" or the "exhale" phase? Or full or dark? What's happening in the cosmos or about to happen? Would a certain astrological influence be advantageous?

Which day of the week is optimal for your ritual? Each day has its own magical symbology and energy, associated with the heavenly bodies in our solar system: Sunday, the sun, success, wealth, fame; Monday, the moon, magic, mystery, intuition; Tuesday, Mars, strength, courage, passion; Wednesday, Mercury, communication, change, planning; Thursday, Jupiter, prosperity, abundance, health; Friday, Venus, love, romance, sexuality; Saturday, Saturn, protection, banishing, cleansing.

Wow! There's a lot to think about! However, making all these considerations, and associated preparations, will give your personal ritual more magic and meaning than if you just slap it out at the last minute. It's not necessary to incorporate every single thing—choose the factors that feel most important to you, those that would make your ritual feel meaningful. Whether simple or elaborate, a solitary ritual should be carefully and thoughtfully planned so you can have the experience you want. Sure, you *could* just walk in cold and do a ritual, but that's like sex without foreplay. Functional, yes, but it's much more pleasurable if you get in the mood first.

Preparing for Ritual

Many solitary practitioners magically cleanse themselves before a ritual by bathing or showering with a salt scrub, often including certain herbs. An herbal saltwater bath by candlelight is exquisite for easing yourself into a magical, metaphysical mode before your ritual. Others do a more metaphorical cleansing with incense or herbal smoke, or magical oil. Some like to dress up in special robes or garments and wear special jewelry. It's like dressing up for a party—it puts you in a festive mood. Dress for being in the presence of the Goddess herself—because you will be. However, the Goddess is completely cool with bare skin too. Some people prefer to forego clothing and work skyclad (naked).

Just as you adorn your body, you can adorn your ritual space too, and create a magical ambiance by closing the curtains, lowering the lighting, burning candles and incense, and playing soft music. I prefer only the glow of fairy lights and candles, which creates an orb of soft, golden light, surrounded in protective darkness.

Before beginning, unplug or turn off all phones, computers, devices, and anything that makes noise. Jangling noise is just as disruptive to a solitary ritual as it is to a group ritual. Make sure all the tools or items you need are already inside your circle space. If you'll be using an altar, set that up in advance, with your handy-dandy emergency magical toolbox or basket underneath.

Getting Started, Solitary Style

In your solitary ritual, follow the same basic ritual template as for a group: Purify yourself with smoke or incense, ground and center, cast a circle, welcome the energies, raise energy, do magical work, release the energies, and uncast the circle. You might like to conclude your ritual with a song, poem, or quiet meditation. You can send a "Merry meet, merry part, and merry meet again" to the universe if you wish, and then indulge in your own post-ritual celebration with a luscious indulgence. As you enjoy your treat, reflect upon your ritual and savor your experience.

Even when working by yourself, if you need to leave your circle, cut yourself an opening with your athame or pointed finger, seal it, do what you need to do, and then reopen and reseal the opening when you return. Passing through the circle without creating an opening pops the magical bubble, even when you're alone. Gotta start over. Exception is given to small children and pets, who can pass back and forth through the bubble without magical disruption.

When you're just starting out, don't expect perfection. If you achieve it, great, but if not, don't beat yourself up. You'll gather confidence as you gain experience. Just conduct your ritual from the heart, with love, honor, and respect, and you'll be fine. The universe has a fantastic sense of humor and will kindly overlook your newbie wobbles. A pure heart, focused intention, and confidence will propel your magic onward to the universe, even if your ritual wasn't picture-perfect.

Activity: Ready, Set, Ritual

The first thing you need before planning or starting a ritual is to set an intention or focus. Here are some things to consider:

Are you attracting or repelling something? Honoring or celebrating something? Connecting to Spirit or the Goddess, or a certain deity? Making change? Beginning or ending something? What exactly do you want to accomplish? Write down your specific intention, and then answer these questions:

- What phase of the moon will enhance your intention?
- What day of the week is most auspicious for your intention?

- What time of day is most auspicious for your intention?
- What element aligns with your intention?
- What colors promote the energy of your intention?
- Do you want an altar? If so, list all the tools or items you need or want to place there.
- Will you do magic in your ritual? Which type? List all the items you'll need.
- Would you like to burn incense or candles? Which ones?
- Would you like to wear something special? List what you'll wear.
- What music might you play?
- What song might you sing?
- What reading, phrase, quatrain, or poem would you like to include?
- How will you cast and uncast your circle?
- How will you raise energy?
- Will you serve yourself cakes and ale and/or indulge afterwards? What will you have?
- How will you cleanse yourself beforehand?
- How do you want the room to look? List all the items you'll need, or changes you'll make.

Now that you've listed everything you need for your ritual, create a program for how you'll do it, using the basic ritual template. For each step, write down what you'll do. When you're finished, check in with yourself—how does that program for your ritual feel? If it feels like a yes in your gut, why not give it a whirl? It's one thing to read about ritual, and even write down details, but quite another to actually experience it. Feel your apprehension and do it anyway! Lean into your fire energy for courage if you need some bolstering. And, if you need to keep your notes with you, that's perfectly fine.

If the ritual you designed seems intimidating, just keep it simple. You don't have to do any magical workings in a ritual if you don't want to. You could simply cast your circle and connect to the Goddess or the universe. Introduce yourself. Express thanks and appreciation. Send some love, receive some love, and just spend some quiet time in that presence. If you're one who prefers baby steps, start there and work your way up to your full ritual, adding things in as you feel comfortable.

The Elements All Play a Part

Did you notice that each of the elements plays a part in planning and conducting a ritual? Earth provides structure—the checklist, the tools needed, making preparations, and setting everything up. Air plans it out, considering all the factors: phases of the moon, days of the week, types of magic. Fire sparks passion, confidence, and showmanship in performing your ritual. Water lends creativity, color, and imagination to the entire process. Spirit is the energy threading through everything, from the moment the circle is cast to the moment it is dissolved.

As you plan and carry out your ritual, call upon these elements to lend their strengths, energies, and talents to you, and express gratitude to them when you welcome them to your circle.

You Make the Magic

Whether creating altars or rituals for yourself, your own energy and intentions make the magic happen. Keep them genuine, comfortable, and meaningful to you. When participating in a group or public ritual, their practices may be different. Take the "when in Rome" approach, and flow along with it. You can make wonderful discoveries with an open mind and a willingness to let others show you how they do things, rather than becoming overly attached to always doing things your own way.

Recommended Reading

K, Amber and Azrael Arynn K. *Ritualcraft: Creating Rites for Transformation & Celebration.* Woodbury, MN: Llewellyn Publications, 2016.

LeFae, Phoenix and Gwion Raven. *Life Ritualized: A Witch's Guide to Life's Most Important Moments.* Woodbury, MN: Llewellyn Publications, 2021.

Mankey, Jason and Laura Tempest Zakroff. *The Witch's Altar: The Craft, Lore & Magick of Sacred Space* (The Witch's Tools Series 7). Woodbury, MN: Llewellyn Publications, 2018.

CHAPTER 13
Deity

Deity is an expression of the divine spiritual life force of the universe. Deity gives Spirit shape. Some people view deities—gods and goddesses—as independent, individual divine beings; separate and unique containers of that universal spirituality. Others view deity as facets of that singular divine force, like the facets of a disco ball or mosaic Tiffany lamp, each of its own shape and color, all illuminated by the same energy. I'm amongst the latter. I enjoy experiencing the divine Spirit as particular personas—deities—that resonate with me, supplemental to my own direct connection with the universe. Deity puts Spirit into easily identifiable, bite-sized packages that humans can comprehend more readily than an invisible, infinite, amorphous divine energy.

Like the Pantheists and some indigenous cultures, I believe that spiritual energy exists in every living thing—even in things we perceive as not living, like streams, wind, rocks, and mountains. For me, it's an easy leap to accept that Spirit can present itself in divine forms—particular facets, manifestations, personas, or deities—just as it does in nature. Embracing a deity and including it in spiritual practices and daily life is a way to single out particular spiritual aspects that I wish to reinforce or amplify. However, I don't consider it "worship." I consider it "inclusion." My relationship with deity is spiritual, not religious. *I* am spiritual—not religious.

Religion vs. Spirituality

Religion is man-made. It's something you *do*. What delicious irony that the first two letters in *dogma* are *d* and *o*. Dogma is the defining character of religion. Religion has prescribed rules, practices, and traditions, accepted as irrefutably true, and conducted or worshipped on certain days or dates, at certain times, in certain ways. The consequences for defying this dogma can range from judgmental side-eyes at church to a death sentence depending on the religion. Religion, unless being practiced by a solitary, usually has a designated leader or authority figure—priest, minister, pastor, etc.—who conducts the services and ceremonies, functioning as the middleman between God (or Spirit or the universe) and everyone else. That authority figure interprets God's words, and transmits them to parishioners or followers, and is the conduit for connecting to God. In some religions, you're expected to contribute financially to "do God's work" (support the church).

In Pagan religions, there's no central authority figure—no Pagan pope to decree what is acceptable and what isn't, no one outlining how everyone shall live, believe, and worship, no one dispensing punishment or worse for those who disobey. However, within groups and covens, there are leaders, sometimes called high priests or high priestesses, who are the authority figures for their group. Groups and covens also have rules, particular practices, and traditions. If you want to be a member of that group, you're expected to play by the rules. In my eyes, this is still dogma. I don't need someone else to provide a spirituality template to me, nor do I need a middleman. I prefer direct connection with Spirit.

Spirituality is internally self-directed, as opposed to religion, which is externally other-directed. Spirituality isn't man-made. In fact, it isn't even made at all, because Spirit just *is*. Spirituality isn't something you do. Spiritual is something you *are*. Spirituality is your connection to Spirit. Spirituality doesn't have artificial categories, like Methodist or Buddhist, because Spirit is one universal energy, available to everyone, on equal terms, no middleman required. There's no dogma in spirituality. Spirituality isn't structured or prescribed by someone else—it's up to each individual to shape their spiritual course. Everyone's a freelancer.

If you're conscious and breathing, Spirit is available to you—whether or not you connect to it. Unlike religion, which only exists if people participate in it, Spirit exists whether humans participate or not. Our belief in Spirit is irrelevant. The universal spiritual force is like sunshine. The sun shines on everything, regardless of what people are doing. If you keep yourself cooped up inside in a darkened room, the sun still shines anyway. All you have to do to experience it is simply open the door. And, you certainly don't need someone else to interpret what the sun intends for you, or funnel it to you through a tube, and then hold out a donation plate. That would be preposterous.

Some people are able to straddle both sides of the religion/spirituality fence. Being religious doesn't negate spirituality. A religious person can be quite spiritual, even if that spirituality is dictated by someone else—there's still a connection to Spirit. A spiritual, non-religious person may have religious practices, or not. Religion and spirituality can coexist, but they aren't synonymous. For example, every person is human (spiritual), but every human isn't an American (religious). One need not be American, or Ethiopian, or Chinese, to be human. One need only *be*.

Religion left such a horrible taste in my mouth that I avoid all of it. However, I absolutely appreciate and respect that others feel differently. Many people, Pagan and non-Pagan alike, feel that their religion brings them closer to God or Spirit, that they get comfort and inspiration from religion, that it works for them, and that it's very precious to them and central to their lives. I'm just not amongst them.

Honoring Deity

Honoring deity isn't part of all Pagan traditions, but it's definitely a presence in many of them, particularly those associated with certain cultural traditions, like Celtic or Egyptian practices. A group of deities associated with one particular culture is called a *pantheon*. In the Pagan community, there's a lot of pantheon mixing and matching. Celtic, Egyptian, and Greek/Roman deities in particular seem to drift across cultural lines and Pagan traditions. It's not uncommon to find a hodgepodge of deities in many Pagan traditions and at public rituals. It's also very common to hear the more generic "God and Goddess" across traditions and practices, or just "the Goddess" alone. Most Pagans seem to be comfortable with "deity shopping" and embracing the gods and goddesses that resonate with them, but there are also purists who only worship one particular pantheon. In other words, whatever your comfort level with deity, there's a Pagan group for that—even if you don't want to include deity at all. Some Pagans approach Paganism as a skill or craft rather than a religion, and deity isn't central, or necessarily present in their practices.

It's absolutely not necessary to include deity in your Garden-Variety Pagan practice. However, it doesn't hurt to be familiar with some of the more common Pagan deities so you'll be able to understand what others are talking about, and their perspective.

Divine Pantheons

There are thousands upon thousands of deities and pantheons across all cultures; however, a few in particular seem to be Pagan rock stars. Following are very brief descriptions of the attributes, qualities, and lore most commonly associated with deities found in the Big Pagan Garden:

Celtic

Brigid: One of the Celtic great mother goddesses, Brigid is associated with healing, poetry, storytelling, creativity, the forge, smithcraft, fire, the hearth, and protection of farm animals. Her Christianized name is St. Bridget. She is honored on Imbolc by Pagans, which is called St. Bridget's Day by Christians, which is still practiced in Ireland. Also known as Brid, Bride, Brighid, and Brigit.

Cerridwen: Crone goddess associated with the cauldron, magic, witchcraft, shape-shifting, transformation, rebirth, hawks, and hens. The "Tale of Taliesin" tells of her shape-shifting as she pursued her servant, Gwion, who transformed himself into a single grain of corn to evade Cerridwen, who transformed herself into a hen and swallowed him, whereupon she became pregnant. The child of this union grew up to be the famed Welsh poet, Taliesin.

Cernunnos: The horned god of fertility, male energy, nature, wild places, the forest, forest animals, and all horned animals, particularly stags. He is associated with the Pagan allegory of the cycle of life and death and is the male counterpart to the Goddess—both her son and her consort.

(The) Dagda: The original male god and father of Celtic deity, he is associated with masculinity, strength, fertility, seasons, and agriculture. He is often depicted wearing only a shirt and carrying a large club of life and death. He also possessed a cauldron of plenty, and a harp that could control men and the seasons. Despite being depicted as rather unkempt and thick-bodied, with an unruly beard, he was allegedly irresistible to women. The Dagda is a major Druidic deity, and chief of the Tuatha Dé Danann, an ancient culture that inhabited the land later known as Ireland. He is the father of many deities, including the goddess Brigid.

Danu: The original Celtic mother goddess and Earth-mother goddess, from whom all life flowed. She is associated with fertility, fruitfulness, wisdom, flowing water (rivers and streams), the wind and fairy hills, and known as the mother of the Tuatha Dé Danann. She is the mother goddess of Irish gods and goddesses, and is associated with the Danube River. Danu is a major Druidic deity.

(The) Morrigan: Fierce goddess of war who shape-shifted into a crow or raven to hover over battlefields, and could instill fear with her cries. She is associated with both life and death, particularly death on the battlefield. She is a triple goddess, with Maiden, Mother, and Crone aspects, as well as a major goddess of the Tuatha Dé Danann. Her name is interpreted as "great queen" or "phantom queen." She is associated with rivers and lakes, and protected her people by blowing a layer of fog over the land to conceal them. She is a consort of the Dagda, and is associated with Samhain. Other variations on her name are Morrigu, Morgane, and Morrighan, and Morgan le Fay of the Arthurian legends.

Lugh: This solar god is one of the original Celtic deities and king of the Tuatha Dé Danann. He was believed to bring light to the world, and is celebrated on Lughnasadh, a sabbat showered in summer sunlight. He is considered to be a powerful warrior, master of all arts and crafts, and a trickster. He is known for being victorious in battle.

Egyptian

Anubis: Depicted as a man's body with a jackal's head, Anubis is the god of embalming and mummification, and was the original god of the dead (this was later relegated to Osiris). He also guided the souls of the deceased to the underworld. He oversaw the embalming of deceased bodies, and is believed to physically and spiritually guard tombs.

Bastet: Depicted as a cat adorned with rings in its ears or nose, or a woman with a cat's body, Bastet is associated with the motherly instincts of a cat protecting and caring for her kittens. She specifically was the protectress of cats, which were sacred in ancient Egypt, and killing one was punishable by death. She is a gentler aspect of Sekhmet. Also known as Bast, Baast, Baset.

Isis: Mother goddess, wife of Osiris and mother of Horus, and amongst the most worshipped of Egyptian deities. Isis is the goddess of motherhood, medicine, marriage, fertility, and magic. A myth says that her tears created the annual flooding of the Nile River. Isis is the feminine aspect of divinity itself.

Osiris: God of the underworld, symbolizing death and resurrection; husband of Isis. He is also associated with fertility and agriculture. Because of his association with the dead and afterlife, he is depicted as partially in mummy wrap, with green skin.

Ra: The sun god Ra (also Re) is depicted with a human body and head of a hawk. He sailed across the sky each day in a boat, then passed through the underworld each night, battling and defeating the snake god Apophis (Apep, Aphoph) to return and make the sun rise again.

Sekhmet: This fierce warrior goddess is depicted as a lioness or a human body with the head of a lioness. Associated with battle, she could breathe fire or cause plagues, and is depicted in blood-red attire. Also Sachmis, Sakhmet, Sekhet, Sakhet.

Greek/Roman

Greek gods and goddesses, and stories about them, predate the Roman versions. The Romans changed the Greek names to suit their own empire, but the deities are the same. The Greek name is listed first, and the Roman second. The original Greek lore comes from the Homeric Hymns, believed to have been written in the seventh century BCE by the Greek poet, Homer. However, that authorship has recently been challenged and remains in question.

Aphrodite/Venus: Goddess of love, passion, pleasure, sexuality, and beauty. She is famously portrayed nude, standing on a half shell, with long, flowing hair, and first appeared from the sea foam, as a full-grown adult. Her name is the root of *aphrodisiac,* and her festival in Greece was called the Aphrodisia.

Artemis/Diana: Goddess of the hunt. Associated with the full moon, the bow and arrow, hounds and deer, as well as chastity, Diana has been adopted by Wiccan traditions as the goddess of witchcraft and magic, and is seen as a protectress of women and witches. Dianic witchcraft gets its name from her.

Athena/Minerva: Goddess of war, war strategy, and wisdom, she is often depicted wearing a helmet and carrying a spear, with an owl on her shoulder that whispered into her ear to inform her when someone was trying to deceive her.

Dionysys/Bacchus: Love child of Zeus and a mortal woman, he is associated with wine, grapevines, winemaking, drunkenness, happiness, and joy. He is often depicted wearing a wreath of grapes.

Hecate/Trivia: Goddess of wild places, childbirth, the crossroads, ghosts, necromancy, magic, knowledge of herbs and poisonous plants, and witch-craft. She is considered to be a virgin triple goddess, and is also associated with hounds and the new/dark moon. Also Hekate.

Pan/Faunus: God of the wild and the woods, fields, shepherds, flocks, and music. Depicted with the hindquarters, legs, and horns of a goat, and often holding a flute, he is affiliated with sex and fertility.

Poseidon/Neptune: God of the sea and protector of all aquatic animals, and creator of sea storms. He is often depicted holding a trident with which he could cause earthquakes, and carried on a sea chariot pulled by creatures with the upper body of a horse and the lower body of a fish, known as a hippocampus.

Zeus/Jupiter: Ruler and god of the sky and thunder, he was the king of the gods on Mount Olympus. He hurled thunderbolts at anyone who disobeyed or defied him, and could cause storms or darkened skies. Married to Hera, he is the father of many of the major gods and goddesses, including Ares, Athena, Heracles, Apollo, and Artemis.

Hindu

Hinduism is one of the oldest religions in the world, and amongst the most practiced, particularly in India, Pakistan, Nepal, Indonesia, and Southeast Asian countries. Many Hindu deities have found their way into the Pagan community, and many Pagans include these deities in their practices and on their altars. However, that does not make them Hindu. Those who are drawn to Hindu deities must treat this widespread and very current religion—and its deities—with respect, recognizing that they are sacred to Hindus worldwide.

Ganesha: "The Remover of Obstacles." He is a pot-bellied god with the head of an elephant. Ganesha is one of the best-known and most widely worshipped Hindu deities, and also known as Ganapati. His name means "Lord of the People." He is associated with the arts and sciences, and is the patron of intellectuals, bankers, scribes, and authors. He is the son of Parvati and Shiva.

Kali/Kali Ma: Four-armed goddess of time, death, doomsday, violence, and sexuality. Kali is a fierce divine mother figure, depicted with blue or black skin, wearing a garland of skulls, and many arms that hold weapons. A consort of Shiva, she is sometimes depicted angrily standing over his dead body, her pointed tongue thrust out. She is also known as the Dark Mother or Goddess of Destruction, and destroys what is necessary for creation and rebirth to occur.

Krishna: God of compassion, tenderness, and love, and known to be playful and mischievous, Krishna is often depicted with a flute in his hands. He is amongst the most popular of the Hindu gods, and one of the avatars (incarnations) of the god Vishnu.

Lakshmi: Four-armed goddess of prosperity, luxury, and wealth. Lakshmi is the wife of Vishnu, and is often depicted sitting upon a lotus, in ornate gold and red garments. She represents fulfillment, contentment, and an auspicious life. She is worshipped at the Hindu festival of Diwali, a celebration of light over darkness.

Saraswati: Four-armed goddess of music, knowledge, learning, the arts, and the river of consciousness. She is often depicted sitting on a lotus, and in her hands holds a book of the Vedas (ancient texts containing the Hindu scriptures), a stringed musical instrument called a *veena*, a pot of purifying water, and a garland or wand of crystals for self-reflection.

Shakti: Consort of Shiva, divine mother; pure, divine, female power, Shiva is all of the female Hindu deities in their different manifestations, and is sometimes simply called Devi (Goddess). She has her own sect within Hinduism, called Shaktism.

Shiva: "The Destroyer." He is empowered to create, protect, transform, or destroy the world to prepare for its renewal. Shiva is amongst the most prominent of Hindu gods, and may represent goodness, but also has a dark side. He is believed to destroy the universe at the end of each of its cycles (more than two billion years each), and is therefore associated with time and destruction.

Vishnu: "The Preserver." Vishnu protects the earth from being destroyed and is affiliated with order and harmony. He is one of the principal Hindu deities, with 10 avatars (incarnations).

Norse

Freya: Goddess of femininity, beauty, fine possessions, magic, divination, war, and fertility. Freya is Odin's wife, one of the principal deities of the Norse pantheon, and has a gentler nature than some of the other Norse gods. She travels in a glittering chariot pulled by two cats. Friday—Freya's Day—is a tribute to her. Also Freja, Freyja.

Loki: Mischievous god known as "the trickster," associated with fire, magic, shape-shifting, and chaos. His relationship with the other gods is variable—sometimes friend, sometimes not. His lore includes shape-shifting into a mare, being impregnated by a stallion, and giving birth to Odin's eight-legged horse, Sleipnir.

Odin: One-eyed father of the Norse gods, creator of the universe, discoverer of the runes. He rules Valhalla, where slain warriors reside in the afterlife, and watches over the worlds. Associated with wisdom, war, magic, poetry, prophecy, victory, riches, and death, Wednesday—Woden's or Odin's Day—is a tribute to Odin.

Thor: God of the sky, weather, lightning and thunder, whose hammer could crush mountains; strong protector of law and community. Thursday—Thor's Day—is a tribute to him.

Tyr: God of battle, victory, sacrifice, justice, and courage. He was amongst the principal Norse war gods, including Odin and Thor. Tuesday—Tyr's Day—is a tribute to him.

Embracing Deity

Although deity is central to many Pagans and their traditions, whether or not you include it in your own Garden-Variety Pagan walk is entirely up to you. If religion and deity aren't your thing, no problem. If you're drawn to understanding the various facets of the divine energy of the universe, follow your curiosity and see where it leads you. There's an immense amount of information and resources on each culture, tradition, and individual deity. Start wandering and exploring and see which deities intrigue you or call to you.

Don't worry about picking the "right" cultural pantheon to explore. There's no right or best one, and there multiple representations of the same energy, such as divine mother or fertility god, across several pantheons. Whether it's Isis or Shakti or Danu, it doesn't really matter, ultimately. They're the same Great Mother Goddess energy in different aspects. Imagine worshipping the Great Mother Goddess as a car trip: We want to go to GMGville. There are six roads leading to GMGville. Pick the road you like best—they all lead to the same place. It's just the journey that looks different.

There are some "starter deities" that are fairly straightforward and gentle if deity is new to you. You don't want to cut your deity teeth on Kali-Ma, Sekhmet, or the Morrigan. They might cut you back. Thor, Shiva, and Zeus might be more of a handful than you bargained for. Let's start with some easygoing deities.

In the Celtic pantheon, Brigid is an excellent beginner's deity. She is powerful, multi-talented, and protective. She even has a specific day to honor her—Imbolc—and information about her will be easy to find. The fair and powerful Lugh also has his own holiday, Lughnasadh. Besides harvest imagery, this warrior god is also associated with craftsmanship. If you like working with your hands, Lugh may channel inspiration to you. Gentle Danu, of the serene, flowing energies of water and nature, is so very easy to love, although images of her are sparse. She's a goddess you *feel*. She is wonderful for connecting to peacefulness, serenity, and connection to nature.

In the Egyptian pantheon, cat lovers will find their goddess in Bastet—beautiful, feline, protective, and joyful. Isis is amongst the great mother goddesses, and magic and medicine are her domain. In the Greek/Roman pantheon, look no further than Aphrodite/Venus—goddess of love, romance, sensuality, and beauty—for your first steps. Iris, known as the Goddess of the Rainbow, is a personal Greek favorite of mine. Her swift color and precision, and task of swiftly communicating between the gods and humanity, lends itself to colorful, creative, crisp writing.

In the Hindu pantheon, Ganesha offers change and positive progress, Krishna is playful and joyful, and Saraswati, devoted to wisdom, music, and self-reflection, seems so down-to-earth for a deity. All of these energies are easy to embrace. Amongst the Norse pantheon, there are some pretty gruff hombres. Lovely Freya, goddess of femininity, beauty, and magic, would be a relatively gentle starting point. There are also some loving, kind, and peaceful goddesses in the Buddhist pantheon, like Tara (she has various hues, representing different aspects), and Kwan Yin. Like Hinduism, Buddhism is a worldwide, active religion—approach these deities with respect for that.

As you're exploring the divine landscape, you may get nudges that a certain deity wants to get to know you. That deity may be popping up all over the place, trying to get your attention, like a second grader frantically holding up one hand in class, saying, "Me, me, me!" when the teacher's looking for an answer. Don't be shy—find out why.

Are you suddenly seeing owls all over the place? Maybe Athena has some wisdom for you. Images of the full moon? Diana or Selene may be eager to reveal their many mysteries to you. Suddenly horses are everywhere. The Celtic Epona may be hinting that some "git 'er done" energy could benefit you. Be open to repetitive images and synchronicities. These meaningful coincidences are often the universe shining a light on something.

Activity: Meeting Deity

Pick a deity from any pantheon that tickles your curiosity and find out more. (If you aren't interested in including deity in your Pagan explorations, you can skip this activity.) You can pick from those I mentioned or research deities online.

If you don't find a deity that appeals to you, do a reverse search online. Pick something you really need or want, such as good luck, better health, courage, romance, and search that plus "goddess" or "god." For example, type "love goddess" into your search window, and about a hundred different names from a variety of cultures and traditions will pop up. That one's easy—

everybody loves love goddesses! If there are too many, refine the search: marriage goddess, romance goddess, sexy goddess, loving-kindness goddess, etc. What exact kind of love do you seek?

For every goal, every need, every desire, there's a god or goddess to assist and inspire you. When you discover "the one," find out everything you can about that deity, in books, online, or at the library. In your journal, make a page for that deity and note all the details: What is this deity's facet of divine spirit? What does this deity represent? What do they do? What symbols are associated with this deity? What is this deity's mythology or story? What is it about that deity specifically that appeals to you?

Download an image of this deity or draw your own and set aside a spot to get acquainted. Set the image where you'll see it every day, like your dresser or desk. Greet them in the morning and say good night before you go to bed. Talk to this deity when the mood strikes you. If they send a message or participate in your life that day, say thank you. Add any significant experiences, observations, or synchronicities to your journal page on this deity.

If you wish to take a next step, place an offering near that image—a snifter of brandy or share your cinnamon toast (always give the deity the first piece). You could adorn their spot with items you think they'd enjoy, and express gratitude for any insight or inspiration this deity inspired. Treat them like a new next-door neighbor that you're getting to know, and let the relationship evolve naturally.

Give it a couple weeks, and evaluate that relationship. If it feels like something's blossoming between you and that deity, keep going: talk with this deity, and if you feel ready, create an altar. If it seems that you and this deity aren't clicking, express gratitude for meeting them, and move on to a different deity. Repeat the exploration process mentioned above. Before bailing on that deity entirely, however, put the image away, maybe in a "Deities" folder. You may discover later that it just wasn't the right time to engage with that deity. Yet.

Deity Altars

An altar for honoring deity is your mini-temple to be in the presence of deity, communicate with them, ask for blessings or assistance, or simply express love, gratitude, and devotion. It's a place to meditate, or just be still and peaceful with these divine facets of the universe. Those who prefer a more structured, religious relationship with deity might say they worship there. I prefer to say I commune with deity at my altar. It's where I spend quality time and feel close to my special goddesses. I'm quite unfond of the very common Pagan term "working with" deity or goddesses. It strikes me as presumptuous and vain—putting them on par with me, a simple human, as if they were coworkers. That's so insulting. My goddesses and I are not coworkers. We are not peers. They are deity, channeling divine energy to me, and should they choose to participate in my life and my work, and grant my special requests, I am deeply grateful.

An altar might be devoted to just one deity, or it may be a grand altar where all your deities gather. I have both. Whether large or small, elaborate or minimalistic, it's the vibrancy of your connection to that deity that's the most important thing.

My main altar is a divine "girls' club" where I interact with my goddesses. Every morning, I light a candle there and bring my goddesses some coffee in a little porcelain espresso cup. My special pantheon includes Gaia, Diana, Aradia, Bastet, Kwan Yin, Green Tara, Brigid, Eiocha, Epona, and Danu, each represented by a small statue or figurine. Why coffee? Because nothing says "I love you" like somebody bringing me a cup of coffee in the morning. It's so comforting and cozy. So honest and genuine. Then, I greet my goddesses, tell them good morning, thank them for participating in my life, and make any special requests I have for the day.

I love my goddesses. They channel divine energy into my life and work, and I'm grateful for that. I don't wait for certain dates or occasions to appreciate and interact with them. I interact with them every day—not just when I want something. We all know people who show up when they want something, and disappear the rest of the time—particularly when you need a favor—and aren't they just a drag? You don't want to be one of "those people" with your deities.

My mini-temple sits upon a red velvet brocade cloth, and is adorned with candles, crystals, fairy lights, singing bowls, an antique temple urn, incense burners, and representations of the four elements. I often embellish it with seasonal items for the sabbats. I've created a place where deity would enjoy spending some time.

Besides my main altar, I have two small ones near my computer for my writing goddesses: one for Brigid, and one for Iris. Brigid's has an image of her blowing on her sacred flame, and some of her symbols: a tiny iron anvil, a glittering orange sunstone, and a figurine of a lamb and ewe. From where I sit, Brigid blows her fiery passion to me as I write, supervising me, keeping me focused, and fending off the Wicked Squirrel of Distraction.

Iris is represented by a cradled collection of small abalone shells and some aura quartz crystals that shimmer with rainbow iridescence. I want my writing to shimmer too. Iris—the winged Greek goddess of the rainbow who transmitted messages from the gods of Olympus to humanity—transforms my rainbow of ideas into coherent communication. Her little altar sits right in front of my keyboard—literally front and center when I'm writing. She's been my writing goddess for many years, and if I don't include her in the process, writing feels thick, like trying to run while waist-deep in mud.

All my deity altars are visual reminders of my divine connection to Spirit. Honoring my goddesses, showing them appreciation and gratitude, visiting them every day, and requesting their divine participation *matters* to me. I don't do this because I feel obligated to, I do it because it enhances my spiritual experience and enriches my life.

Activity: Create a Deity Altar

Pick a deity you feel drawn to, or whose energy you need in your life, and find out about the stories and symbols of that deity. It can be from those I mentioned, or one you've discovered on your own.

Find a spot for your altar to serve as a miniature temple where you'll spend time with this deity, and share your concerns, your appreciation, and your heart. It's a place for ritual, meditation, study, and communicating and bonding with that deity. You may petition your deity for particular needs or requests there, and express your gratitude and appreciation.

Everything on your deity altar is meant to please that deity. For example, Bastet loves and protects cats, so feline imagery would please her. Lakshmi is associated with wealth and luxury. She would appreciate an altar adorned with some of the finer things, like velvet, silk, gold, silver, and jewels. Dionysus is closely associated with the grape harvest and wine, so an altar to honor him would include grape clusters and wine. Multi-talented Brigid is associated with all sorts of things: farm animals (particularly sheep), forging, poetry, storytelling, courage, strength, creation, and more. She might appreciate fire symbology for her forging talents and passionate spirit, wool from her beloved sheep, or things forged from steel.

Begin with a representation of this deity—a statue, figurine, artwork, or symbolic representation—and embellish it with your own special touches. What colors, flowers, crystals, plants, or animals would harmonize with this deity's symbolism? How about fresh flowers or vanilla incense? What sort of gifts and offerings would be appreciated? Make your altar creative and special, infused with imagery that facilitates a spiritual connection between you and that deity. And, a little bling on your deity altar doesn't hurt! They are deities, after all.

Prepare your altar as you would a lovely dinner table for a special guest. Just tossing a pizza onto the table with some napkins for plates wouldn't make that person feel special, honored, or even welcome. You'd get out the good china and shiny flatware, make sure the wine glasses were spotless, make a beautiful centerpiece, and light candles. When you want to shower someone with love and adoration, you prepare special food and create an atmosphere and ambiance that conveys your feelings for them. Deity is no different. It responds to creativity, effort, attention, and most of all, genuine love and devotion. Let it flow freely.

When you've finished assembling your altar, cleanse it with incense or herbal smoke, light the candles, and place your hands there. Welcome that deity to your life and your altar, and dedicate it to them. Express gratitude for this divine presence and participation. This isn't a "one and done" visit. It's not a decoration. Your altar is a vessel for your ongoing spiritual relationship with that deity.

Pour out love and gratitude there on a regular basis—not just when you need something. Thank this deity for participating in your life. Bring offerings to them, just as you would a special guest. Deities are like humans in that regard—they appreciate being welcomed and pampered. They aren't shy about being fussed over.

Honoring Deity Is Your Choice

Honoring deity is not a compulsory component of Pagan life, but for many, it deeply enhances it. It's like looking at Spirit, the universe, or "God" through Diana-colored glasses. Or Freya or Pan or Hathor, or whichever deity appeals to you. If you prefer to make your connection with deity via organized religion, that's perfectly fine. If you prefer to go it alone, that's perfectly fine. If you prefer to do neither—also perfectly fine. Your own approach to spirituality—and deity—is unique to you, and represents a divine connection to a facet of Spirit.

Recommended Reading

Freeman, Philip. *Celtic Mythology: Tales of Gods, Goddesses, and Heroes.* New York, NY: Oxford University Press, 2017.

Monaghan, Patricia. *Encyclopedia of Goddesses & Heroines.* Novato, CA: New World Library, 2014.

CHAPTER 14

Pagan Traditions

The time has come! You know your Pagan ABCs and 123s, and you're ready to explore all those colorful flower beds in the Big Pagan Garden! Most of the things we've explored will wind their way through many traditions, often with some variation on the exact methods and practices. Some traditions focus on religion, others on mastering skills. Some have a loosey-goosey approach, others have quite strict practices. Some Pagans practice in groups or covens, others alone as solitaries. None of them are right, and none of them are wrong. They're just different choices.

That said, as you explore this wondrous garden, you may come across folks who sniff, "Well, we are geraniums, and that's not how *we* do it." Just like the non-Pagan world, there are some folks who are very invested in their "rightness," and may try to convince you of your "wrongness." You can still listen, and consider what they have to say, but you're under no obligation to accept it. However, you may gather valuable insight from perspectives that you aren't totally aligned with. Take what resonates with you and leave the rest—sort of like picking all the cashews out of the mixed nuts. Tuck those "cashews" in your pocket and continue exploring. All paths and traditions have something to offer. Just remember that everyone doesn't need to agree with you, and you don't need to agree with them. The only one you need to agree with is you.

If you're exploring a tradition and get a surge of "Yes!" in your gut … trust it. Follow it. See where it leads. Like me, that unidentifiable "something" you've been searching for may be right there in front of you. However, to reiterate, there's no requirement to commit to any tradition or practice.

You can continue on as a Garden-Variety Pagan forever if you like, and create your own unique traditions and practices.

Alrighty, then. Let's head out into the garden.

The Structure of Paganism

Paganism is structured like Christianity. Under the Christian umbrella, there is Catholicism, Mormonism, Presbyterianism, and so forth. Within each, there are different beliefs and many subcategories, such as many dioceses within Catholicism. All of them are Christian, regardless of specific religion or diocese. All Catholics are Christian, but not all Christians are Catholic.

Likewise, under the Pagan umbrella, there are specific religions, such as Wicca or Druidism. There are also traditions that are practiced as a craft or skill, such as magicians, non-Wiccan witches, cultural Pagans (like us Garden-Variety Pagans), and Neopagans. The New Age community, which shares many beliefs and language with the Pagan community, often dovetails under the Pagan umbrella, as do those who are just randomly Paganish. Just like Christianity, all Wiccans are Pagan, but not all Pagans are Wiccan.

One of the main differences between Christianity and Paganism is monotheism vs. polytheism. Christianity, like Judaism and Islam, is monotheistic, and worships a sole male god: God, YHWH/Yahweh, and Allah, respectively. These three religions are called Abrahamic, as they are linked to the God of Abraham exclusively. Polytheistic religions worship more than one god, and sometimes many, all of which are non-Abrahamic in origin. Besides Paganism, other polytheistic religions include Buddhism, Hinduism, Shintoism, and some indigenous religions and practices.

There's a third umbrella in the belief system world that's not Christian, Pagan, or polytheistic: atheism, which does not recognize any deity at all, and agnosticism, which is non-committal about the existence of deity. This set of people is more inclined to believe in science than spirituality.

Religion vs. Practice

Some of the most basic contrasts between Pagan traditions are those that are practiced as religion and those that focus upon gathering magical knowledge and skill. The line sometimes blurs—one may be both a religious devotee and also a magical practitioner. This is the beauty of Paganism: you can shape your own spirituality and practices to suit your own interests and needs, and will likely find a group where you fit in—*if* you want one. There are likely as many solitary practitioners in the Pagan community as there are those who follow a certain path—maybe more.

Pagan religions embrace deity worship and a structure for rituals, gatherings, and celebrations of particular sabbats or sacred days. When practiced in a group or coven, there is a leader, such as a High Priestess or Priest, and a hierarchy, and possibly degrees as one progresses in knowledge, skill, and experience.

Those who approach Paganism as a practice—magicians, sorcerers, shamans, and some witches—devote themselves to mastering magic, spells, or states of consciousness that usually require extensive research, practice, and dedication. They are perpetual students of metaphysical spirituality, mysticism, and magic. They may study ancient formulas for spells in books known as *grimoires*, and are more focused on magical proficiency than spiritual practice or deity worship. Some may include deity in their practice, but it's not usually their main focus.

Magicians

Magicians, as the word implies, focus on magic specifically, mastering mysterious, prescribed, and often ancient magical practices and formulas to achieve certain results, and may work in groups or alone. Ceremonial magicians perform structured, elaborate, and complex rituals, sometimes called High Magic, and may include others in their rituals, or work as solitaries.

Sorcery is associated with black magic, sometimes called "baneful magic," which may involve malevolent intent, cursing, and hexing. This is the sort of "witchcraft" Hollywood exploits and embellishes to terrify us and sell lots of theater tickets. That said, many witches know how to curse or hex. As I mentioned in the chapter on magic, baneful magic, hexing, and cursing is like owning a handgun. It just sits in the gun cabinet. Should you ever need to protect yourself or your loved ones, you know where it is and how to use it—and, if you don't know how to use it, don't touch it.

Yes, black magic is part of the Big Pagan Garden too, but you don't spend any energy worrying about that. If that's not your jam, just walk on by. Those magicians aren't going to try to lure you in. In fact, quite the opposite.

In contrast to Christians, Pagans don't proselytize, in particular those who are really invested in secrecy and the occult, which means supernatural, mystical, magical, or alchemical practices that are kept hidden from view—not evil—as the word is commonly misconstrued in mainstream society.

Witches and Witchcraft

Witches are the largest group overall in Paganism, straddling both sides of the religion vs. practice fence. And it can get a little confusing: All Wiccans are witches, but not all witches are Wiccan. Both call themselves "witch," but only Wiccans call themselves Wiccan because they practice witchcraft as a religion. Wicca has several sects, such as Gardnerian or Dianic, and often specify themselves as such. Nonreligious witches approach witchcraft as a practice. They may include deities in their magic, but their main focus is the Craft, not deity worship or religious practices—ritual, yes; religion, not necessarily.

Many solitaries identify generically as witches, and there has recently been a mainstream surge of interest in witchcraft, particularly amongst people searching for an alternate lifestyle and belief system.

What Is a Witch?

So, what is a witch, anyway? An ugly old hag in black pointed hat and gown, hovering over a steaming cauldron, chanting "Boil, boil, toil and trouble" and dropping in eye of newt and ear of toad and whatnot? Well, it could be, but most likely not—although that classic stereotype is sort of oddly beloved in the Pagan community.

Many non-Pagan folks equate *witch* with "Devil worshipper," but this is a slur. The Devil is part of the Christian pantheon, and isn't a figure in Pagan spirituality, except in Satanic groups. Satanic groups do exist in the Pagan world, but as with sorcerers, if you don't want to participate in that—just don't. They're way less interested in convincing people to join them than Hollywood would like us to believe. That's just more Hollywood nonsense.

Witches are probably all around you and you don't even realize it. They're just regular people—your next-door neighbors, coworkers, the librarian, your computer technician, or the cashier at the bank. They may wear flowy skirts and way too much silver jewelry or be entirely too obsessed with J. R. R. Tolkien, but all in all—just people, like anyone else. Unless you learned about witches and witchcraft from Pagans, most of what you believe is probably erroneous.

Witch can mean many things. Some witches are Wiccan, some aren't. Some witches are mystics. Some are scholars. Some are performers. Some are teachers. Some are herbalists. Some are psychics. Some are community leaders. Some are healers. Some are clergy. Some are naturalists. Some are environmentalists. Some wear a lot of black makeup and clothing and seek to impress/intimidate others with their witchy badassery. Some are a little of this, and a little of that. Whatever it is, there's a witchcraft for that.

What do witches do? Simple: They practice witchcraft! For many, it's a full-time endeavor. A calling. A passion. Witchcraft is their life, their path, and their way of interacting with the seen and unseen worlds, whether they call themselves witches or Wiccan. Consider the word *witchcraft*. Witch*craft*. It's like any other craft: blacksmithing, carpentry, masonry. There are skills involved, with increasingly experienced levels, from apprentice to master. With any skill, mastery is an ongoing endeavor, and witchcraft is no different. There's a constant sharpening and honing of skills, formulas, spells, magic, and practices, which some witches write down in a Book of Shadows, a personal record of their magical discoveries and achievements.

In centuries past, *witch* meant female and *warlock* meant male, but that terminology has fallen out of usage. The division is considered rather archaic now. Nowadays, both genders are called witches. The word *witch* comes from Old English words, *wicca* (pronounced *witch-ah)* meaning male, and *wicce* (*witch-eh*) meaning female. What the word means depends on who you're asking and what time period you're asking them in. *Witch* and its root words could mean anything from "wise one" (a common translation of *wicca* and *wicce*) to "herbalist" to "sorceress" to "fortune-teller" to "hag" to "scary Halloween character" to "crazy cat lady."

Religious Persecution

Where did all the negative press about witches and witchcraft come from? We can thank the Roman Catholic Church for that. The early Church became powerful during its unholy alliance with the Roman Empire beginning in the fourth century CE. The teachings of the Roman Catholic Church were a great tool for the Roman Empire to bulldoze across Europe in the centuries that followed, in a calculated effort to obliterate any teachings or practices that didn't align with the Holy Bible, particularly polytheistic Pagan practices. As the Empire gained power, so did the Church. Remember how most of the Pagan sabbats have Christian equivalencies? That's why. Both the Empire and Church sought to crush Pagan disobedience and stamping out Pagan celebrations with Christian holidays and tearing down Pagan temples and rebuilding Christian churches on top of them was part of the strategy.

As the Roman Empire began collapsing under its own weight in the mid-fifth century, several European kingdoms aligned themselves with the powerful Roman Catholic Church, as its teachings provided convenient methods for controlling the masses with fear and terror. The persecution of witches in the onslaught that followed was merciless, perverse, cruel, and frequently arbitrary. In the Middle Ages, you could be "guilty" of witchcraft simply because someone called you a witch, and the onus was then on you to prove your innocence. Sadly, the tests for determining if someone was a witch or not involved torture and were often fatal. Accused women would scream out confessions of witchcraft while in agony, and then be sentenced to death so they could be cleansed of sin. Often the transgression of these "witches" was nothing more than practicing herbal medicine, having certain patterns of moles on their skin, being old, widowed, and/or unattractive, or owning a cat.

A horrific manual written in Germany in 1486 by Catholic clergyman Heinrich Kramer and Jakob Sprenger, called *Malleus Maleficarum* (translated as *Hammer of Witches*) detailed a legal process for convicting and murdering witches under the crime of heresy. This vicious, cruel handbook for slaughter cemented the erroneous link between witchcraft and Satan, creating a binary world in which everything was either of God or the Devil. Kramer fixated upon women, declaring them more carnal than men and therefore easily seduced by the Devil. Meanwhile, the Spanish Inquisition was proliferating and also obsessed with exterminating heretics, fueled by the power of the Church and its alliances with rulers in several countries. The term "witch hunt" comes from these cruel, bloody years of accusing and executing innocent people to squash resistance to the Catholic Church and allied kingdoms. The Church split into two factions in 1517 during the Reformation, giving rise to the Protestant Church, which was equally obsessed with persecuting and prosecuting "witches."

The history of witchcraft in medieval Europe is saturated in blood, torture, and murder. The exact number executed for witchcraft varies between resources, but it ranges from 40,000 to 200,000 hanged, beheaded, or burned alive between 1300-1850.[47] Although witchcraft trials ended in England with the Witchcraft Act of 1735, witchcraft remained illegal there until 1951. Persecution for witchcraft was exported to colonial America in the 1600s. The notorious Salem Witch Trials condemned nineteen people to death in Massachusetts in 1692 amid witchcraft hysteria. When the United States was born in 1776, there were no laws against witchcraft. However, it wasn't until 1985 that witchcraft received protection under the First Amendment of the U.S. Constitution as a religion in the court case Dettmer v. Landon.[48]

The word *witch* is stained with prejudice, misinformation, and hysteria, all rooted in medieval church and state persecution. It's important to know the historical facts and defang that word, particularly if you're confronted by someone spouting nonsense about witches or witchcraft. A witch is simply one devoted to knowledge and skill in herbalism, healing, divination, and magic, and may have Goddess- or nature-based spiritual beliefs and practices, or certain beloved deities. A witch may love getting together with those interested in the same. Singing, drumming, and frivolity may be involved. Probably chocolate.

Pagan Paths and Traditions

Pagan paths and traditions can be practiced in groups or alone as a solitary. However, Pagans in certain groups won't accept you as legitimate if you didn't enter their tradition in a specific way. You can't call yourself a British Traditional Witch if you have no connection to a BTW coven, for example. However, you could follow Wiccan practices on your own and call yourself Wiccan without any objections.

---

47. Niall McCarthy, "The Death Toll of Europe's Witch Trials," Statista, last updated October 29, 2019, https://www.statista.com/chart/19801/people-tried-and-executed-in-witch-trials-in-europe/; Ellen Castelow, "Witches in Britain," Historic UK, accessed August 18, 2020. https://www.historic-uk.com/CultureUK/Witches-in-Britain/.

48. Patti Wigington, "American Witchcraft Laws," Learn Religions, accessed August 18, 2020, https://www.learnreligions.com/american-witchcraft-laws-2562884.

If you're a joiner, and having a group to learn, practice, and celebrate with appeals to you, reach out to a local group and find out how to get involved. Most every tradition can be found online or on social media, and may be able to point you toward a group or coven that meets near you. Don't be surprised if some seem a bit standoffish at first. Many Pagans need to determine if your intentions are genuine before inviting you into their inner circle. You can't just show up at a coven meeting and declare yourself a member. You have to be invited. If freelancing on your own and creating your own path as a solitary seems more your style, you can still learn a lot from those who follow specific traditions. Either choice is fine. And, it's non-committal. You can always change your mind later on.

The following is just a sampling of Pagan traditions, particularly those you're likely come across in the Big Pagan Garden:

Asatru: This tradition focuses upon ancient Norse, Germanic, and Viking Paganism, and is a form of Heathenry. The beliefs come from the pre-Christian Scandinavian peoples, and are outlined by the "Nine Noble Virtues": Courage, Truth, Honor, Fidelity, Discipline, Hospitality, Industriousness, Self-Reliance, and Perseverance. There are three types of deities in Asatru: the Aesir (gods of the tribe or clan; leadership), the Vanir (representing Earth and nature), and the Jotnar (giants always at war with the Aesir; destruction and chaos). The deities of Asatru are Norse.[49]

Atheopaganism: This tradition is nature- and science-based, and does not honor any deities, only the earth. Atheopaganism doesn't have intermediaries (priests or priestesses) between the sacred Earth and humans, but there is clergy. According to founder Mark Green, Atheopagan clergy act as group facilitators who plan rituals, meetings, or functions, rather than people with elevated status. Atheopagan values include healthy skepticism, reverence for the earth, gratitude, humility, inclusiveness, responsibility, curiosity, integrity, kindness, compassion, and embracing pleasure, and, Mark adds, keeping a sense of humor.

British Traditional Wicca: To follow this path, you must be formally initiated by an existing BTW member, and are expected to pursue a specified

---

49. Patti Wigington, "Asatru — Norse Heathens of Modern Paganism," Learn Religions, last updated July 6, 2019, https://www.learnreligions.com/asatru-modern-paganism-2562545.

course of training and practice based upon the practices and beliefs of European witchcraft common from the 1500s through 1800s. Those who progress in the practices and training earn degrees: First, Second, and Third. You cannot just join a British Traditional Wicca coven; you must be formally accepted into the coven to participate.[50]

Brujería: Brujería is a system of folk magic with roots in Mexican and Mexican-American witchcraft, Judeo-Christianity, Catholicism, Hoodoo, and Vodou. Its workings are determined by whether magical work is "justified" or not, and magical work is conducted as healing for the client. One of the central deities in Brujería is Santa Muerte—Nuestra Señora de la Santa Muerte (Our Lady of the Holy Death), Mexican goddess of death and the dead. Although Brujería is a growing Pagan presence, it's not a truly Pagan tradition or religion due to its association with Catholic practices, and is more correctly considered a quasi-Christian system of folk magic.[51]

Ceremonial Magic: This practice combines Western Qabbalah, astrology, and tarot, with roots in the Hermetic Order of the Golden Dawn, founded in 1888. Aleister Crowley adapted their teachings and merged them with those of the Ordo Templi Orientis (OTO). This tradition involves elaborate, complex, and precise rituals, and one must be accepted into a group to participate. Ceremonial magic is linked to Hermetic Qabbalah (focusing upon the nature of divinity, the Tree of Life amongst its symbols), Enochian magic (evoking and commanding spirits), and Thelema (spiritual philosophy and practice created by Crowley). Practitioners of this tradition are simply called magicians. If members of the Golden Dawn or OTO, they are called members or initiates.

Dianic Wicca/Witchcraft: Founded by Zsuzsanna Budapest in 1971, this tradition is feminist in its approach, sometimes radically so, and devoted to celebrating the divine feminine in all women, who are viewed as the physical embodiment of the Goddess. The Goddess is worshipped in

50. Witches of the Craft, "British Traditional Witchcraft," accessed August 22, 2020, https://witchesofthecraft.com/2018/04/13/various-paths-of-witchcraft-british-traditional-witch-craft/.

51. Katrina Rasbold, "10 Things You (Probably) Didn't Know About Brujería," Llewellyn.com, accessed August 31, 2020, https://www.llewellyn.com/blog/2019/01/10-things-you-proba-bly-didnt-know-about-brujeria/.

three aspects: Maiden, Mother, Crone. Dianic witches are predominantly female. A male Dianic witch is very rare. Dianic practice includes magic, visualization, meditation, and unlike some other traditions, embraces cursing and hexing against abusers of women. Dianic Wiccans synchronize their magic and rituals with the phases of the moon. This tradition gets its name from its central deity, the Roman goddess Diana.[52]

Druid: Associated with ancient Celts, the true practices of Druidism aren't entirely known because the original Druids didn't keep written records. Their practices and lore were passed orally from person to person and generation to generation, and modern-day Druids attempt to recreate these Celtic origins. Within the Druid Order, stories are preserved and passed along by Bards. Ovates study herbalism, healing, and divination. Druids have a deep connection to nature and a spiritual connection to the land. Their gods and goddesses are ancient Celtic deities.[53]

Feri (Faery/Faerie/Fairy): Feri has 1960s connections to Californians Victor and Cora Anderson, and a spiritual pantheon of its own. It is a path of ecstatic witchcraft, differing from Wicca in structure, says Faery initiate and Pagan author Storm Faerywolf: "We don't have a dogmatic ritual structure, and we do not place emphasis on fertility or agriculture." He adds that Feri is nebulous, with lore, lineages, and deity differing from one Feri group to the next. The fae—nature-dwelling sprites, faeries, elves, gnomes—are associated with this tradition (but not included by every group), and aren't always sweet, delicate, and good-natured. They are very powerful and not always amiable toward humans. Feri spiritual practices include magic, meditation, and energy work.[54]

Gardnerian Wicca/Witchcraft: This tradition gets its name from its founder, Gerald Gardner, sometimes called "the father of modern Wicca and witchcraft." He is credited for bringing Wiccan practices out into the open in the 1950s, after being initiated into the New Forest Coven in 1939, and

---

52. WiseWitch, "Types of Wicca: Dianic Wicca," Wise Witches & Witchcraft, accessed August 22, 2020, https://witchcraftandwitches.com/types-of-wicca/dianic-wicca/.

53. "Experience the Power of an Ancient Tradition," Druidry.org, accessed August 22, 2020, http://www.druidry.org.

54. "Feri: American Traditional Witchcraft," Feri Tradition, accessed August 22, 2020, http://www.feritradition.com/index.html.

was a contemporary of Aleister Crowley. Gardnerian Wicca is practiced in covens, led by a high priestess and a high priest. According to Lady Argante, a 25-year Gardnerian and third-degree High Priestess of Coven Daoine Sidhe in the San Francisco Bay Area, Gardnerian Wicca is an initiatory mystery tradition, and many aspects are oathbound, meaning coven members take an oath of secrecy before joining and engaging in their practices. She says this tradition is also distinctive in that Gardnerian initiates may not charge money for teaching witchcraft.

Heathenry: One of the Neopagan traditions, this path centers on reconstructing ancient, pre-Christian belief systems adhered to by the Germanic peoples of the Iron Age and early Middle Ages, and encompasses the same deities as Asatru. Runic divination is commonly practiced in Heathen groups, and a connection to wild nature, and harmony with it, is a main focus of this tradition. "Heathen" was a derogatory term early Christians used, sometimes interchangeably with "Pagan," to identify followers of Pagan or polytheistic religions rather than the "God of Israel," as well as a slur against the "Godless" or "uncivilized." In ancient Norse cultures, the "heath" was simply uncultivated, wild land, like forests and moors, where the "heathen" dwelled.[55]

Hoodoo: Hoodoo's origins in the U.S. come from enslaved Africans, kidnapped and brought here against their will. These people sometimes found themselves working alongside indigenous peoples, from whom they learned about local native herbs, plants, and medicine.[56] Hoodoo's other influences include Conjure, which also originates with African Americans; Vodou, with its origins in Haiti; and, ironically, Christianity. Magical work encompasses the use of herbs, roots, plants, and oils, as well as magical tools called "curios," and can also embrace cursing and hexing. The practice of using Mojo bags originates with Hoodoo.

Neopagan: This broad term applies to various traditions that strive to revive ancient Pagan beliefs and practices. Because much of ancient Pagan history is guesswork and imagination due to the lack of written documentation,

---

55. "Heathen, Origin and Meaning," Mimir's Brunnr, accessed September 8, 2020, https://mimirsbrunnr.com/2019/03/14/heathen-origin-and-meaning/.

56. "Introduction to Hoodoo," Carolina Conjure, accessed August 31, 2020, https://www.carolinaconjure.com/introduction-to-hoodoo.html.

Neopagans do their best to recreate ancient traditions, often with a relationship with nature at their core. Some Pagans simply identify as generically Neopagan, and form their own practices and traditions.

Reconstructionist: These traditions focus on researching the religious practices and beliefs of ancient cultures, such as Celtic, Norse, Greek, Roman, or Egyptian, and recreating a similar spirituality or religious practice. Academic study is central to these traditions.

Stregheria: Early Italian witchcraft is the heart of this tradition and is famously outlined in *Aradia: Gospel of the Witches* by Charles Leland. Aradia, daughter of Roman goddess Diana, was sent to Earth by her mother to teach humans the ways of magic and protect women and witches. Aradia is central to Stregheria, which is a blend of ancient Etruscan spiritual practices, Italian folk magic, and even some hints of early Catholicism.[57] Amongst its sacred symbols is the cimaruta, an ancient charm that features the moon, a rooster, a serpent, a key, and a flower, all positioned on a rue branch, meant to represent the Goddess in her triple form: Hekate (key), Diana (moon), and Proserpina (serpent).[58]

Thelema: This spiritual practice is based upon the philosophies and teachings of Aleister Crowley. Thelemic beliefs span from atheism to polytheism. Its basic belief is to ascend to higher states of existence, uniting oneself with higher powers, and understanding and embracing one's true Will, which is a Thelemite's ultimate goal. The Law of Thelema states, "Do what thou wilt shall be the whole of the law" (one's own will is one's sole deciding factor). Thelemic deities include Nuit, Hadit, and Ra Hoor Khuit, which correspond to Egyptian deities Isis, Osiris, and Horus.[59]

Wicca: Wicca has several subcategories, including Alexandrian, Dianic, Gardnerian, and Seax, each with their own version of Wiccan practices. Wiccans may call themselves "Wiccan" or "witch." Although there is a lot of focus on ancient Celtic practices and traditional witchcraft, Wicca

57. Patti Wiginton, "What is Stregheria?" Learn Religions, last updated May 20, 2018, https://www.learnreligions.com/about-stregheria-traditions-2562552.

58. "The Cimaruta," Stregheria.com, accessed August 21, 2020, http://www.stregheria.com/Cimaruta-Article.htm.

59. Catherine Beyer, "Understanding the Religion of Thelema," Learn Religions, last updated January 27, 2019, https://www.learnreligions.com/thelema-95700.

is a "neo" religion, publicly appearing in the US and Great Britain with the 1954 publication of *Witchcraft Today* by Gerald Gardner, from whom Gardnerian witchcraft gets its name. One can follow a generically Wiccan path as a solitary, worshipping the Goddess, working with phases of the moon, and celebrating the sabbats, along with doing magic and ritual. However, solitaries cannot properly identify as Dianic, Gardnerian, or British Traditional without joining a coven, being initiated, and following a structured training process. There are also "hedgewitches" or "green witches," which follow a nature-based path, often embracing folk magic.

A Little Bit Paganish

There are lots of folks wandering around the Big Pagan Garden who don't identify with a particular tradition—cultural Pagans, New Agers, Burners, and the much-maligned fluffy bunnies—yet they're there nonetheless, often to the chagrin of Very Serious Pagans and the Witchier Than Thou.

Cultural Pagans are freelancers. They *may* loosely follow a particular tradition, participate in sabbats, observe full moon rituals, and/or feel aligned with the Goddess—or not. Some are quite serious about their practices and view it as religion, while others have eclectic spirituality, beliefs, and practices. Cultural Paganism is more lifestyle than religion. Garden-Variety Pagans fall into this group.

The New Age movement constantly evolves and changes, and embraces mystical knowledge and practices. Its eclectic influences include Theosophy, the Aquarian Age, Eastern philosophies and religions, Gnosticism, and altered states of consciousness. Yoga, veganism, and enlightenment are part of their groove. New Agers get a lot of side-eye and sometimes outright disdain from Very Serious Pagans. I find them quite colorful and interesting.

Also drifting in and out of the Pagan community are the Burners. Burning Man is their annual Mecca, and altered states of consciousness are totally acceptable. If it's wearing fur chaps, hula-hooping to throbbing rave music on a desert playa, and it's really high, it probably falls in the Burner camp. Burners are mostly there for the party. But that's okay. I like parties.

At the lighter end of this lighter end of the Pagan spectrum are the fluffy bunnies. Joyful, random, and unfocused, they're all about love and light, crystals and sparkly things, and everybody's a goddess! They adore rainbows, angels, fairies, and unicorns that poop glitter (sometimes the unicorns are caticorns), and are disdainfully labeled "Playgans" by Very Serious Pagans. Poor little fluffy bunnies. They aren't hurting anyone. They're just happy to be there—little Pagan toddlers, putting everything in their mouths to see how it tastes. Fluffy bunnies—sparkle away! It's okay!

Ready to Take Root

What did you think of all those colorful flower beds? Are you curious about one? Go find out more. You have enough information to have a coherent conversation with someone dedicated to that path. If it was all very interesting, but you'd rather continue on as a solitary eclectic Garden-Variety Pagan, that's okay too. Just keep exploring the topics and techniques you found fascinating or intriguing and shape your own practices.

Whatever your preference, there are social media groups, blogs, websites, and resources galore with more information. Pagan festivals and conventions, both in person and virtual, are also excellent learning opportunities. To get started, just Google. Google is the gateway for curiosity to get out and play.

Congratulations, little wildflower—you're ready to take root and blossom!

Recommended Reading:

Adler, Margot. *Drawing Down the Moon—Witches, Druids, Goddess-Worshippers, and Other Pagans in America*. New York, NY: Penguin Books, 1986.

Higginbotham, Joyce and River. *Paganism—An Introduction to Earth-Centered Religions*. Woodbury, MN: Llewellyn Publications, 2019.

Conclusion

And So, Our Journey Comes to an End

Wow. We've already arrived at the end of our stroll through the Big Pagan Garden. But this isn't an ending, really, because one journey's end is where the next one begins. Going forward, you'll walk your own path.

We are richer for having made this journey together. I'm joyful for that—but a bit tearful as I realize that our time together is done. I've written this book from my heart, to yours—not because I'm a preeminent Pagan scholar, or multi-generational 10th-Degree Wiccan High Priestess, or Pagan rock star with a massive following, but simply because I know how deeply my Pagan perspective has enriched my own life, and I wanted to share it with you, my sweet friend.

May you come away from this journey with a rejuvenated sense of the amazing, talented, miraculous, unique being you truly are, fearless in expressing your true, genuine self. May you feel connected to our planet, the life on it, and the cosmos as well, trusting and relying upon your instincts and intuition. May everything you've explored and discovered on our walk together be a springboard for discoveries of your own.

You began this journey with me because you were curious. Curiosity brought us together, and it will guide you onward. Pay attention to curiosity—it's the root of intuition. Curiosity pokes you and says, "What if…" and brings you to doorways you might not have considered—or even noticed. Stay curious, my friend.

May the words in this book bring you inspiration, validation, wonder, and magic. May your heart rejoice in the everlasting love of the Goddess, and your spirit soar and dance with the energies of the universe. May you always be well, safe, happy, and healthy.

So mote it be.

Glossary

Altar: An assemblage of items intended to draw magical energy or to serve as a worktable for magical work and ritual.

Athame: A double-edged blade used in ritual to represent the God, or masculine or projective energy.

Beltane: The midpoint between the spring equinox and summer solstice, ocurring on May 1; a celebration of love and romance.

Besom: A broom, often handmade, with a brush made of twigs or bristles attached to a natural branch or stave. It is used in to cleanse and purify a ritual space.

Biocongruence: In perfectly balanced harmony with nature, the earth, and the natural world.

Boline: White-handled knife with a curved, crescent-shaped blade, used for harvesting magical herbs.

Celtic Cross: One of the oldest and most well-known layouts for tarot cards, with ten positions, resembling a plus sign on the left and a straight line on the right.

Chalice: A goblet or glass used in ritual to represent the Goddess, or feminine or receptive energy.

Congruence: In harmony; perfectly balanced.

Cosmocongruence: In perfectly balanced harmony with the cosmos and the energies of the universe.

Deosil: Clockwise, associated with building up.

Equinox: Days of equal night and day, occurring on or around March 21 and September 22.

Esbat: One of thirteen full moons per year, at which time covens or Pagan groups will meet for magical work and ritual.

Familiar: A living animal that is unusually drawn toward magical work and lends its energy to it.

Four Elements, The: The necessary components of both the earth and one's temperament: earth, air, fire, and water.

Gaia: Another name for Mother Earth; in Greek mythology, the earth goddess (also Gaea).

Goddess, The: The divine, spiritual energy of the earth.

Guardian Animal: A metaphysical animal spirit that appears in one's life without being called and offers protection and guidance.

Imbolc: The midpoint between the winter solstice and the spring equinox, occurring on or around February 1; associated with the Celtic goddess Brigid and the birth of spring lambs.

Litha: The summer solstice, occurring on or around June 21; the longest day of the year in the northern hemisphere; also called Midsummer, a time when the veil between this world and the fae world is most thin.

Lughnasadh: The midpoint between the summer solstice and fall equinox, occurring around August 1; the first of three harvest festivals.

Mabon: The fall equinox and second harvest festival, occurring on or around September 22.

Ostara: The spring equinox, occurring on or around March 21; a celebration of spring and fertility.

Pagan: A follower or practitioner of a non-Abrahamic religion, tradition, or lifestyle, often in rhythm with nature, the earth, and the seasons; often polytheistic.

Pentacle: A protective symbol comprised of a five-pointed star drawn from one continuous line, surrounded by a circle. Its points represent earth, air, fire, water, and Spirit, as well as the five points of the human body, protected by the circle.

Quatrain: A four-line poem or chant; the first and third line, and second and third line, may rhyme, or the first and second, and third and fourth.

Ritual: A formal ceremony, done alone or in a group, where magical work is done.

Sabbat: One of eight Pagan seasonal holidays: Yule, Imbolc, Ostara, Beltane, Litha, Lughnasadh, Mabon, Samhain.

Samhain: The third harvest festival on October 31, the midpoint between the fall equinox and winter solstice, signifying the end of the Pagan year; a time to honor and remember beloved dead, when the veil between this world and the afterworld are most thin.

Seeker: One who seeks a spiritual Pagan path.

Solar Cross: A four-pointed cross within a circle, resembling a plus sign. The points represent the summer and winter solstices, and the spring and fall equinoxes.

Solitary: One who practices a Pagan tradition or religion alone, without joining a group or coven.

Solstice: The longest and shortest days of the year, occurring on or around December 21 and June 21, respectively.

Spirit Animal: A metaphysical animal that provides insight, challenges, wisdom, or protection, or carries a message from Spirit.

Spirit: The spiritual energy of the universe.

Totem: A physical representation of a spirit animal—often hand-carved or chiseled from wood or stone—intended to draw that animal's energy to an individual or group, often to protect it.

Tradition: A specific Pagan religion or practice.

Triple Goddess: A symbol comprised of a circle (full moon) with outward-facing crescents attached to each side, representing the phases of the moon as well as the Goddess in her three forms: Maiden, Mother, and Crone.

Wheel of the Year: An eight-pointed wheel representing all eight sabbats, flowing from one to the next, representing the never-ending flow of the seasons.

Widdershins: Counterclockwise, associated with dissolving or tearing down.

Yule: The winter solstice, occurring on or around December 21; the shortest day of the year in the northern hemisphere. A celebration of the birth of the sun, signifying the beginning of the Pagan year.

Bibliography

Books

Adler, Margot. *Drawing Down the Moon: Witches, Druids, Goddess-Worshippers, and Other Pagans in America*. New York, NY: Penguin Books, 1986.

Beckett, John. *The Path of Paganism*. Woodbury, MN: Llewellyn Publications, 2019.

Blake, Deborah. *Everyday Witchcraft: Making Time for Spirit in a Too-Busy World*. Woodbury, MN: Llewellyn Publications, 2015.

Blake, Deborah. *The Little Book of Cat Magic: Spells, Charms & Tales*. Woodbury, MN: Llewellyn Publications, 2018.

Buckland, Raymond. *Wicca For One: The Path of Solitary Witchcraft*. New York, NY: Citadel Press, 2004.

Cabot, Laurie. *The Witch in Every Woman: Reawakening the Magical Nature of the Feminine to Heal, Protect, Create, and Empower*. New York, NY: Dell Publishing, 1997.

Cunningham, Scott. *Earth, Air, Fire & Water: More Techniques of Natural Magic*. Woodbury, MN: Llewellyn Publications, 2005.

Cunningham, Scott. *Wicca: A Guide for the Solitary Practitioner*. Woodbury, MN: Llewellyn Publications, 1989.

Danaan, Victoria David. *The Book of Adeptus*. Woodlands, TX: 7th House, 2013.

Dow, Carolyn. *Tea Leaf Reading For Beginners: Your Fortune in a Tea Cup*. Woodbury, MN: Llewellyn Publications, 2011.

Dugan, Ellen. *Natural Witchery: Intuitive, Personal & Practical Magick.* Woodbury, MN: Llewellyn Publications, 2007.

Green, Mark A. *Atheopaganism: An Earth-Honoring Path Rooted in Science.* Santa Rosa, CA: Green Dragon Publishing, 2019.

Grimassi, Raven. *Grimoire of the Thorn-Blooded Witch: Mastering the Five Arts of Old World Witchery.* San Francisco, CA: Red Wheel/Weiser, LLC., 2014.

Harrison, Paul. *Elements of Pantheism: A Spirituality of Nature and the Universe.* Shaftesbury, Dorset, England: Element Books, 2013.

Higginbotham, Joyce and River. *Paganism: An Introduction to Earth-Centered Religions.* Woodbury, MN: Llewellyn Publications, 2019.

K, Amber and Azrael Arynn K. *How to Become a Witch: The Path of Nature, Spirit & Magick.* Woodbury, MN: Llewellyn Publications, 2018.

LeFae, Phoenix and Gwion Raven. *Life Ritualized: A Witch's Guide to Life's Most Important Moments.* Woodbury, MN: Llewellyn Publications, 2021.

Louv, Richard. *Last Child in the Woods: Saving Our Children from Nature-Deficit Disorder.* Chapel Hill, NC: Algonquin Books, 2006.

Lyle, Jane. *The Cup of Destiny.* New York: Shelter Harbor Press, 2019.

Matthews, Caitlyn. *The Complete Lenormand Oracle Handbook: Reading the Language and Symbols of the Cards.* Rochester, VT: Destiny Books, 2014.

McBride, Kami. *The Herbal Kitchen.* Newburyport, MA: Conari Press/Red-Wheel/Weiser, LLC, 2019.

Murphy-Hiscock, Arin. *The Green Witch: Your Complete Guide to the Natural Magic of Herbs, Flowers, Essential Oils, and More.* Avon, MA: Adams Media, 2017.

Peschel, Lisa. *A Practical Guide to the Runes: Their Uses in Divination and Magick.* St. Paul, MN: Llewellyn Worldwid, 1989.

Pollack, Rachel. *The New Tarot Handbook.* Woodbury, MN: Llewellyn Publications, 2019.

Pollack, Rachel. *Seventy-Eight Degrees of Wisdom: A Book of Tarot.* Hammersmith, London, England: Element/Harper Collins Publishers, 1997.

RavenWolf, Silver. *HedgeWitch: Spells, Crafts & Rituals For Natural Magick.* Woodbury, MN: Llewellyn Publications, 2008.

RavenWolf, Silver. *To Ride a Silver Broomstick: New Generation Witchcraft.* St. Paul, MN: Llewellyn Publications, 1996.

Sams, Jamie and David Carson. *Medicine Cards.* New York, NY: St. Martin's Press, 1988, 1999.

Starhawk. *The Spiral Dance: A Rebirth of the Ancient Religion of the Great Goddesses.* New York, NY: Harper Collins Publishers, 1999.

White, Gregory Lee and Catherine Yronwode. *The Stranger in the Cup: How to Read Your Luck and Fate in the Tea Leaves.* Forestville, CA: Lucky Mojo Curio Company, 2020.

Yronwode, Catherine. *Hoodoo Herb and Root Magic: A Materia Magica of African-American Conjure.* Forestville, CA: Lucky Mojo Curio Company, 2002.

Online

Ancient History Encyclopedia. "Religion Timeline." Ancient History Encyclopedia. Accessed July 8, 2020. https://www.ancient.eu/timeline/religion.

Atkinson, Nancy. "Confirmed: We Really are Star Stuff." Universe Today. Last updated January 11, 2017. https://www.universetoday.com/132791/confirmed-really-star-stuff/.

BBC. "Meet the Ancestors of All Plants and Animals." Last updated September 5, 2014. http://www.bbc.com/earth/story/20140905-meet-the-ancestors-of-all-plants-and-animals.

Beer, Colin. "Instinct/Behavior." Encyclopaedia Britannica. Accessed June 15, 2020. https://www.britannica.com/topic/instinct/Freuds-Trieb.

Beyer, Catherine. "Understanding the Religion of Thelema." Learn Religions. Last updated January 27, 2019. https://www.learnreligions.com/thelema-95700.

Bible Hub. "Exodus 3:14." Accessed July 8, 2020. https://biblehub.com|/exodus/3-14.htm.

Brooke, Lindsay. "A Universe of 2 Trillion Galaxies." Phys.org. Last updated January 16, 2017. https://phys.org/news/2017-01-universe-trillion-galaxies.html.

Carolina Conjure. "Introduction to Hoodoo." Accessed August 31, 2020. https://www.carolinaconjure.com/introduction-to-hoodoo.html.

Castelow, Ellen. "Witches in Britain." Historic UK. Accessed August 18, 2020. https://www.historic-uk.com/CultureUK/Witches-in-Britain/.

Celtic Connection. "Sacred Trees of the Celts and Druids." Wicca.com. Accessed July 9, 2020. https://wicca.com/celtic/sacred-trees.html.

Cholle, Francis P. "What Is Intuition, And How Do We Use It?" Psychology Today. Last updated August 31, 2011. https://www.psychologytoday.com/us/blog/the-intuitive-compass/201108/what-is-intuition-and-how-do-we-use-it.

Clemens, Colleen. "What We Mean When We Say 'Toxic Masculinity.'" Teaching Tolerance. Last updated December 11, 2017. https://www.tolerance.org/magazine/what-we-mean-when-we-say-toxic-masculinity.

DivinationByTeaLeaves.com. "What is My Future for 2021?" Accessed January 29, 2020. http://www.divinationbytealeaves.com/a-dictionary-of-symbols-a.htm.

Druidry.org. "Experience the Power of an Ancient Tradition." Accessed August 22, 2020. https://druidry.org.

Feri Tradition. "Feri - American Traditional Witchcraft." Accessed August 22, 2020. http://www.feritradition.com/index.html.

Flowing Data. "History of Earth in 24-hour Clock." October 9, 2012. Accessed July 8, 2020. https://flowingdata.com/2012/10/09/history-of-earth-in-24-hour-clock/.

Forte Academy. "5 Things You Should Know About the 'Evil Eye' (and How to Protect Yourself)." Medium. Accessed January 28, 2020. https://medium.com/forte-academy/5-things-you-should-know-about-the-evil-eye-and-how-to-protect-yourself-3a01605cc303.

Genzer, Peter. "Scientists Pinpoint Energy Flowing Through Vibrations in Superconducting Crystals." Phys.org. Last updated April 30, 2018. https://phys.org/news/2018-04-scientists-energy-vibrations-superconducting-crystals.html.

Good Health Academy. "Manuka Honey for the Skin—What Does the Science Say?" Last updated January 27, 2020. https://www.goodhealthacademy.com/health-benefits/manuka-honey-for-skin/.

GoTopless.Org. "Topless Laws." Accessed February 23, 2021. https://gotopless.org/topless-laws.

Greshko, Michael and National Geographic Staff. "Origins of the Universe, Explained." National Geographic. Last updated January 18, 2017. https://www.nationalgeographic.com/science/space/universe/origins-of-the-universe/.

Hadhazy, Adam. "Why Do We Always See the Same Side of the Moon?" Discover. Last updated October 29, 2014. https://www.discovermagazine.com/the-sciences/why-do-we-always-see-the-same-side-of-the-moon.

Healthline. "How To Do an Elimination Diet and Why." Accessed June 12, 2020. https://www.healthline.com/nutrition/elimination-diet.

Healthline. "The What, Why, and How of Epsom Salt Baths." Accessed June 10, 2020. https://www.healthline.com/health/epsom-salt-bath#bath.

Hunt, Tam. "Could Consciousness All Come Down to the Way Things Vibrate?" The Conversation. Accessed February 25, 2021. https://theconversation.com/could-consciousness-all-come-down-to-the-way-things-vibrate-103070.

Kahn, Nina. "This is the Real Difference Between Your Sun, Moon, & Rising Zodiac Signs." Bustle. Last updated September 9, 2019. https://www.bustle.com/life/a-sun-moon-rising-zodiac-sign-explainer-that-will-help-astrology-make-so-much-more-sense-12222972.

Kahn, Nina. "Your Guide to the Planets in Astrology & How They Affect You." Bustle. Last updated July 23, 2020. https://www.bustle.com/life/how-each-planets-astrology-directly-affects-every-zodiac-sign-13098560.

Leveilee, Nicholas P. "Copernicus, Galileo, and the Church: Science in a Religious World." *Inquiries Journal.* Last updated 2011. http://www.inquiriesjournal.com/articles/1675/copernicus-galileo-and-the-church-science-in-a-religious-world.

Logan, Ryan W. and Colleen A. McClung. "Rhythms of Life: Circadian Disruption and Brain Disorders Across the Lifespan." *Nature Reviews Neuroscience.* Last updated November 20, 2018. https://www.nature.com/articles/s41583-018-0088-y.

Maclin, Ellie. "Dark Moon vs. New Moon." Sciencing. Last updated April 24, 2017. https://sciencing.com/dark-moon-vs-new-moon-5082.html.

Merton, Mary. "What is Lenormand?" The Tarot Conservatory. Last updated August 31, 2017. https://www.thetarotconservatory.com.au/what-is-lenormand/.

McCarthy, Niall. "The Death Toll of Europe's Witch Trials." Statista. Last updated October 29, 2019. https://www.statista.com/chart/19801/people-tried-and-executed-in-witch-trials-in-europe/.

Mimir's Brunnr. "Heathen, Origin and Meaning." Accessed September 8, 2020. https://mimirsbrunnr.com/2019/03/14/heathen-origin-and-meaning/.

Narr, Karl J. "Prehistoric Religion, the Beliefs and Practices of Stone Age Peoples." Encyclopaedia Britannica. Accessed July 8, 2020. https://www.britannica.com/topic/prehistoric-religion.

Native American Indian Facts. "Totem Pole Facts." Accessed January 19, 2021. https://native-american-indian-facts.com/Native-American-Indian-Art-Facts/Native-American-Indian-Totem-Pole-Facts.html.

Native Land. "Territories." Accessed July 17, 2020. https://native-land.ca.

Neubauer, Simon; Hublin, Jean-Jacques; and Philipp Gunz. "The Evolution of Modern Human Brain Shape." Science Advances. Last updated January 24, 2018. https://advances.sciencemag.org/content/4/1/eaao5961.

Old Farmers' Almanac. "Full Moon Names." Last updated April 27, 2020. https://www.almanac.com/content/full-moon-names.

Sebastiani, Althea. "Dark Moon vs. New Moon: What's the Difference?" Last updated January 14, 2011. https://www.ladyalthaea.com/all-articles/dark-moon-vs-new-moon.

Siegal, Ethan. "The Universe is Disappearing, and There's Nothing We Can Do To Stop It." *Forbes*. August 17, 2018. https://www.forbes.com/sites/startswithabang/2018/08/17/the-universe-is-disappearing-and-theres-nothing-we-can-do-to-stop-it/#19513908560e.

"Sleep and Chronic Disease." Centers for Disease Control and Prevention. Accessed February 26, 2021. https://www.cdc.gov/sleep/about_sleep/chronic_disease.html.

Strauss, Mark. "What's the Difference Between Dark Matter and Dark Energy?" Mentalfloss.com. Last updated September 3, 2015. https://www.mentalfloss.com/article/68083/whats-difference-between-dark-matter-and-dark-energy.

Stregheria.com. "The Cimaruta." Accessed August 21, 2020. http://www.stregheria.com/Cimaruta-Article.htm.

Tetraktys Admin. "The Thirteen Wiccan Esbats Explained—All You Need to Know." Tetraktys. Last updated May 12, 2019. https://www.thetetraktys.com/2019/wiccan-esbats-explained/.

Toomey, Diane. "Exploring How and Why Trees 'Talk' to Each Other." *Yale Environment 360*. Last updated September 1, 2016. https://e360.yale.edu/features/exploring_how_and_why_trees_talk_to_each_other.

Tuttle, Russell Howard. "Human Evolution." Encyclopaedia Britannica. Accessed July 8, 2020. https://www.britannica.com/science/human-evolution.

Wicca Now. "The Wiccan Rede: The Complete Text Version." Accessed January 27, 2020. https://wiccanow.com/the-wiccan-rede/.

Wigington, Patti. "American Witchcraft Laws." Learn Religions. Last updated June 25, 2019. https://www.learnreligions.com/american-witchcraft-laws-2562884.

Wigington, Patti. "Asatru: Norse Heathens of Modern Paganism." Learn Religions. Last updated July 6, 2019. https://www.learnreligions.com/asatru-modern-paganism-2562545.

Wigington, Patti. "What is Stregheria?" Learn Religions. Last updated May 20, 2018. https://www.learnreligions.com/about-stregheria-traditions-2562552.

Williams, Kori. "Billie Eilish Calls Out Sexism During World Tour: Is My Value Based Only on Your Perception?" *Seventeen*. March 10, 2020. https://www.seventeen.com/celebrity/music/a31340779/billie-eilish-body-shaming-world-tour/.

Weizmann Institute of Science. "Quantum Theory Demonstrated: Observation Affects Reality." Science Daily. Last updated February 26, 1998. https://www.sciencedaily.com/releases/1998/02/980227055013.htm.

Wicca Living. "The Oak King and the Holly King: Aspects of the God." Wicca Living. Accessed July 29, 2020. https://wiccaliving.com/ wiccan-oak-king-holly-king./

WiseWitch. "Dianic Wicca." Wise Witches & Witchcraft. Accessed August 22, 2020. https://witchcraftandwitches.com/types-of-wicca/dianic-wicca/.

Witches of the Craft. "British Traditional Witchcraft." Accessed August 22, 2020. https://witchesofthecraft.com/2018/04/13/ various-paths-of-witchcraft-british-traditional-witchcraft/.

To Write to the Author

If you wish to contact the author or would like more information about this book, please write to the author in care of Llewellyn Worldwide Ltd. and we will forward your request. Both the author and publisher appreciate hearing from you and learning of your enjoyment of this book and how it has helped you. Llewellyn Worldwide Ltd. cannot guarantee that every letter written to the author can be answered, but all will be forwarded. Please write to:

Debra DeAngelo
⁒ Llewellyn Worldwide
2143 Wooddale Drive
Woodbury, MN 55125-2989

Please enclose a self-addressed stamped envelope for reply,
or $1.00 to cover costs. If outside the U.S.A., enclose
an international postal reply coupon.

Many of Llewellyn's authors have websites with additional information and resources. For more information, please visit our website at http://www.llewellyn.com